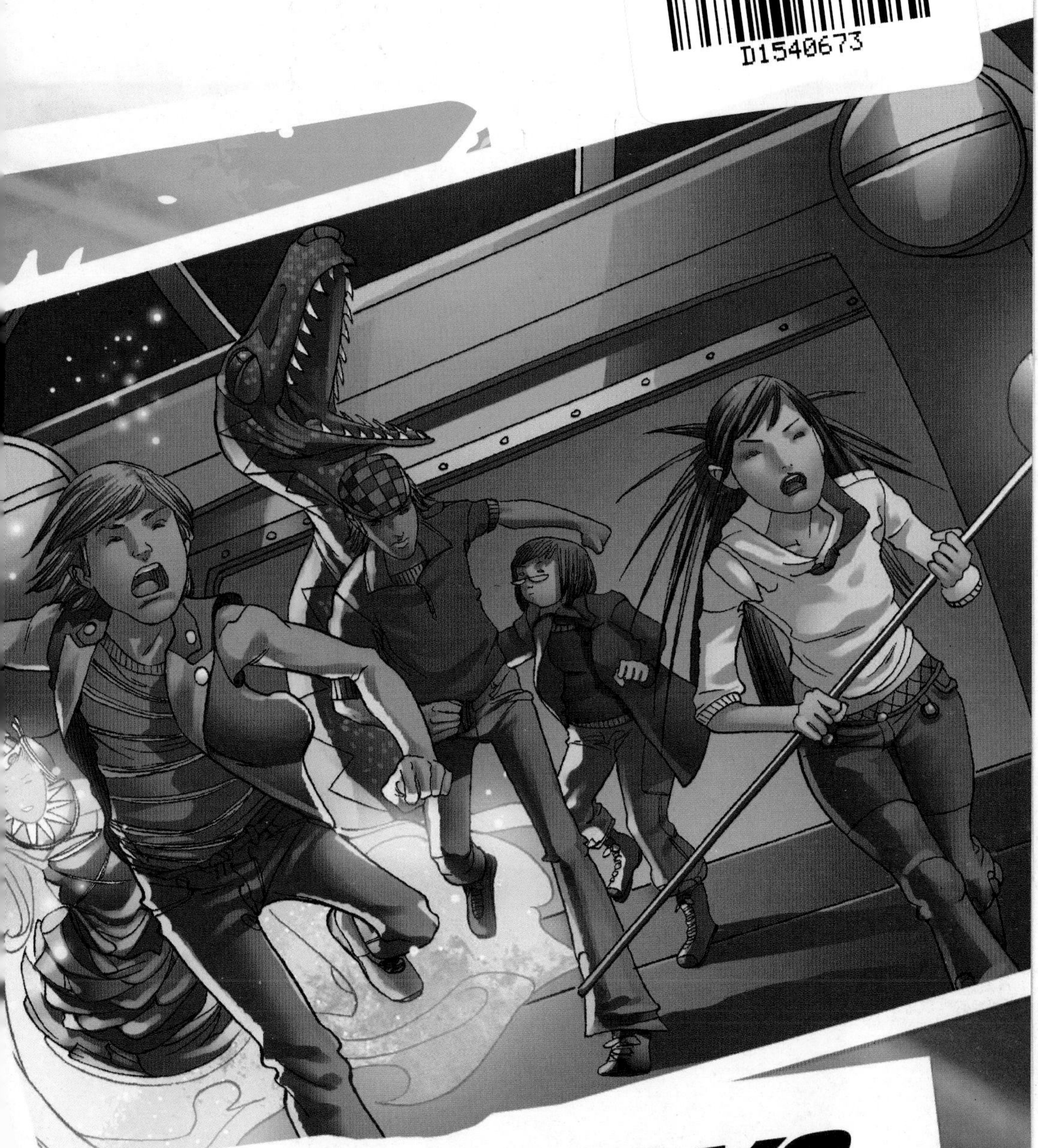

RUNAWAYS

PARENTAL GUIDANCE

RUNAWAYS

PARENTAL GUIDANCE

WRITER: **BRIAN K. VAUGHAN**

PENCILER: **ADRIAN ALPHONA**

INKER: **CRAIG YEUNG**

COLORIST: **UDON'S CHRISTINA STRAIN**

LETTERER: **VC'S RANDY GENTILE**

COVER ART: **MARCOS MARTIN**

ASSISTANT EDITOR: **NATHAN COSBY**

EDITOR: **MACKENZIE CADENHEAD** & **NICK LOWE**

SPECIAL THANKS TO C.B. CEBULSKI

RUNAWAYS CREATED BY **BRIAN K. VAUGHAN** & **ADRIAN ALPHONA**

COLLECTION EDITOR: **JENNIFER GRÜNWALD**

ASSISTANT EDITOR: **ALEX STARBUCK**

ASSOCIATE EDITOR: **JOHN DENNING**

EDITOR, SPECIAL PROJECTS: **MARK D. BEAZLEY**

SENIOR EDITOR, SPECIAL PROJECTS: **JEFF YOUNGQUIST**

SENIOR VICE PRESIDENT OF SALES: **DAVID GABRIEL**

EDITOR IN CHIEF: **JOE QUESADA**

PUBLISHER: **DAN BUCKLEY**

EXECUTIVE PRODUCER: **ALAN FINE**

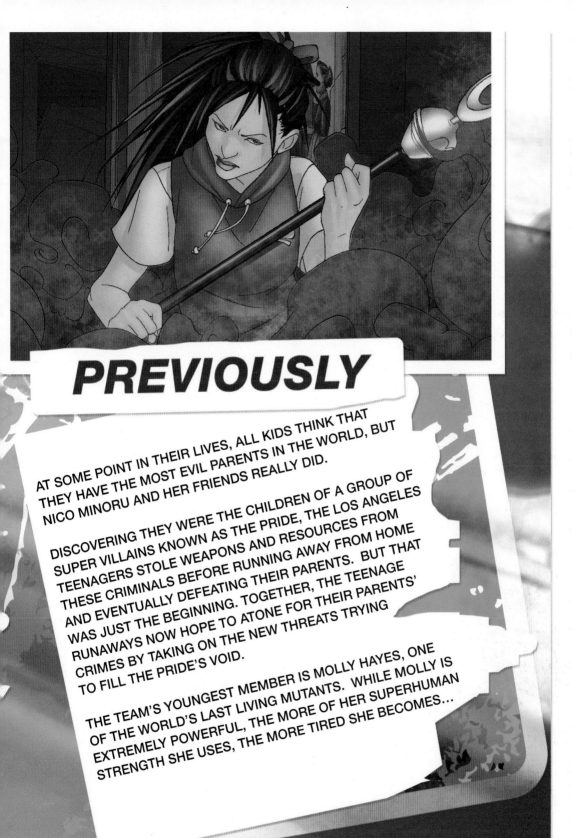

PREVIOUSLY

AT SOME POINT IN THEIR LIVES, ALL KIDS THINK THAT THEY HAVE THE MOST EVIL PARENTS IN THE WORLD, BUT NICO MINORU AND HER FRIENDS REALLY DID.

DISCOVERING THEY WERE THE CHILDREN OF A GROUP OF SUPER VILLAINS KNOWN AS THE PRIDE, THE LOS ANGELES TEENAGERS STOLE WEAPONS AND RESOURCES FROM THESE CRIMINALS BEFORE RUNNING AWAY FROM HOME AND EVENTUALLY DEFEATING THEIR PARENTS. BUT THAT WAS JUST THE BEGINNING. TOGETHER, THE TEENAGE RUNAWAYS NOW HOPE TO ATONE FOR THEIR PARENTS' CRIMES BY TAKING ON THE NEW THREATS TRYING TO FILL THE PRIDE'S VOID.

THE TEAM'S YOUNGEST MEMBER IS MOLLY HAYES, ONE OF THE WORLD'S LAST LIVING MUTANTS. WHILE MOLLY IS EXTREMELY POWERFUL, THE MORE OF HER SUPERHUMAN STRENGTH SHE USES, THE MORE TIRED SHE BECOMES…

RUNAWAYS: PARENTAL GUIDANCE. Contains material originally published in magazine form as RUNAWAYS #13-18. First printing 2010. Hardcover ISBN# 978-0-7851-4149-5. Softcover ISBN# 978-0-7851-4150- Published by MARVEL WORLDWIDE, INC., a subsidiary of MARVEL ENTERTAINMENT, LLC. OFFICE OF PUBLICATION: 417 5th Avenue, New York, NY 10016. Copyright © 2004 and 2010 Marvel Characters, Inc. All rights reserved. Hardcover: $19.99 per copy in the U.S. (GST #R127032852). Softcover: $16.99 per copy in the U.S. (GST #R127032852). Canadian Agreement #40668537. All characters featured in this issue and distinctive names and likenesses thereof, and all related indicia are trademarks of Marvel Characters, Inc. No similarity between any of the names, characters, persons, and/or institutions in this magazine with those of any living or dead person or institution is intended, and any such similarity which may exist is purely coincidental. **Printed in the U.S.A.** ALAN FINE, EVP - Office of the President, Marvel Worldwide, Inc. and EVP & CMO Marvel Characters B.V.; DAN BUCKLEY, Chief Executive Officer and Publisher - Print, Animation & Digital Media; JIM SOKOLOWSKI, Chief Operating Officer; DAVID GABRIEL, SVP of Publishing Sales & Circulation; DAVID BOGART, SVP of Business Affairs & Talent Management; MICHAEL PASCIULLO, VP Merchandising & Communications; JIM O'KEEFE, VP of Operations & Logistics; DAN CARR, Executive Director of Publishing Technology; JUSTIN F. GABRIE, Director of Publishing & Editorial Operations; SUSAN CRESPI, Editorial Operations Manager; ALEX MORALES, Publishing Operations Manager; STAN LEE, Chairman Emeritus. For information regarding advertising in Marvel Comics or on Marvel.com, please contact Ron Stern, VP of Business Development, at rstern@marvel.com. For Marvel subscription inquiries, please call 800-217-9158. Manufactured between 1/25/10 and 2/24/10 (hardcover), and 1/25/10 and 6/30/10 (softcover), by R.R. DONNELLEY, INC., SALEM, VA, USA.

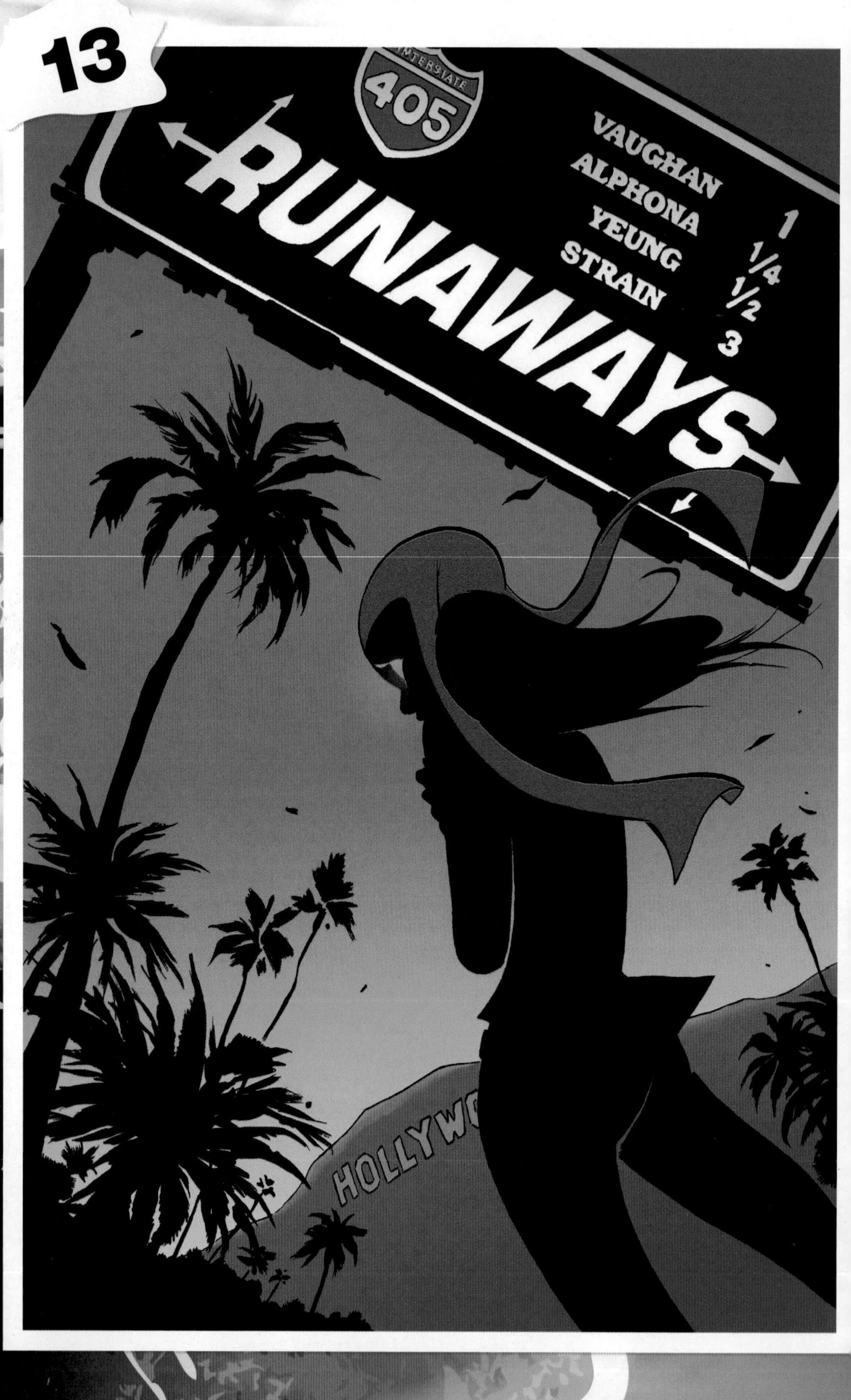
13
INTERSTATE
405
RUNAWAYS
VAUGHAN 1
ALPHONA 1/4
YEUNG 1/2
STRAIN 3

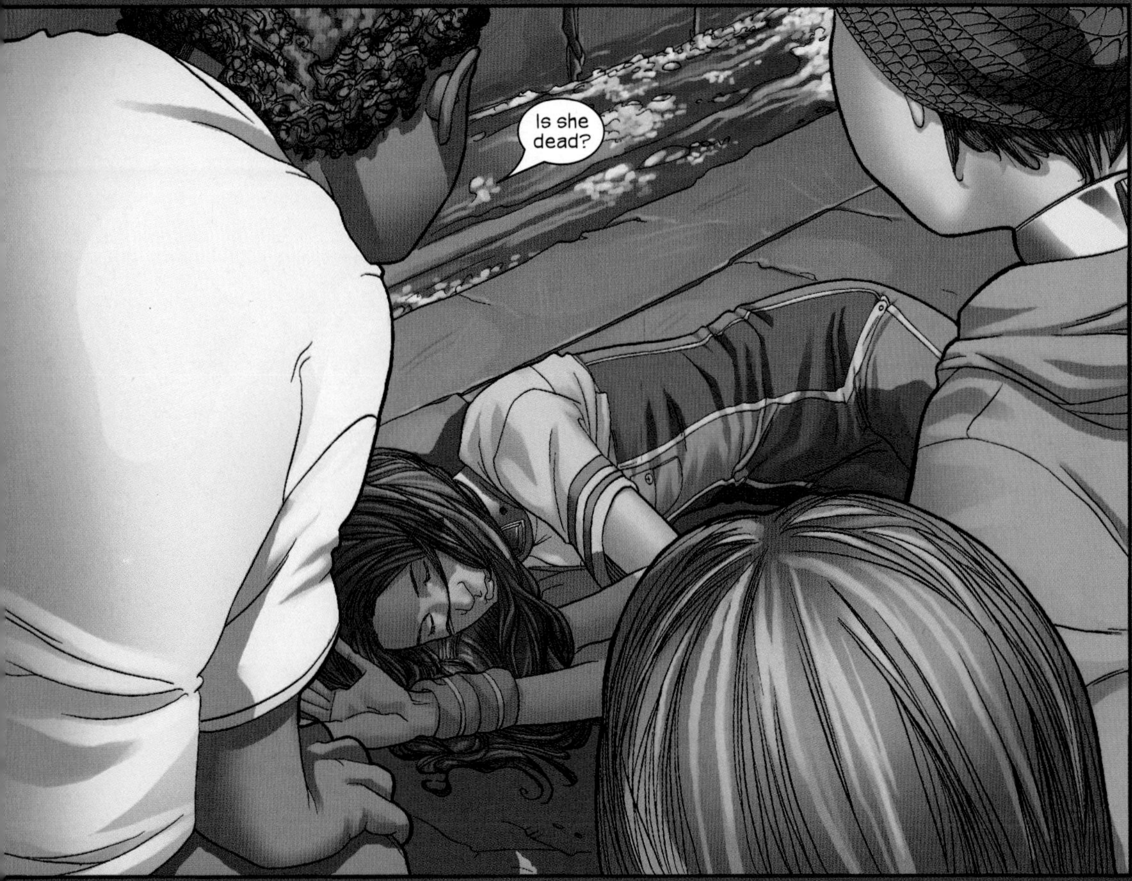
Is she dead?

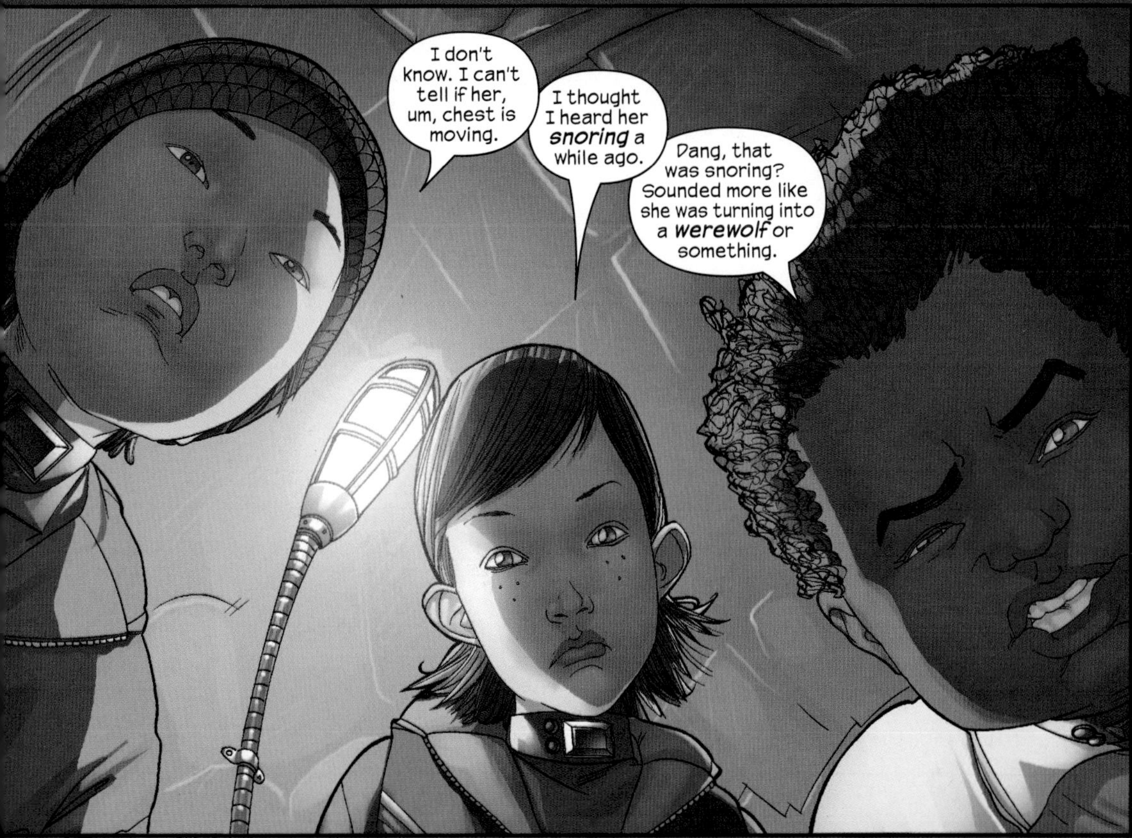
I don't know. I can't tell if her, um, chest is moving.
I thought I heard her *snoring* a while ago.
Dang, that was snoring? Sounded more like she was turning into a *werewolf* or something.

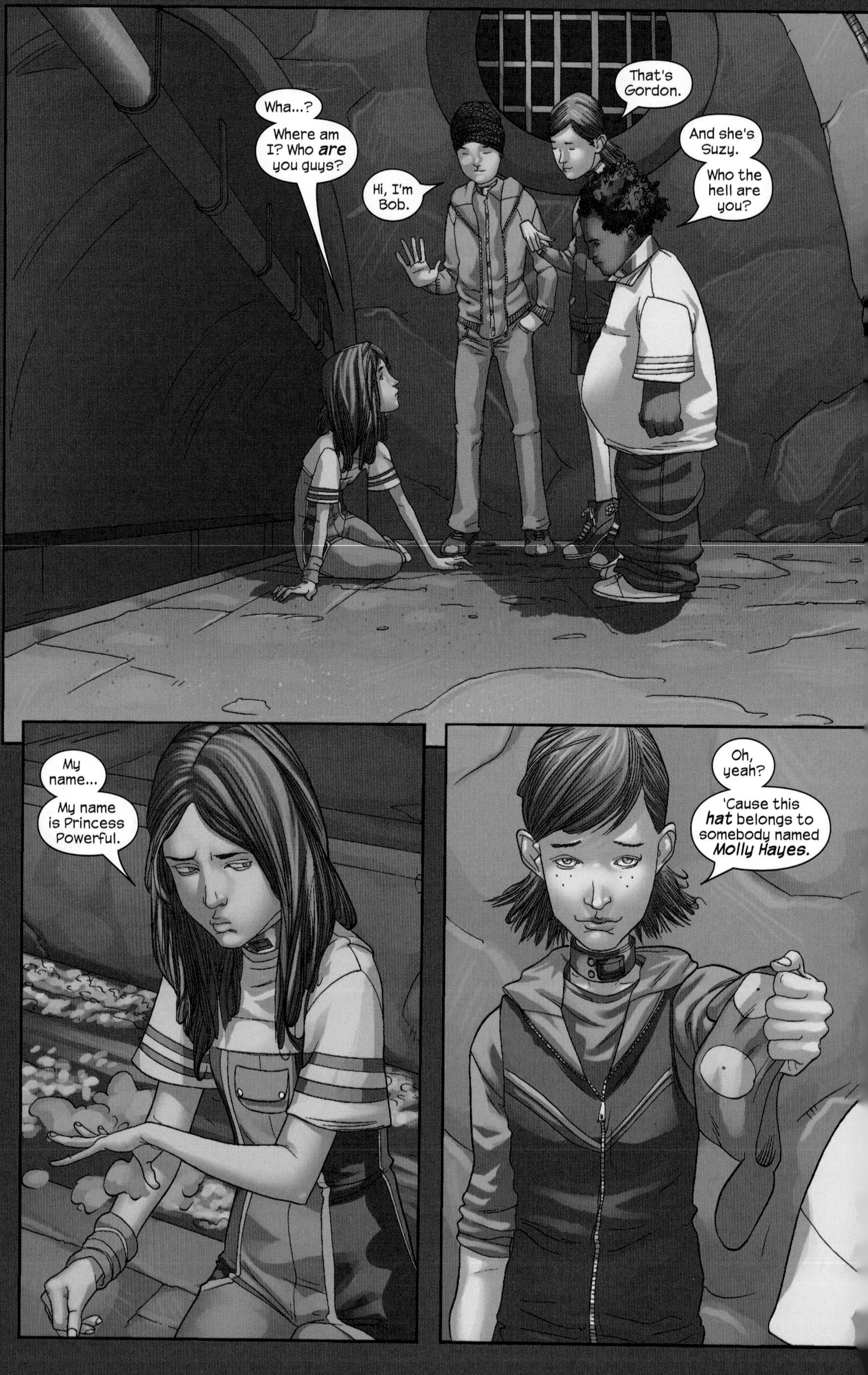
Wha...?
Where am I? Who are you guys?
Hi, I'm Bob.
That's Gordon.
And she's Suzy.
Who the hell are you?
My name...
My name is Princess Powerful.
Oh, yeah?
'Cause this hat belongs to somebody named Molly Hayes.

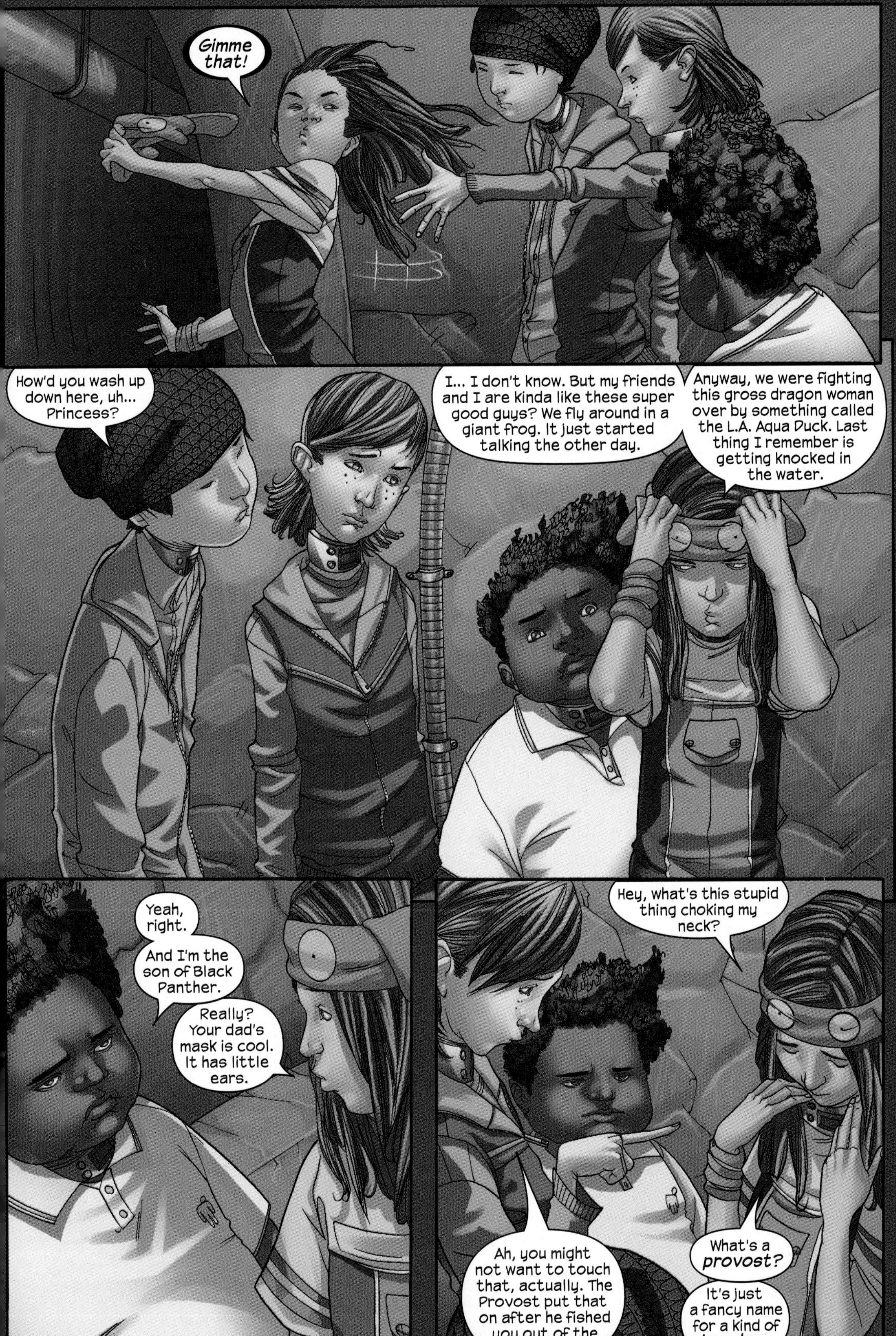
Gimme that!
How'd you wash up down here, uh... Princess?
I... I don't know. But my friends and I are kinda like these super good guys? We fly around in a giant frog. It just started talking the other day.
Anyway, we were fighting this gross dragon woman over by something called the L.A. Aqua Duck. Last thing I remember is getting knocked in the water.
Yeah, right.
And I'm the son of Black Panther.
Really? Your dad's mask is cool. It has little ears.
Hey, what's this stupid thing choking my neck?
Ah, you might not want to touch that, actually. The Provost put that on after he fished you out of the sewer.
What's a provost?
It's just a fancy name for a kind of teacher.

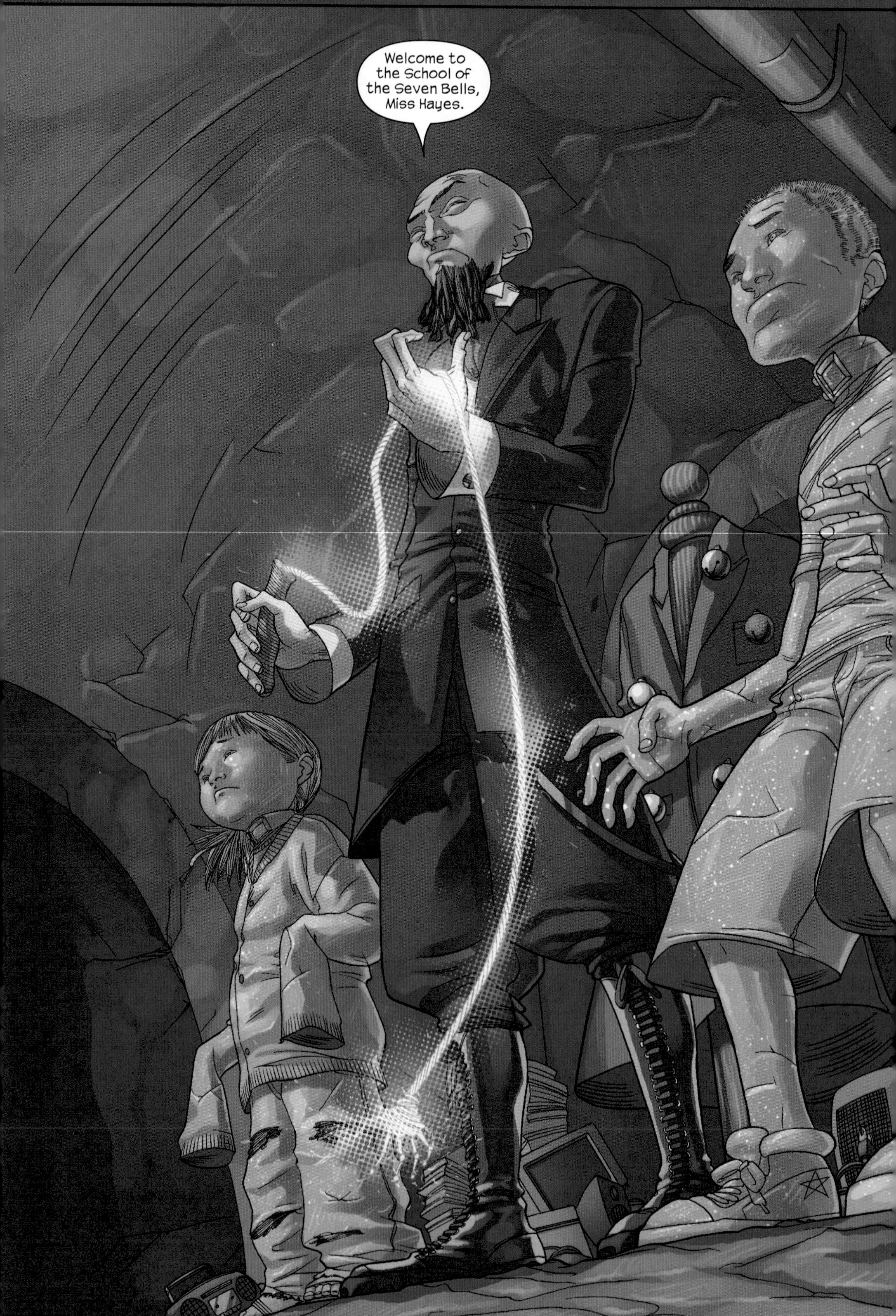
Welcome to the School of the Seven Bells, Miss Hayes.

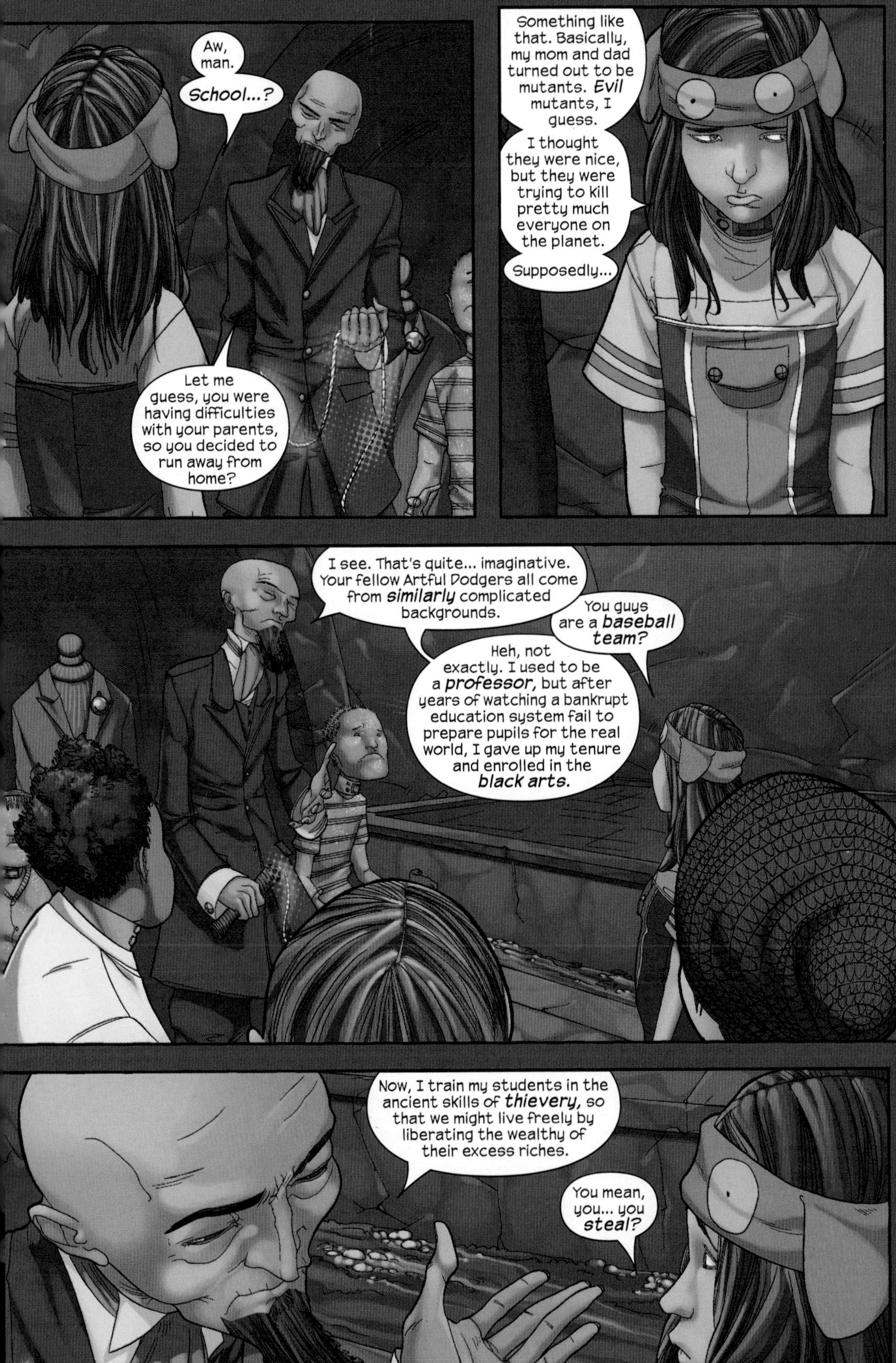

Aw, man.
School...?
Let me guess, you were having difficulties with your parents, so you decided to run away from home?
Something like that. Basically, my mom and dad turned out to be mutants. Evil mutants, I guess.
I thought they were nice, but they were trying to kill pretty much everyone on the planet.
Supposedly...
I see. That's quite... imaginative. Your fellow Artful Dodgers all come from similarly complicated backgrounds.
You guys are a baseball team?
Heh, not exactly. I used to be a professor, but after years of watching a bankrupt education system fail to prepare pupils for the real world, I gave up my tenure and enrolled in the black arts.
Now, I train my students in the ancient skills of thievery, so that we might live freely by liberating the wealthy of their excess riches.
You mean, you... you steal?

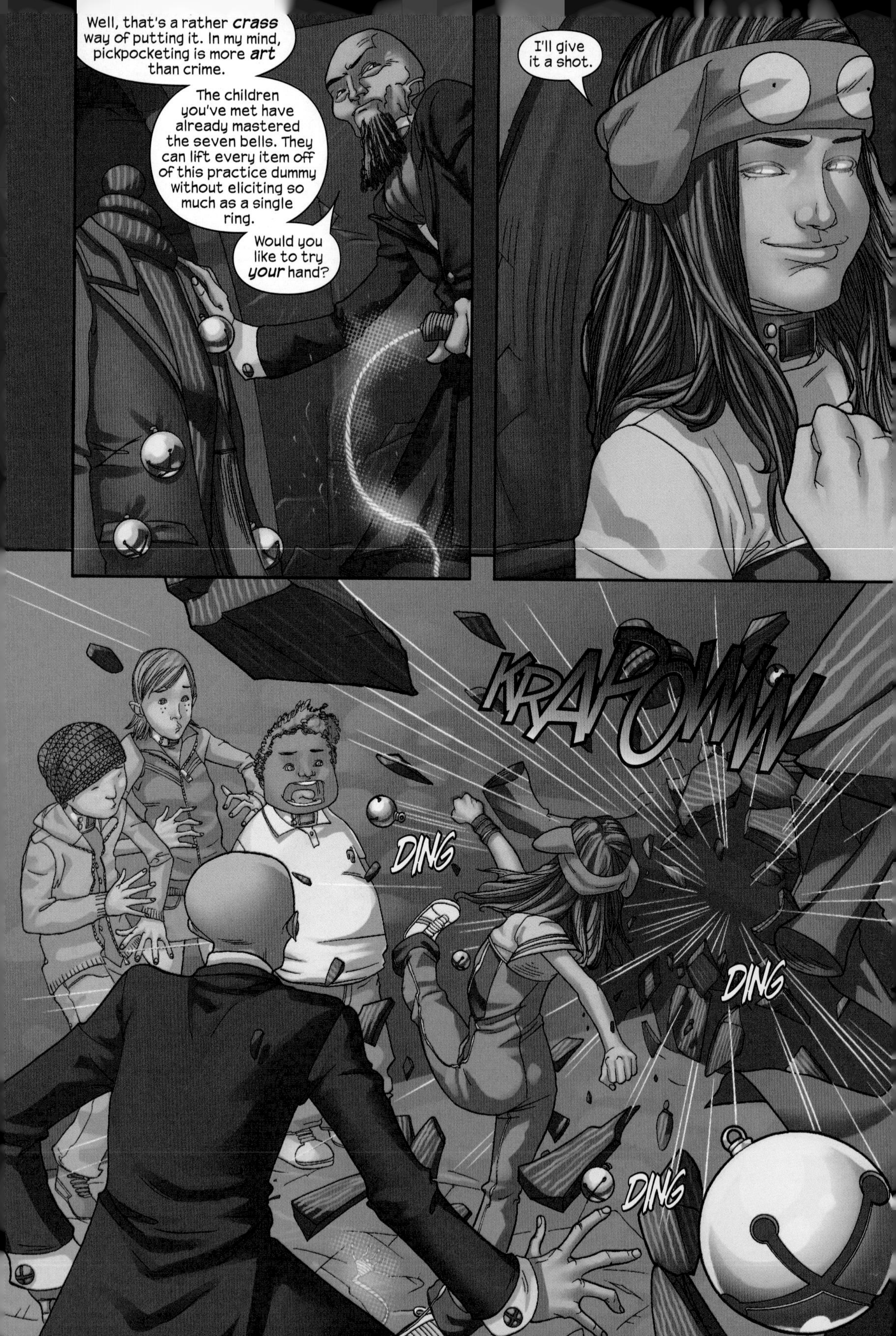
Well, that's a rather *crass* way of putting it. In my mind, pickpocketing is more *art* than crime.
The children you've met have already mastered the seven bells. They can lift every item off of this practice dummy without eliciting so much as a single ring.
Would you like to try *your* hand?
I'll give it a shot.
KRAPOWW
DING
DING
DING

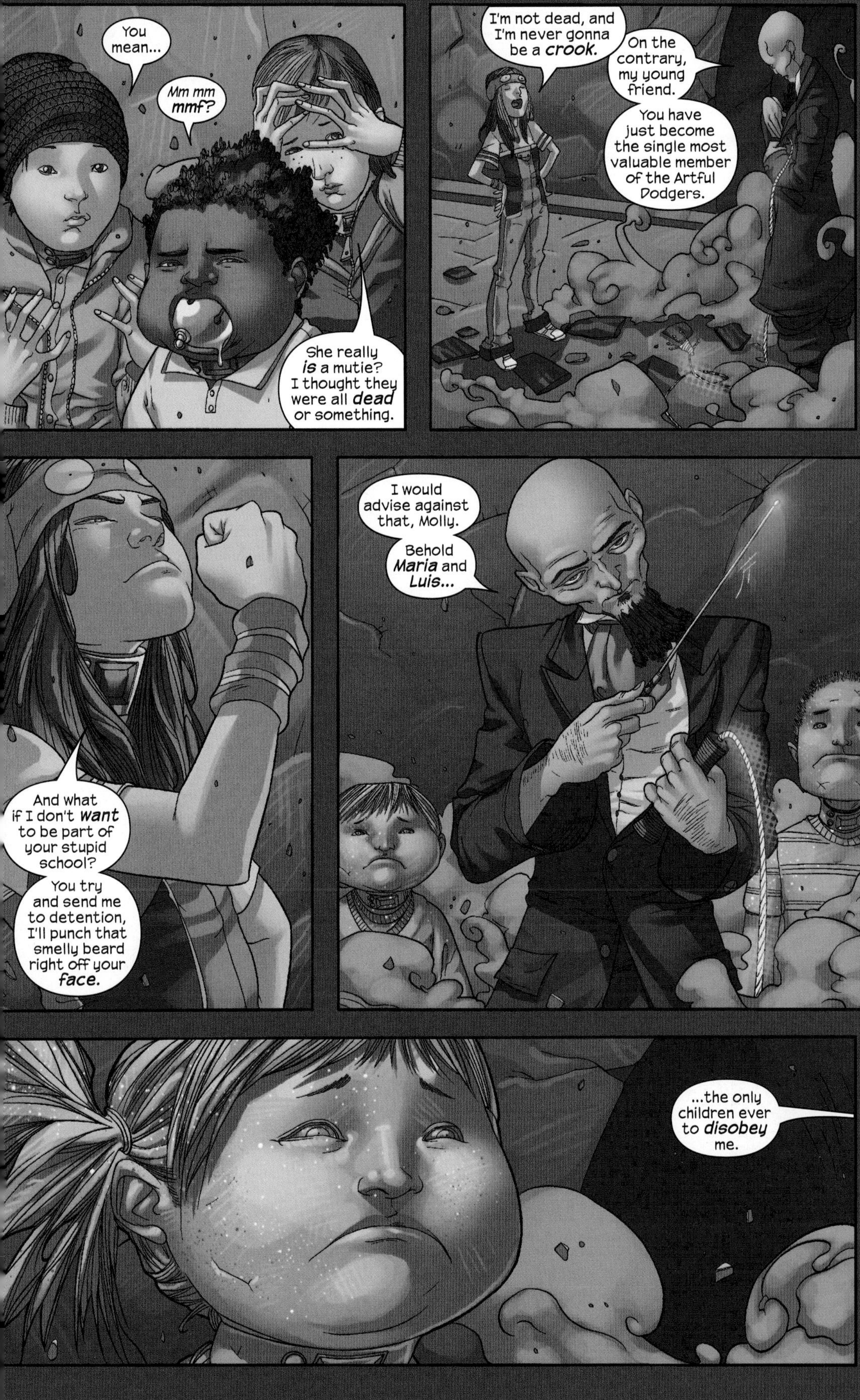
You mean...
Mm mm mmf?
She really is a mutie? I thought they were all dead or something.
I'm not dead, and I'm never gonna be a crook.
On the contrary, my young friend.
You have just become the single most valuable member of the Artful Dodgers.
And what if I don't want to be part of your stupid school?
You try and send me to detention, I'll punch that smelly beard right off your face.
I would advise against that, Molly.
Behold Maria and Luis...
...the only children ever to disobey me.

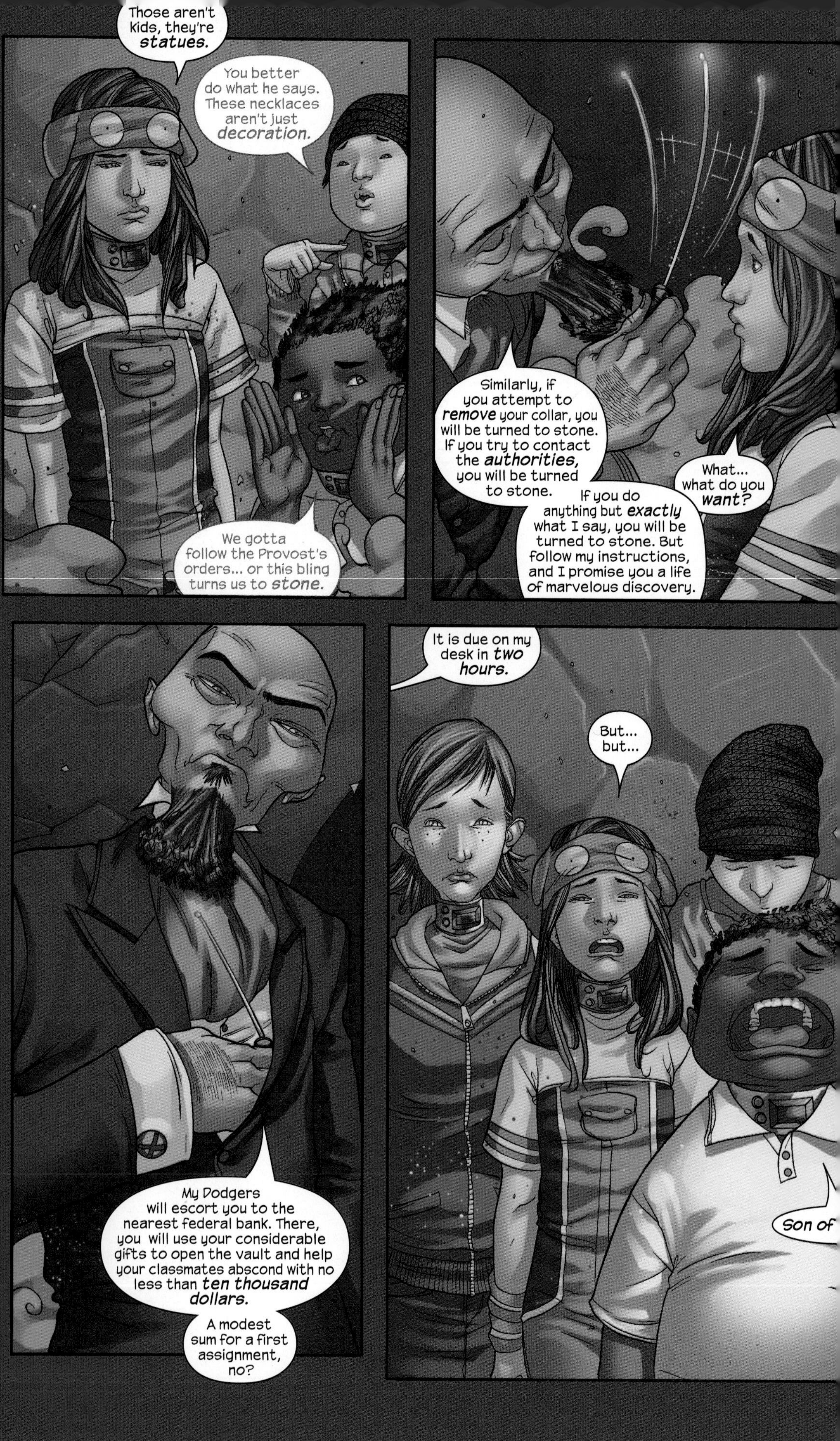

Those aren't kids, they're *statues.*
You better do what he says. These necklaces aren't just *decoration.*
We gotta follow the Provost's orders... or this bling turns us to *stone.*
Similarly, if you attempt to *remove* your collar, you will be turned to stone. If you try to contact the *authorities,* you will be turned to stone.
If you do anything but *exactly* what I say, you will be turned to stone. But follow my instructions, and I promise you a life of marvelous discovery.
What... what do you *want?*
My Dodgers will escort you to the nearest federal bank. There, you will use your considerable gifts to open the vault and help your classmates abscond with no less than *ten thousand dollars.*
A modest sum for a first assignment, no?
It is due on my desk in *two hours.*
But... but...
Son of

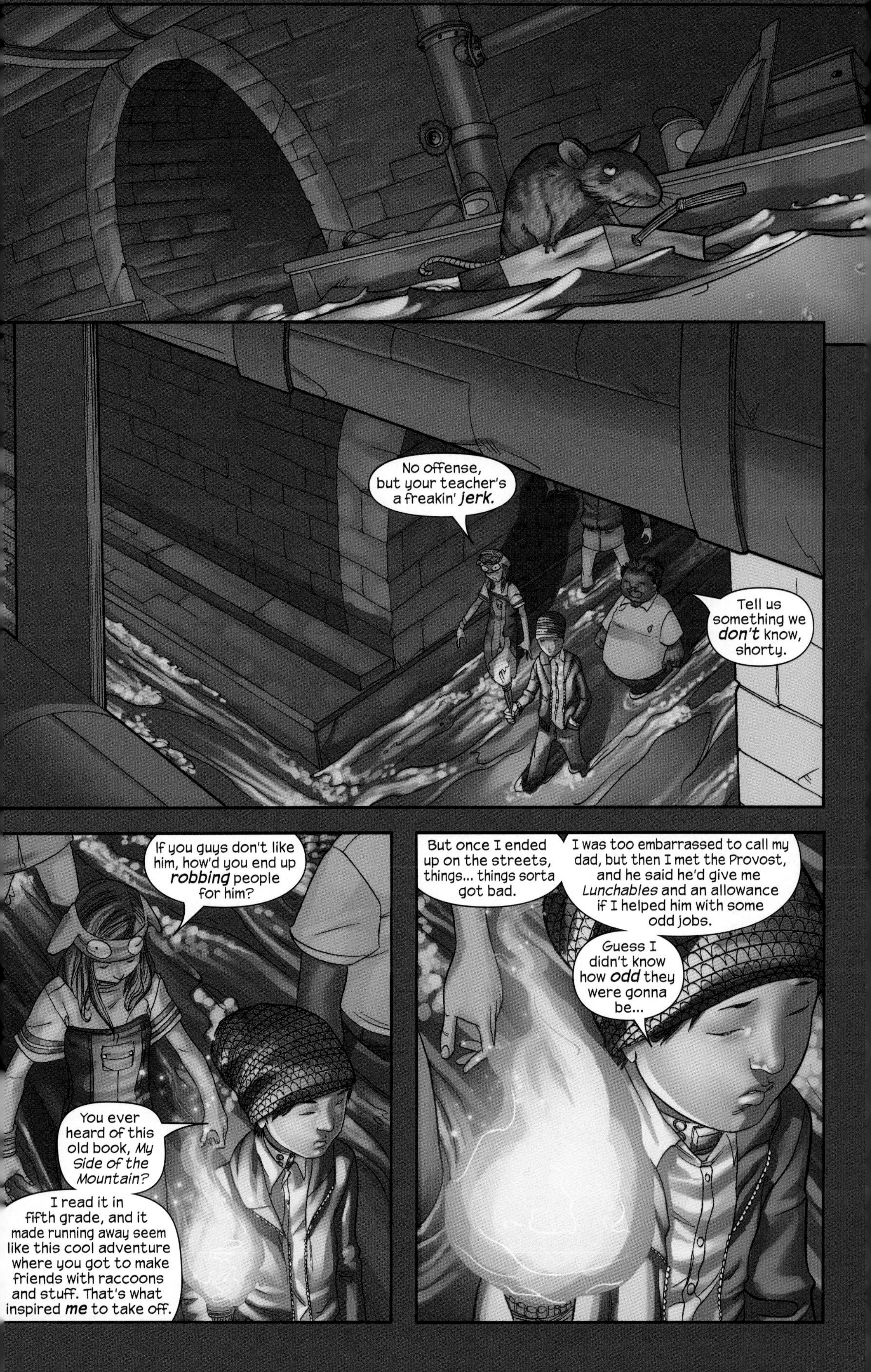
No offense, but your teacher's a freakin' *jerk.*
Tell us something we *don't* know, shorty.
If you guys don't like him, how'd you end up *robbing* people for him?
You ever heard of this old book, *My Side of the Mountain?*
I read it in fifth grade, and it made running away seem like this cool adventure where you got to make friends with raccoons and stuff. That's what inspired *me* to take off.
But once I ended up on the streets, things... things sorta got bad.
I was too embarrassed to call my dad, but then I met the Provost, and he said he'd give me *Lunchables* and an allowance if I helped him with some odd jobs.
Guess I didn't know how *odd* they were gonna be...

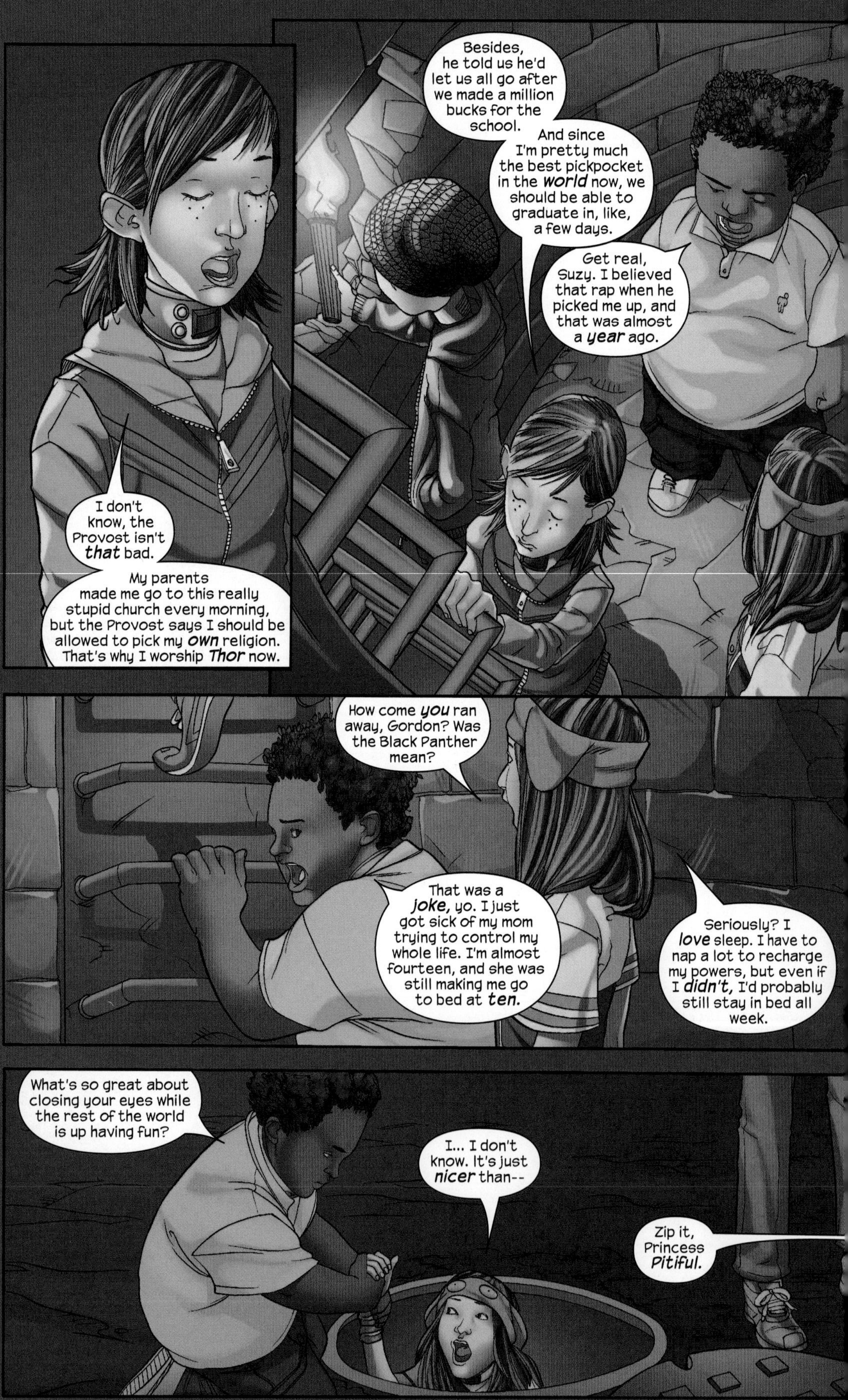

Besides, he told us he'd let us all go after we made a million bucks for the school.
And since I'm pretty much the best pickpocket in the *world* now, we should be able to graduate in, like, a few days.
Get real, Suzy. I believed that rap when he picked me up, and that was almost a *year* ago.
I don't know, the Provost isn't *that* bad.
My parents made me go to this really stupid church every morning, but the Provost says I should be allowed to pick my *own* religion. That's why I worship *Thor* now.
How come *you* ran away, Gordon? Was the Black Panther mean?
That was a *joke,* yo. I just got sick of my mom trying to control my whole life. I'm almost fourteen, and she was still making me go to bed at *ten.*
Seriously? I *love* sleep. I have to nap a lot to recharge my powers, but even if I *didn't,* I'd probably still stay in bed all week.
What's so great about closing your eyes while the rest of the world is up having fun?
I... I don't know. It's just *nicer* than--
Zip it, Princess *Pitiful.*

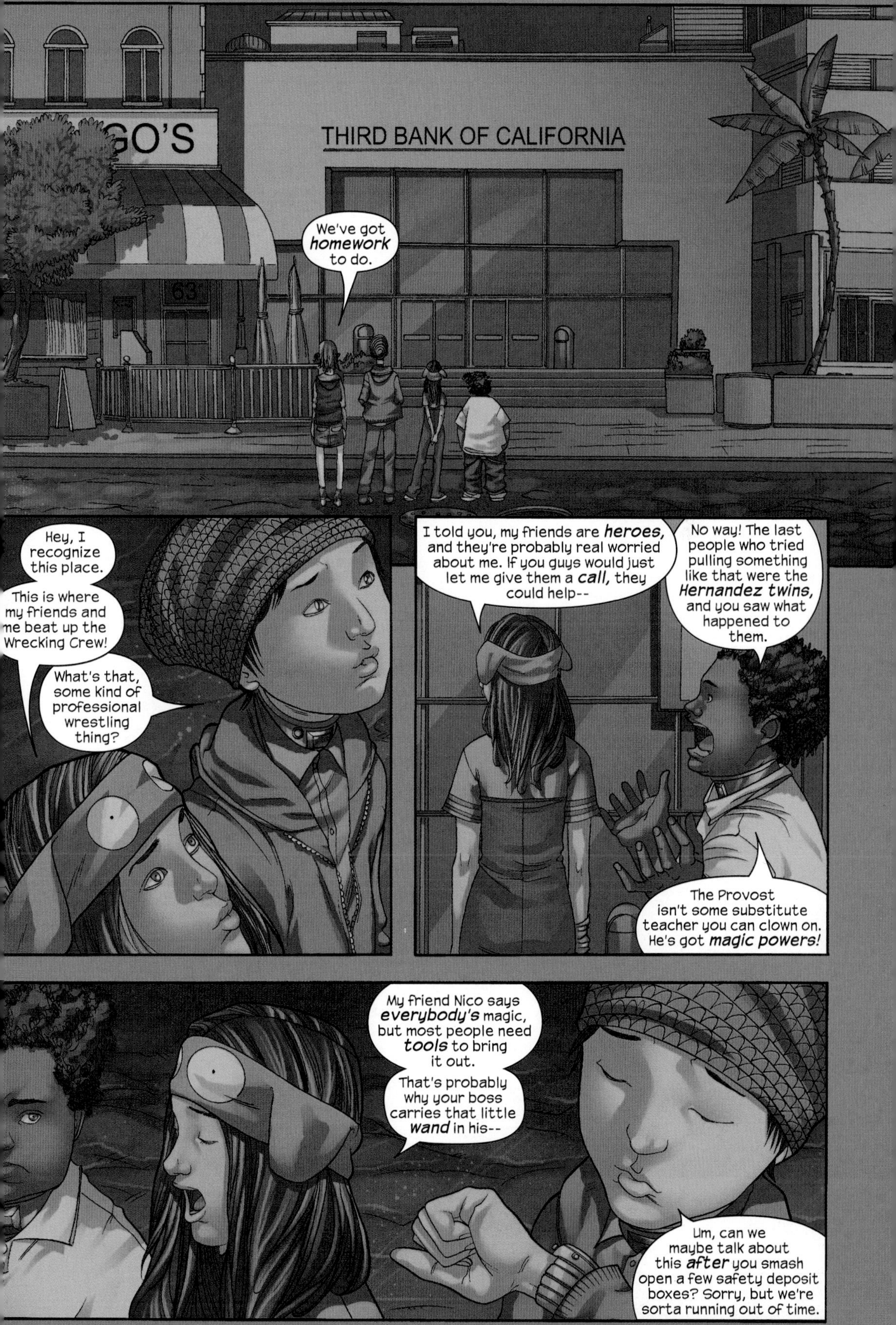

GO'S
THIRD BANK OF CALIFORNIA
63
We've got homework to do.
Hey, I recognize this place.
This is where my friends and me beat up the Wrecking Crew!
What's that, some kind of professional wrestling thing?
I told you, my friends are heroes, and they're probably real worried about me. If you guys would just let me give them a call, they could help--
No way! The last people who tried pulling something like that were the Hernandez twins, and you saw what happened to them.
The Provost isn't some substitute teacher you can clown on. He's got magic powers!
My friend Nico says everybody's magic, but most people need tools to bring it out.
That's probably why your boss carries that little wand in his--
Um, can we maybe talk about this after you smash open a few safety deposit boxes? Sorry, but we're sorta running out of time.

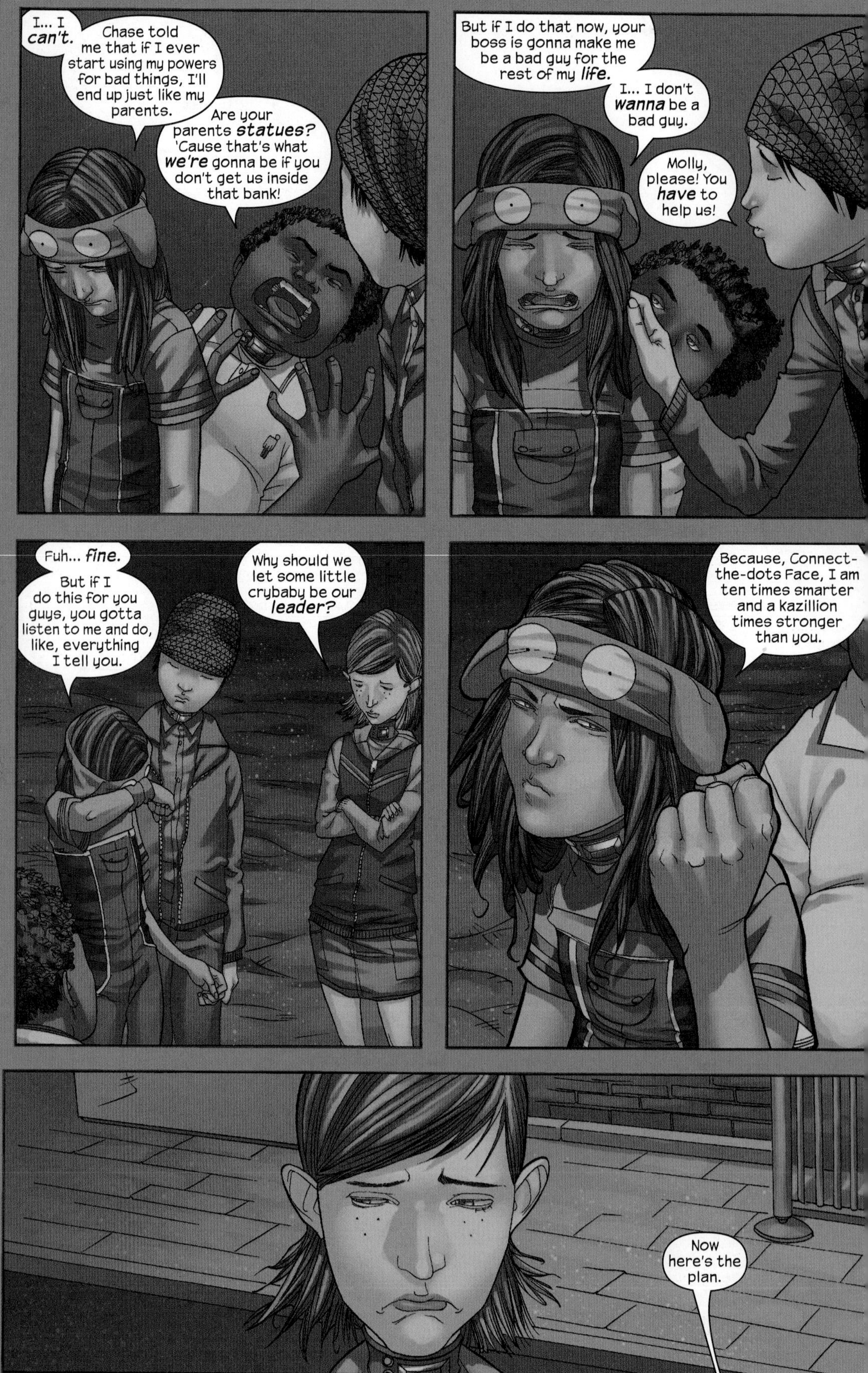
I... I can't.
Chase told me that if I ever start using my powers for bad things, I'll end up just like my parents.
Are your parents statues? 'Cause that's what we're gonna be if you don't get us inside that bank!
But if I do that now, your boss is gonna make me be a bad guy for the rest of my life.
I... I don't wanna be a bad guy.
Molly, please! You have to help us!
Fuh... fine.
But if I do this for you guys, you gotta listen to me and do, like, everything I tell you.
Why should we let some little crybaby be our leader?
Because, Connect-the-dots Face, I am ten times smarter and a kazillion times stronger than you.
Now here's the plan.

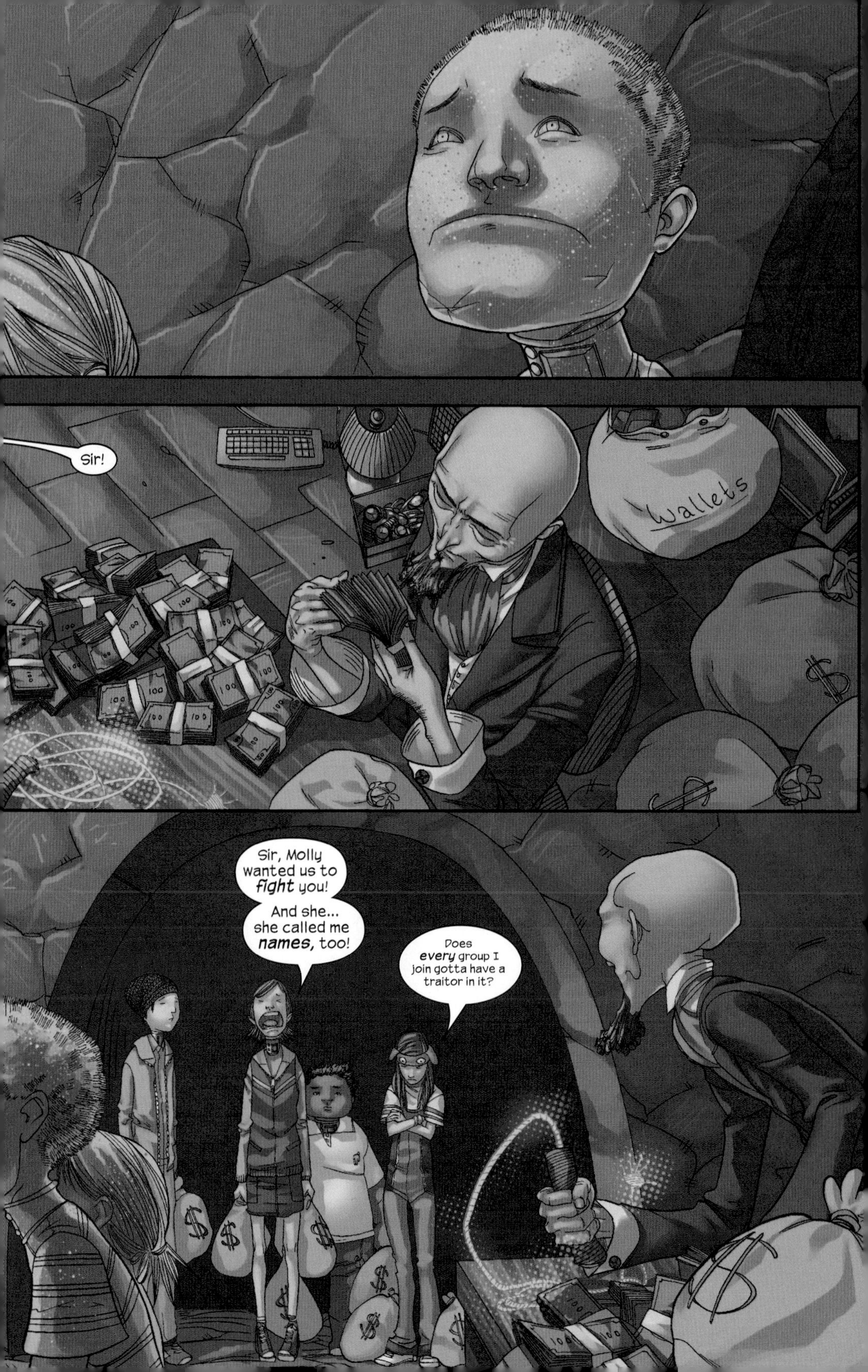
Sir!
Wallets
Sir, Molly wanted us to *fight* you!
And she... she called me ***names,*** too!
Does ***every*** group I join gotta have a traitor in it?

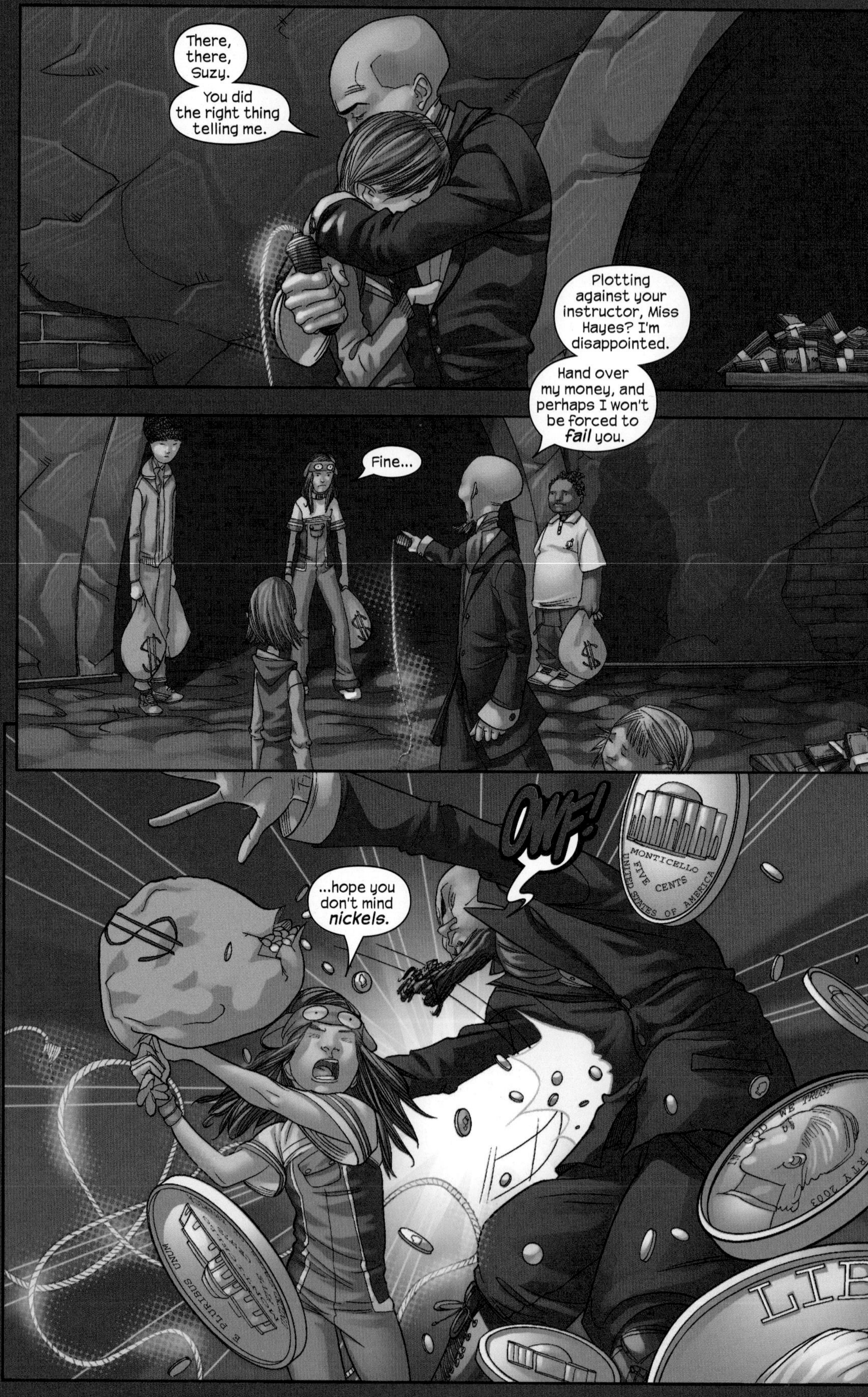
There, there, Suzy.
You did the right thing telling me.
Plotting against your instructor, Miss Hayes? I'm disappointed.
Hand over my money, and perhaps I won't be forced to *fail* you.
Fine...
OWF!
...hope you don't mind *nickels*.
MONTICELLO
FIVE CENTS
UNITED STATES OF AMERICA
IN GOD WE TRUST
2003
E PLURIBUS UNUM

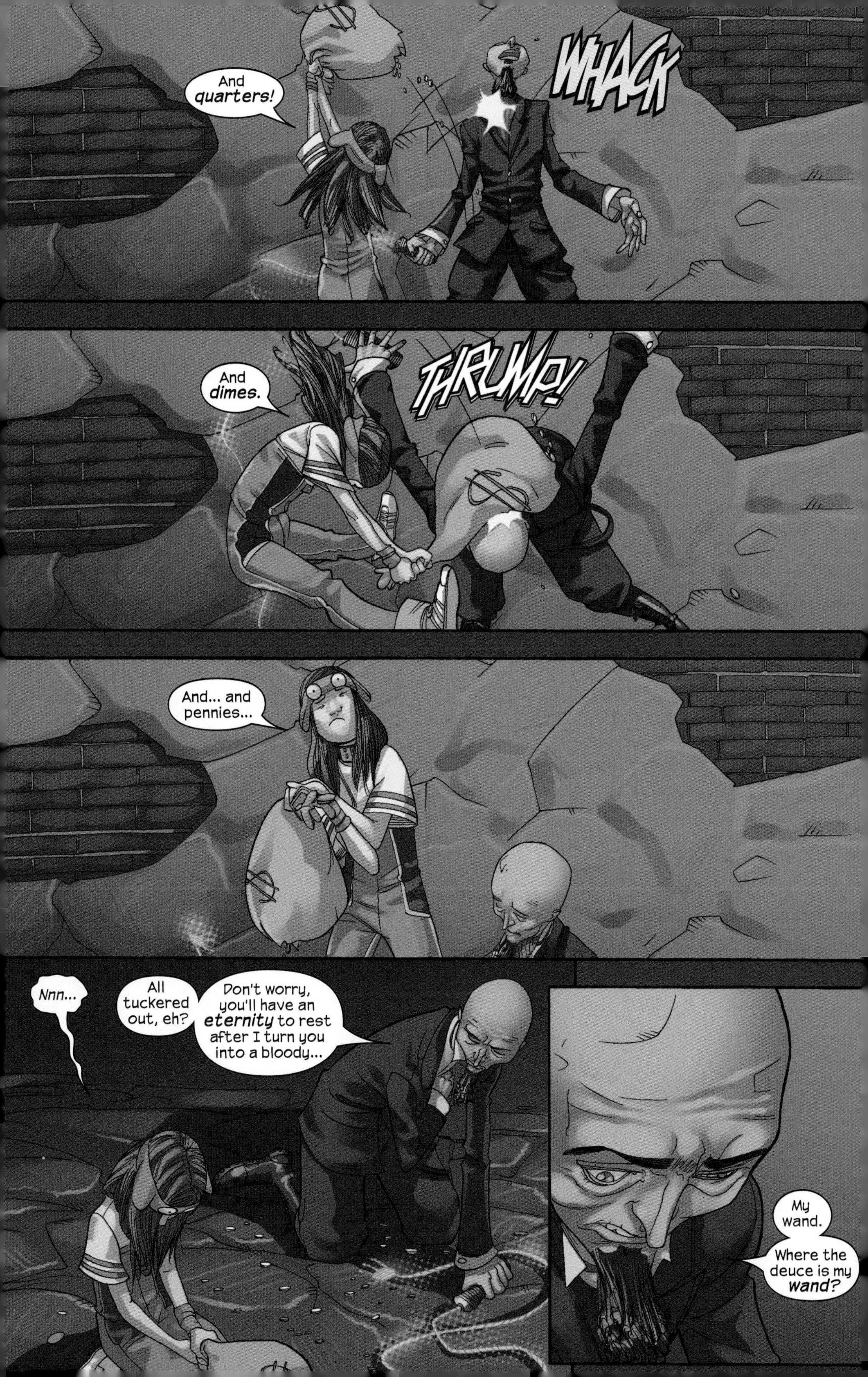
And quarters!
WHACK
And dimes.
THRUMP!
And... and pennies...
Nnn...
All tuckered out, eh?
Don't worry, you'll have an eternity to rest after I turn you into a bloody...
My wand.
Where the deuce is my wand?

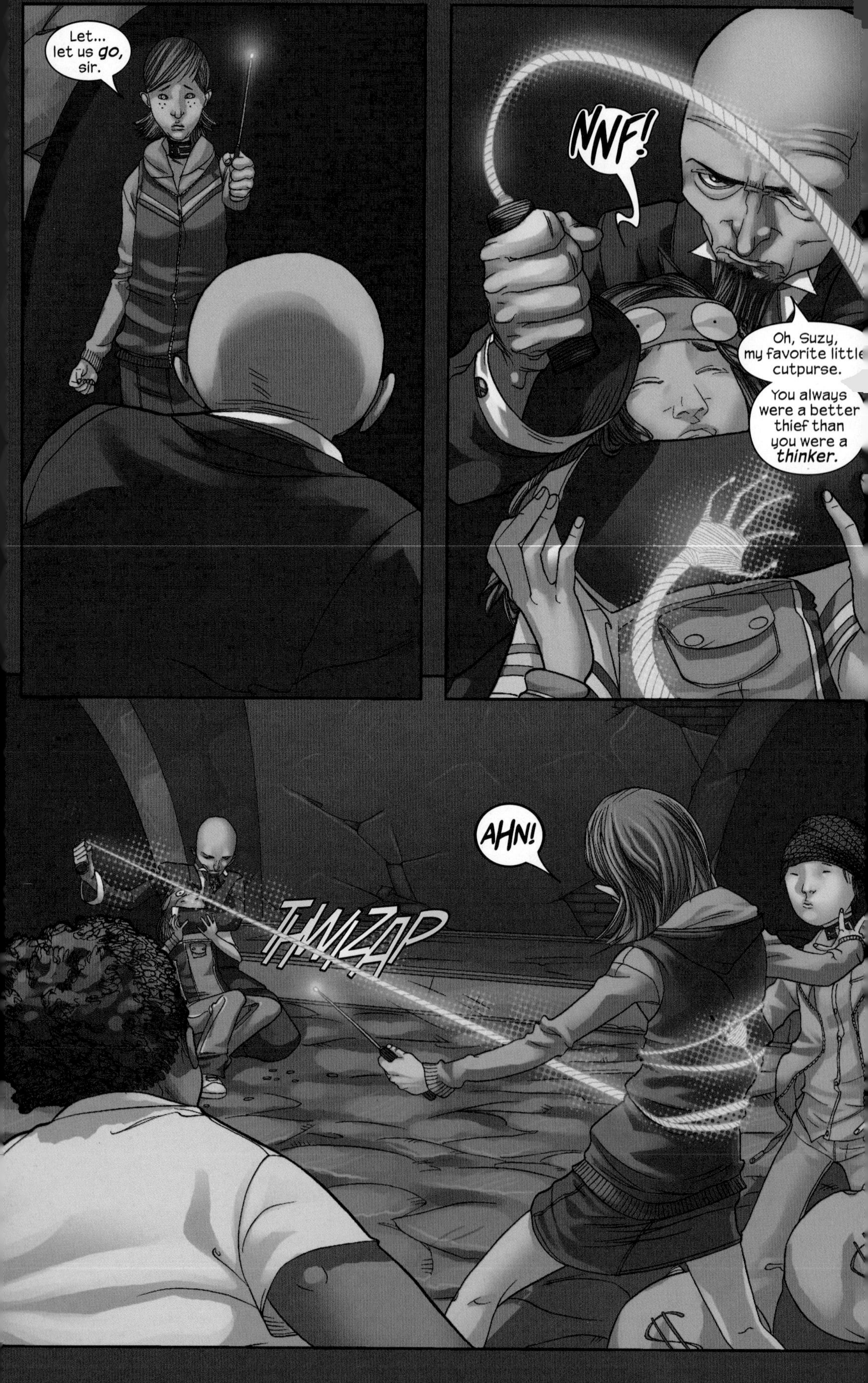
Let... let us go, sir.
NNF!
Oh, Suzy, my favorite little cutpurse.
You always were a better thief than you were a thinker.
AHN!
THWIZAP

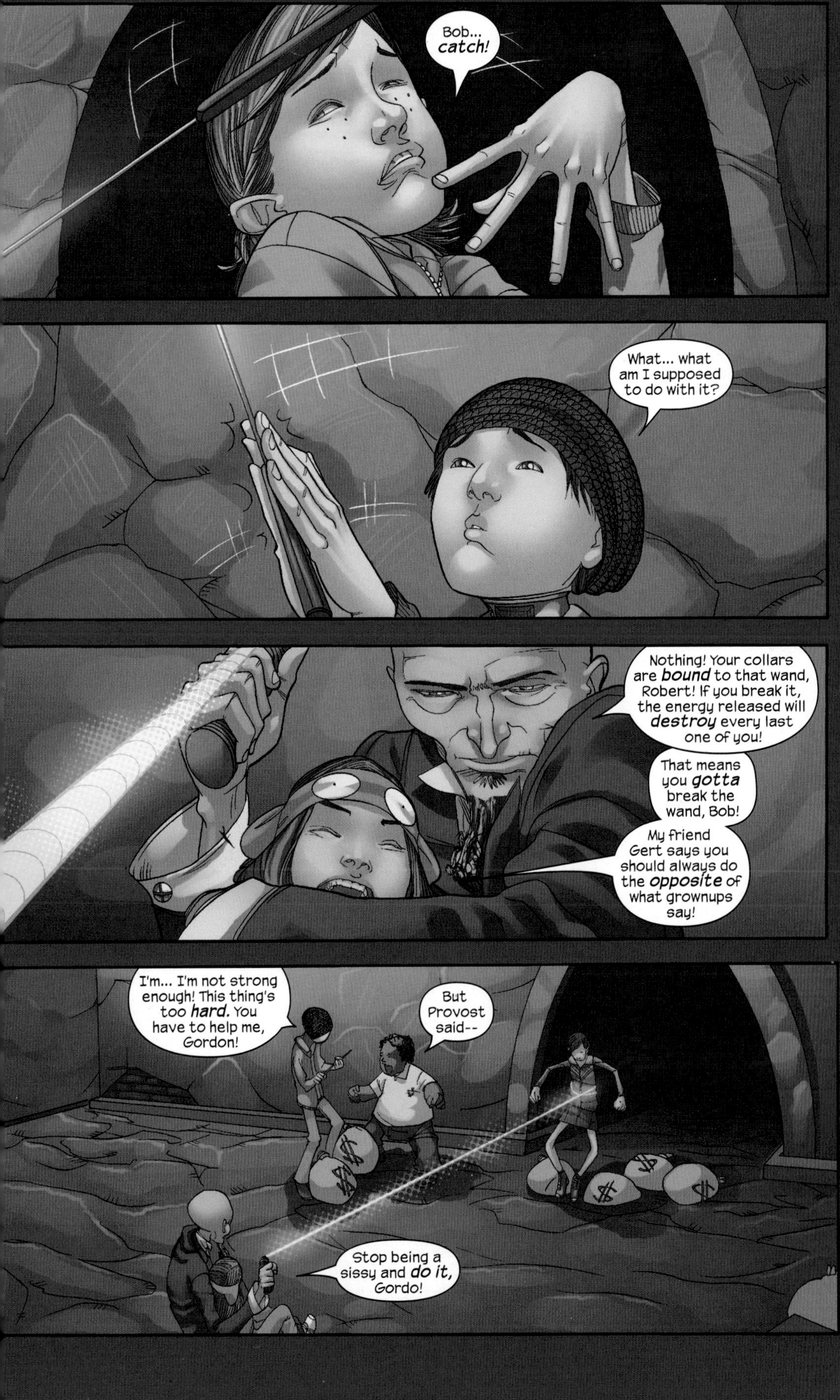
Bob... catch!
What... what am I supposed to do with it?
Nothing! Your collars are bound to that wand, Robert! If you break it, the energy released will destroy every last one of you!
That means you gotta break the wand, Bob!
My friend Gert says you should always do the opposite of what grownups say!
I'm... I'm not strong enough! This thing's too hard. You have to help me, Gordon!
But Provost said--
Stop being a sissy and do it, Gordo!

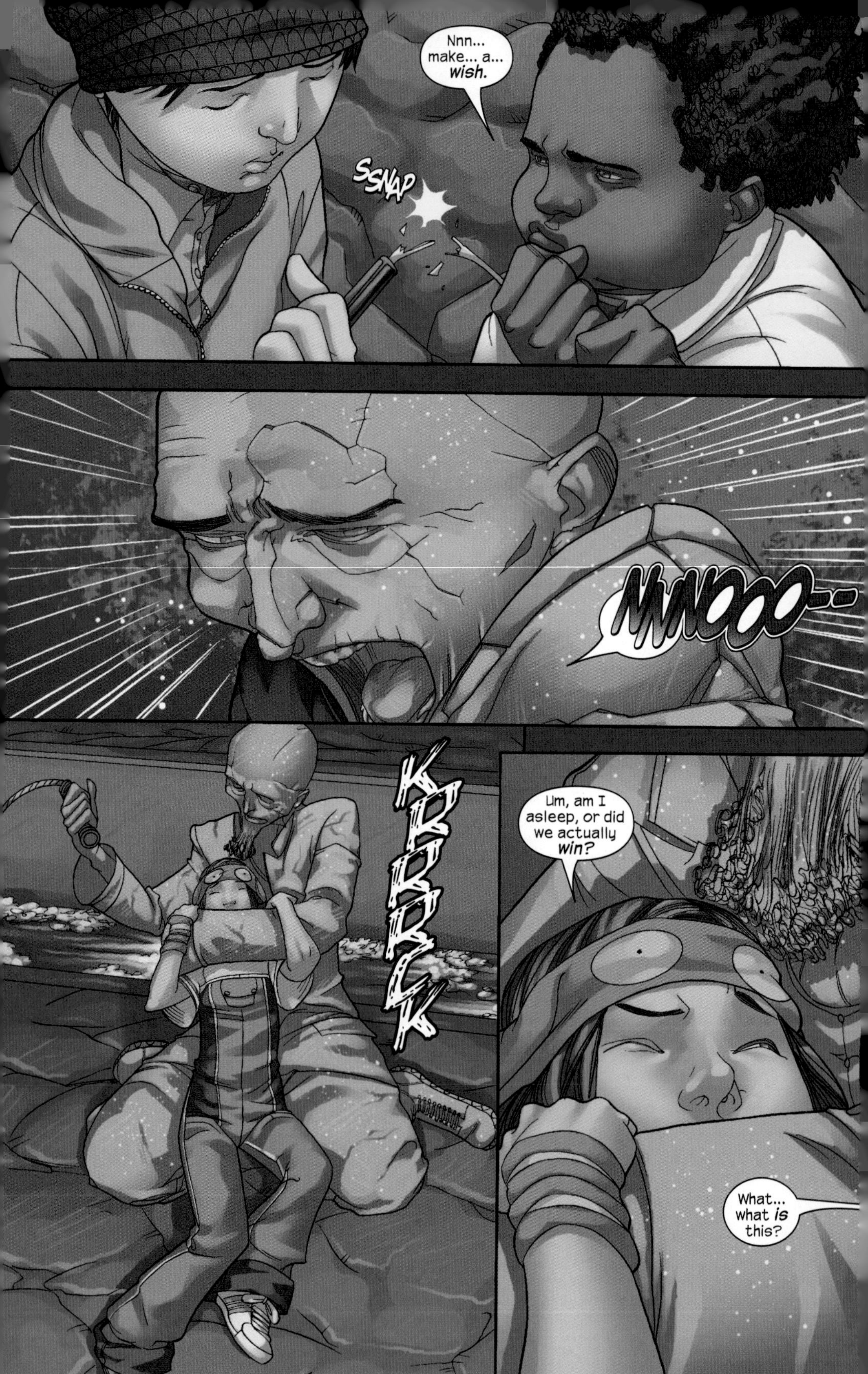
Nnn... make... a... wish.
SSNAP
MMNOOO--
KRRRRCK
Um, am I asleep, or did we actually win?
What... what is this?

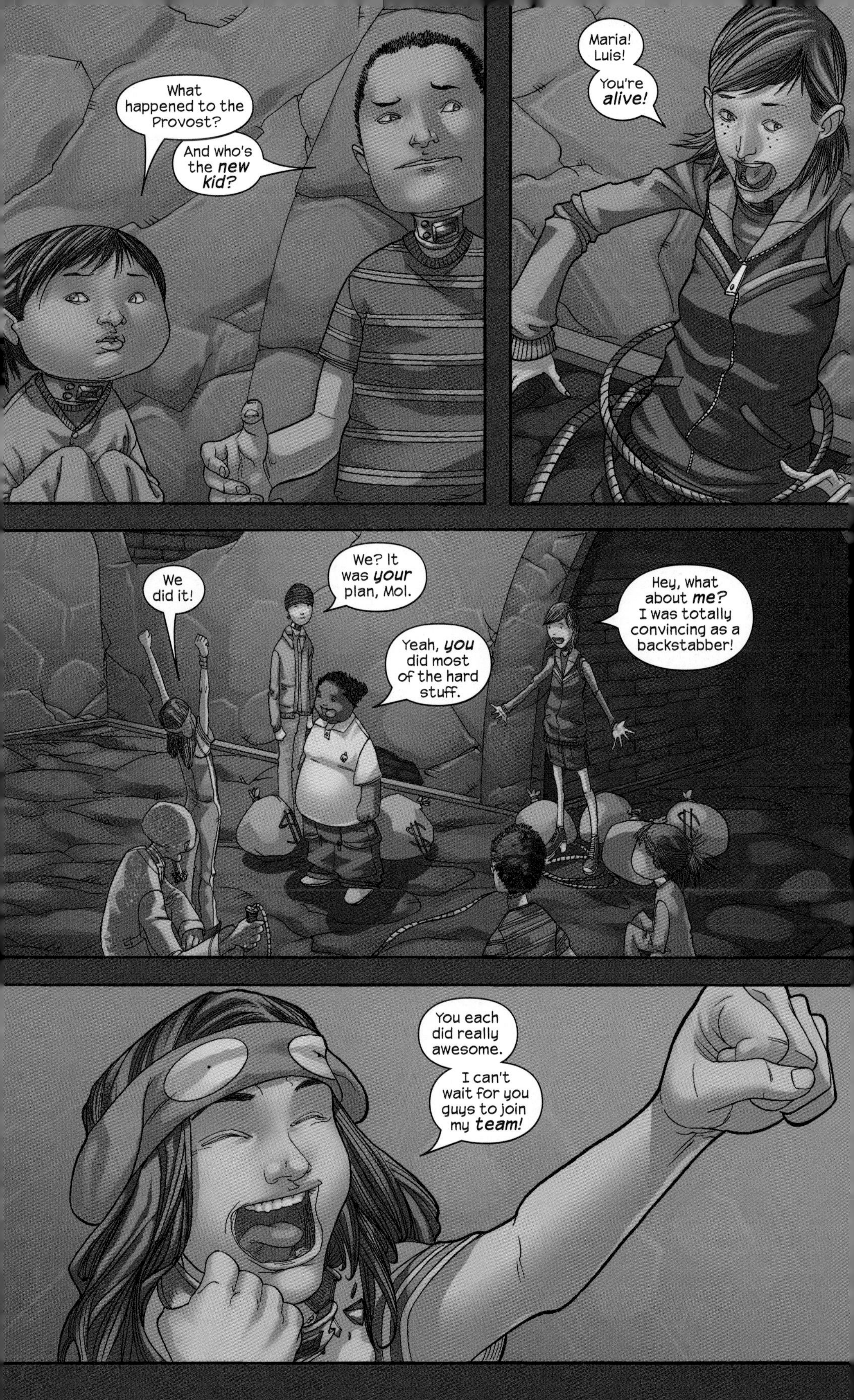
What happened to the Provost?
And who's the *new kid?*
Maria! Luis!
You're *alive!*
We did it!
We? It was *your* plan, Mol.
Yeah, *you* did most of the hard stuff.
Hey, what about *me?* I was totally convincing as a backstabber!
You each did really awesome.
I can't wait for you guys to join my *team!*

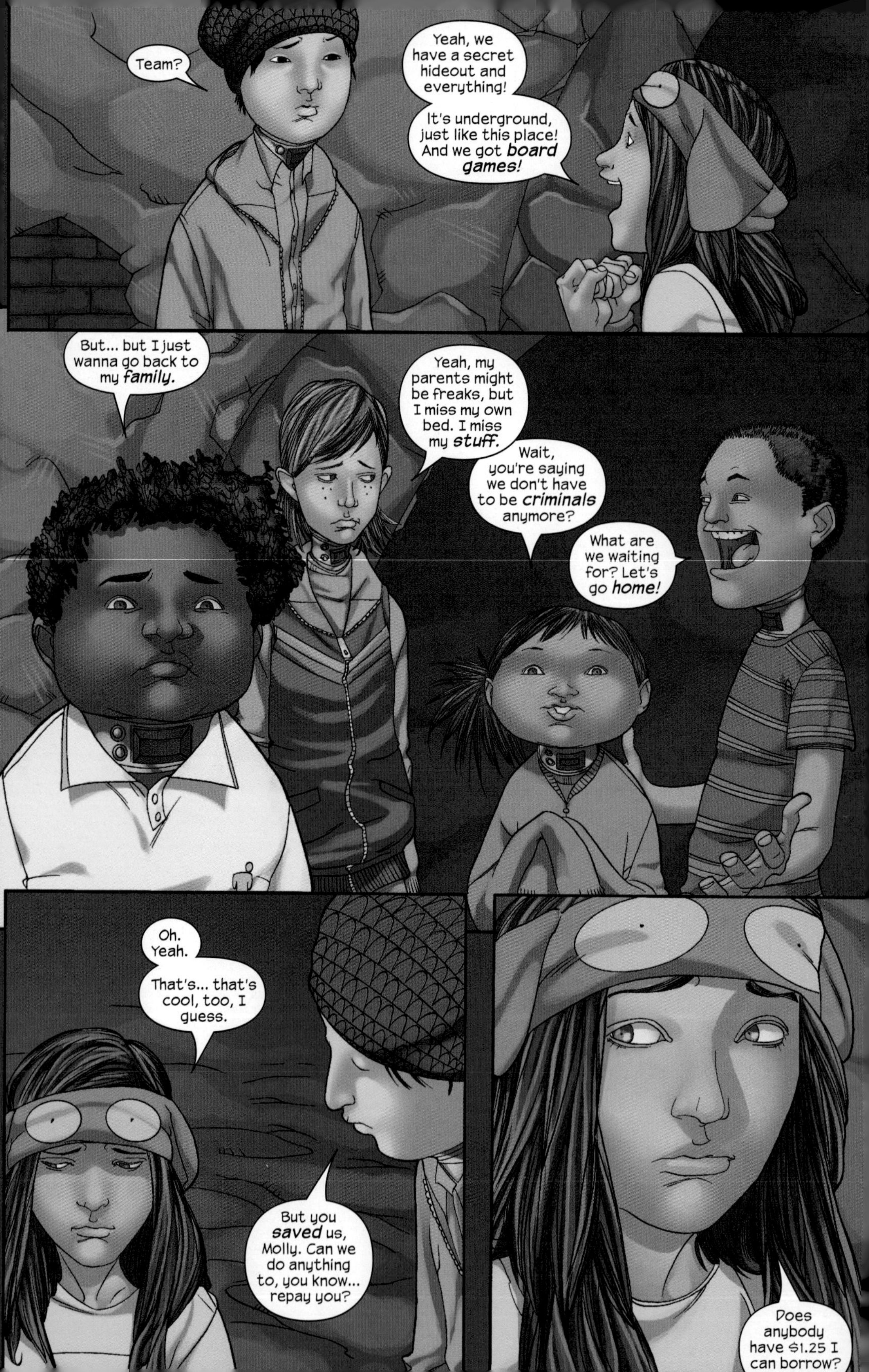
Team?
Yeah, we have a secret hideout and everything!
It's underground, just like this place! And we got *board games!*
But... but I just wanna go back to my *family.*
Yeah, my parents might be freaks, but I miss my own bed. I miss my *stuff.*
Wait, you're saying we don't have to be *criminals* anymore?
What are we waiting for? Let's go *home!*
Oh. Yeah.
That's... that's cool, too, I guess.
But you *saved* us, Molly. Can we do anything to, you know... repay you?
Does anybody have $1.25 I can borrow?

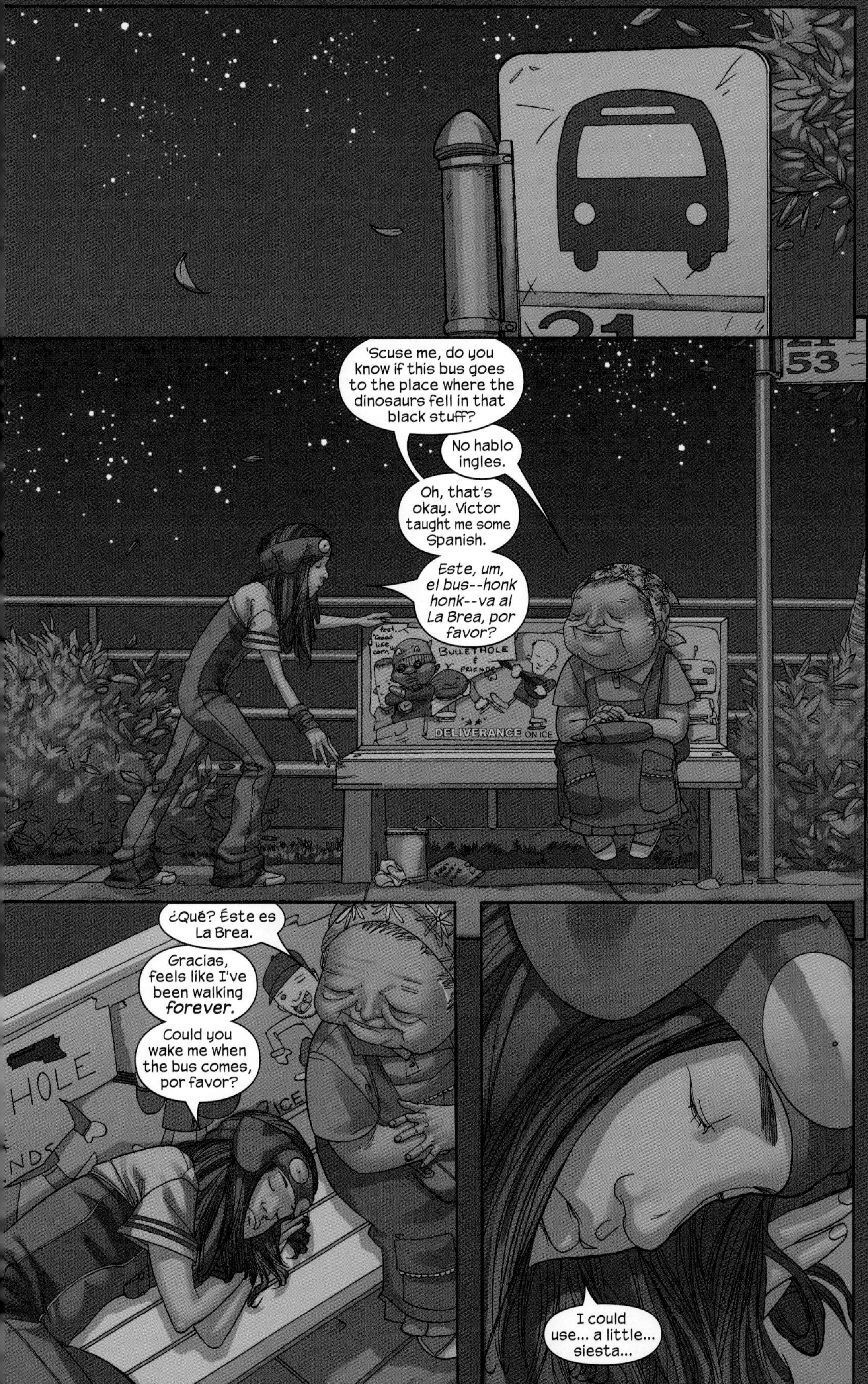
21
53
'Scuse me, do you know if this bus goes to the place where the dinosaurs fell in that black stuff?
No hablo ingles.
Oh, that's okay. Victor taught me some Spanish.
Este, um, el bus--honk honk--va al La Brea, por favor?
BULLETHOLE & FRIENDS
DELIVERANCE ON ICE
¿Qué? Éste es La Brea.
Gracias, feels like I've been walking *forever.*
Could you wake me when the bus comes, por favor?
I could use... a little... siesta...

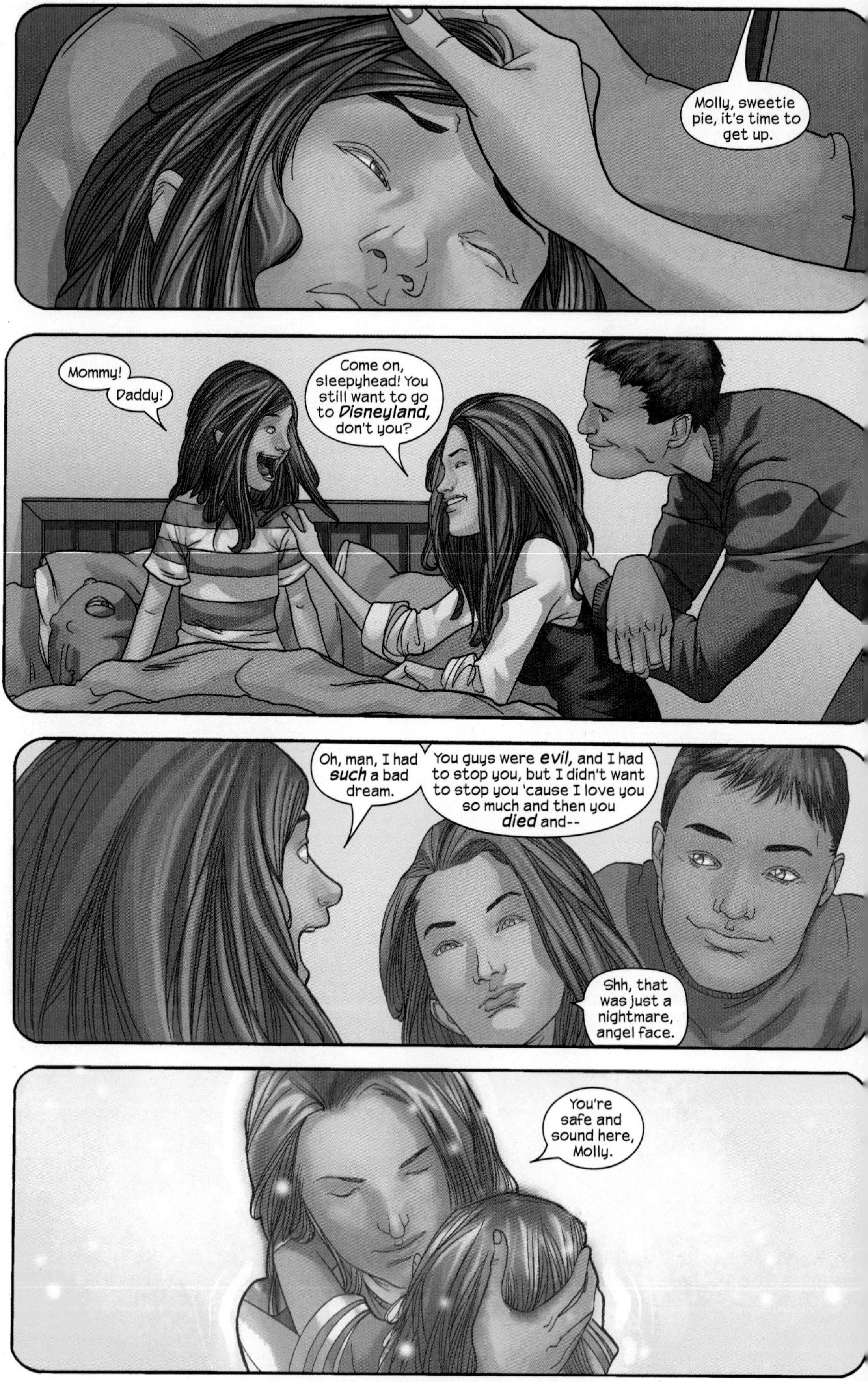
Molly, sweetie pie, it's time to get up.
Mommy!
Daddy!
Come on, sleepyhead! You still want to go to *Disneyland,* don't you?
Oh, man, I had *such* a bad dream.
You guys were *evil,* and I had to stop you, but I didn't want to stop you 'cause I love you so much and then you *died* and--
Shh, that was just a nightmare, angel face.
You're safe and sound here, Molly.

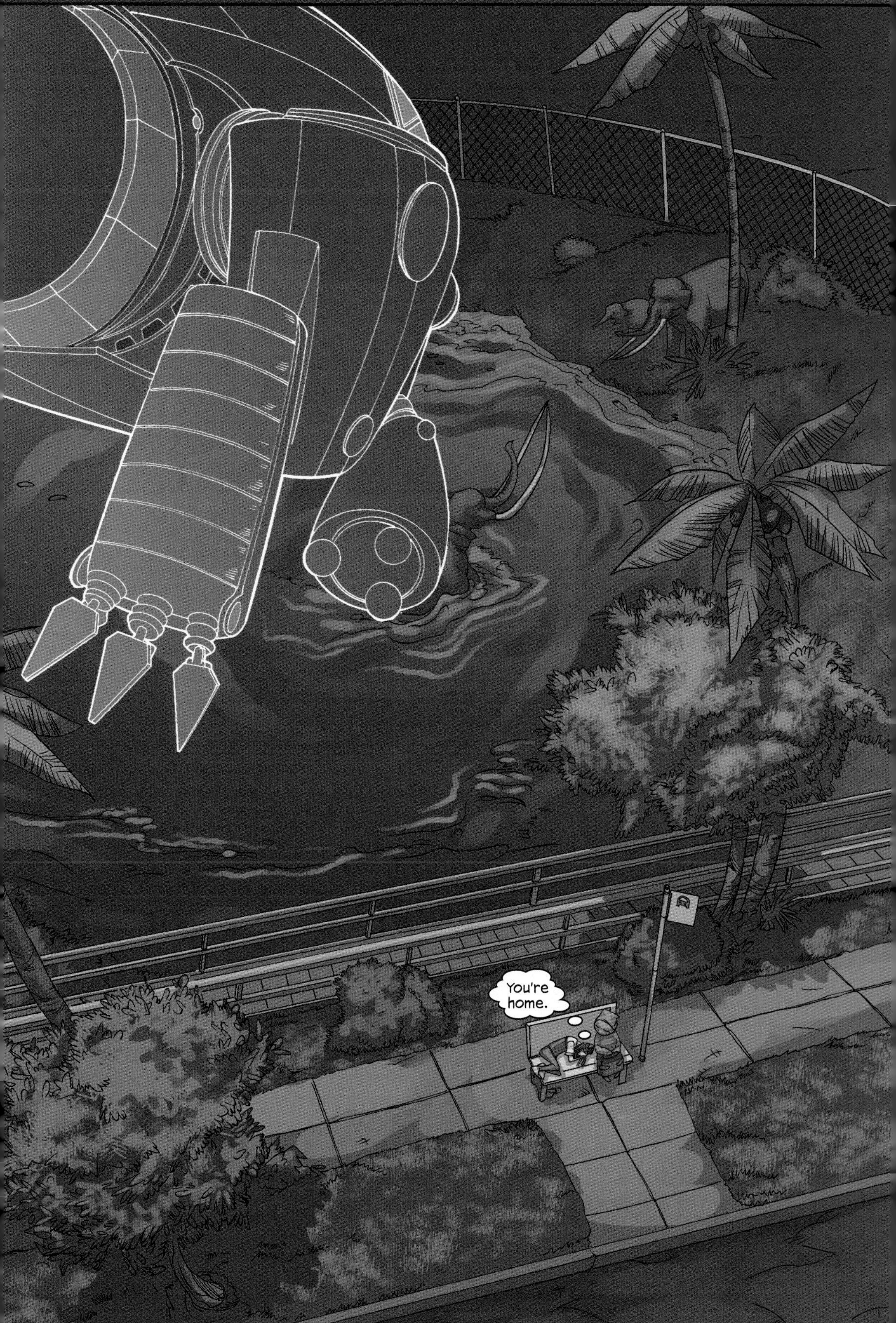
You're home.

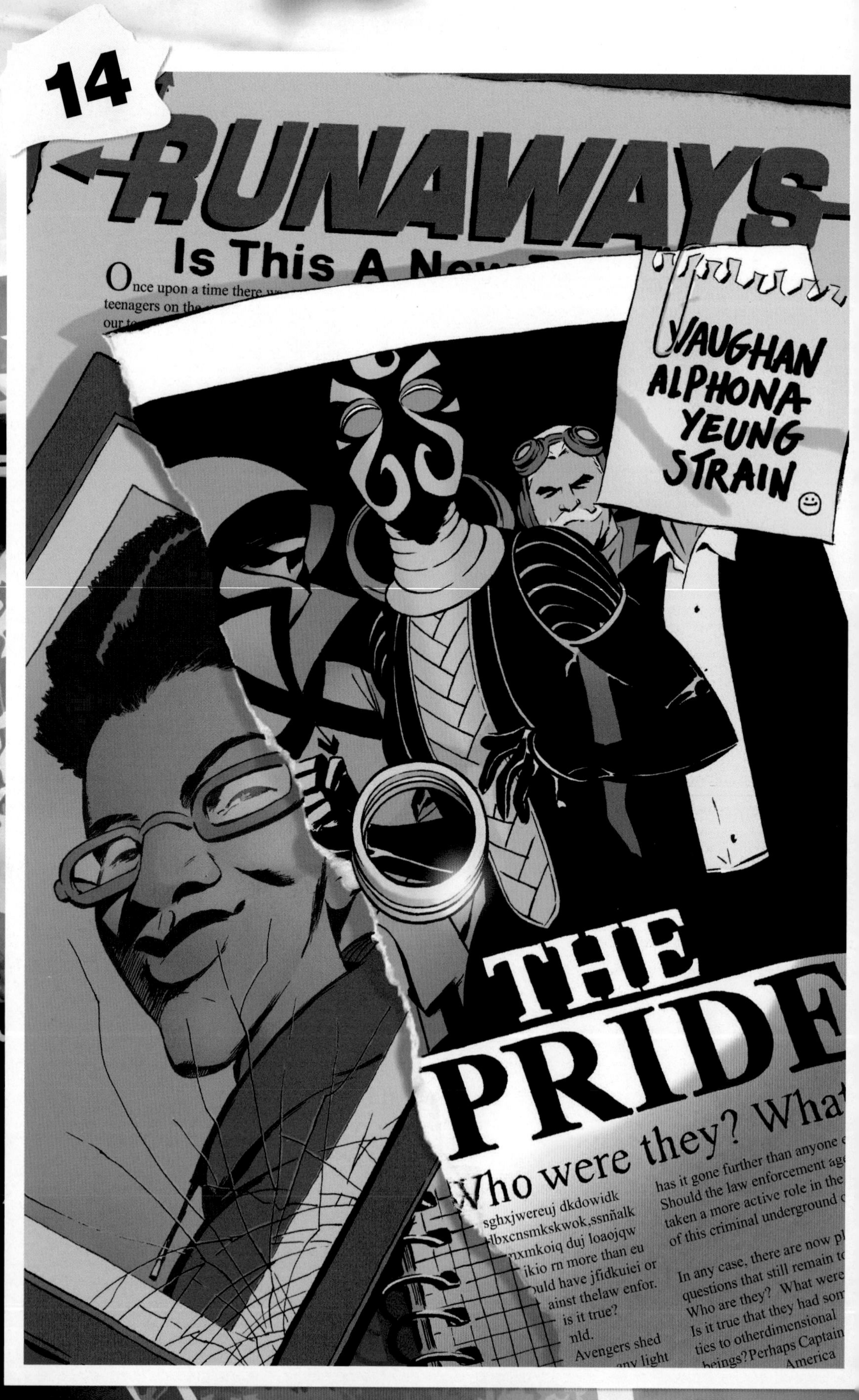
14
RUNAWAYS
Is This A New
Once upon a time there w
teenagers on th
VAUGHAN
ALPHONA
YEUNG
STRAIN
THE
PRIDE
Who were they? Wha
sghxjwereuj dkdowidk
dbxcnsmkskwok,ssññalk
nxmkoiq duj loaojqw
ikio rn more than eu
ould have jfidkuiei or
ainst thelaw enfor.
is it true?
nld.
Avengers shed
has it gone further than anyone
Should the law enforcement ag
taken a more active role in the
of this criminal underground
In any case, there are now p
questions that still remain t
Who are they? What were
Is it true that they had som
ties to otherdimensional
beings?Perhaps Captain
America

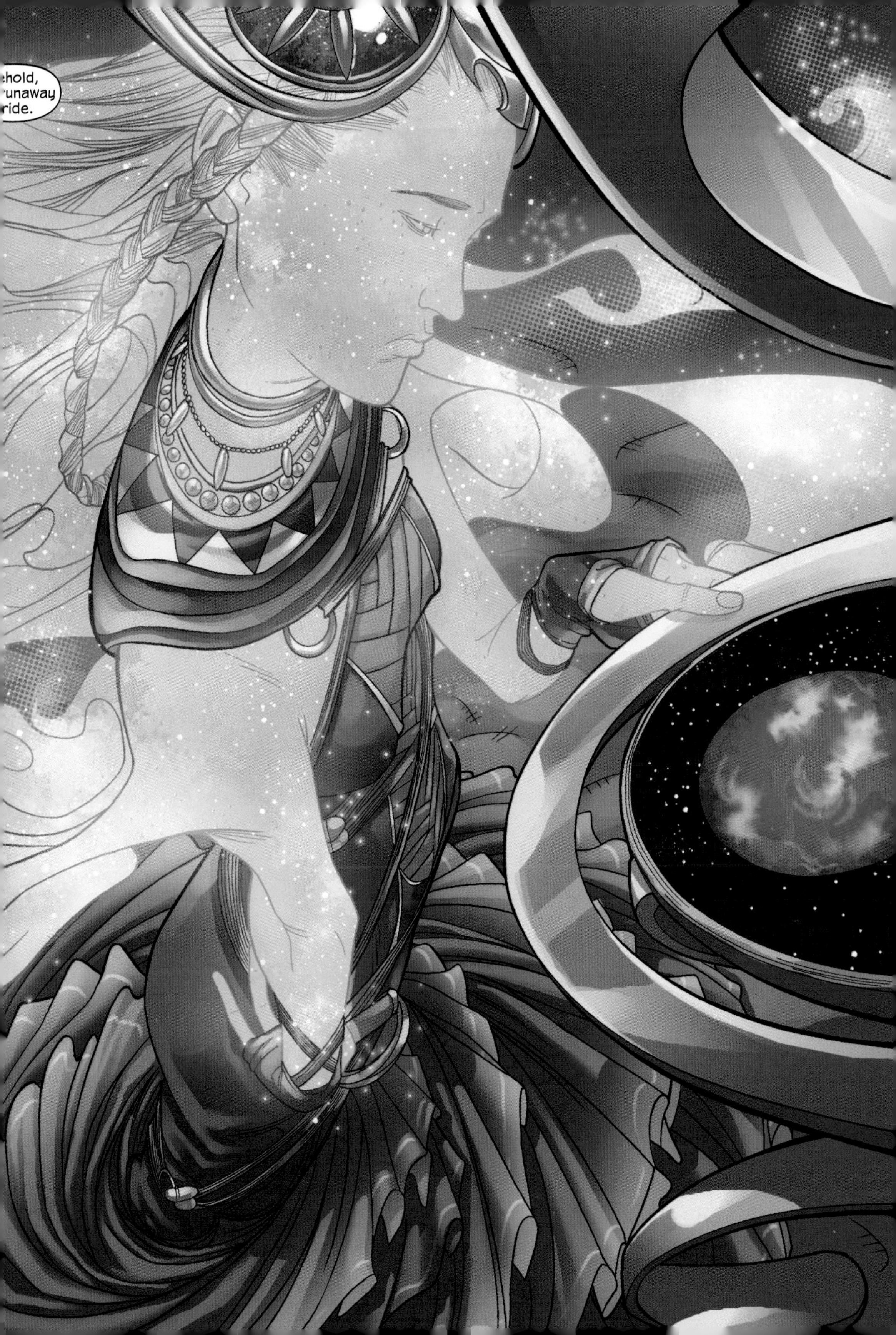
ehold,
runaway
ride.

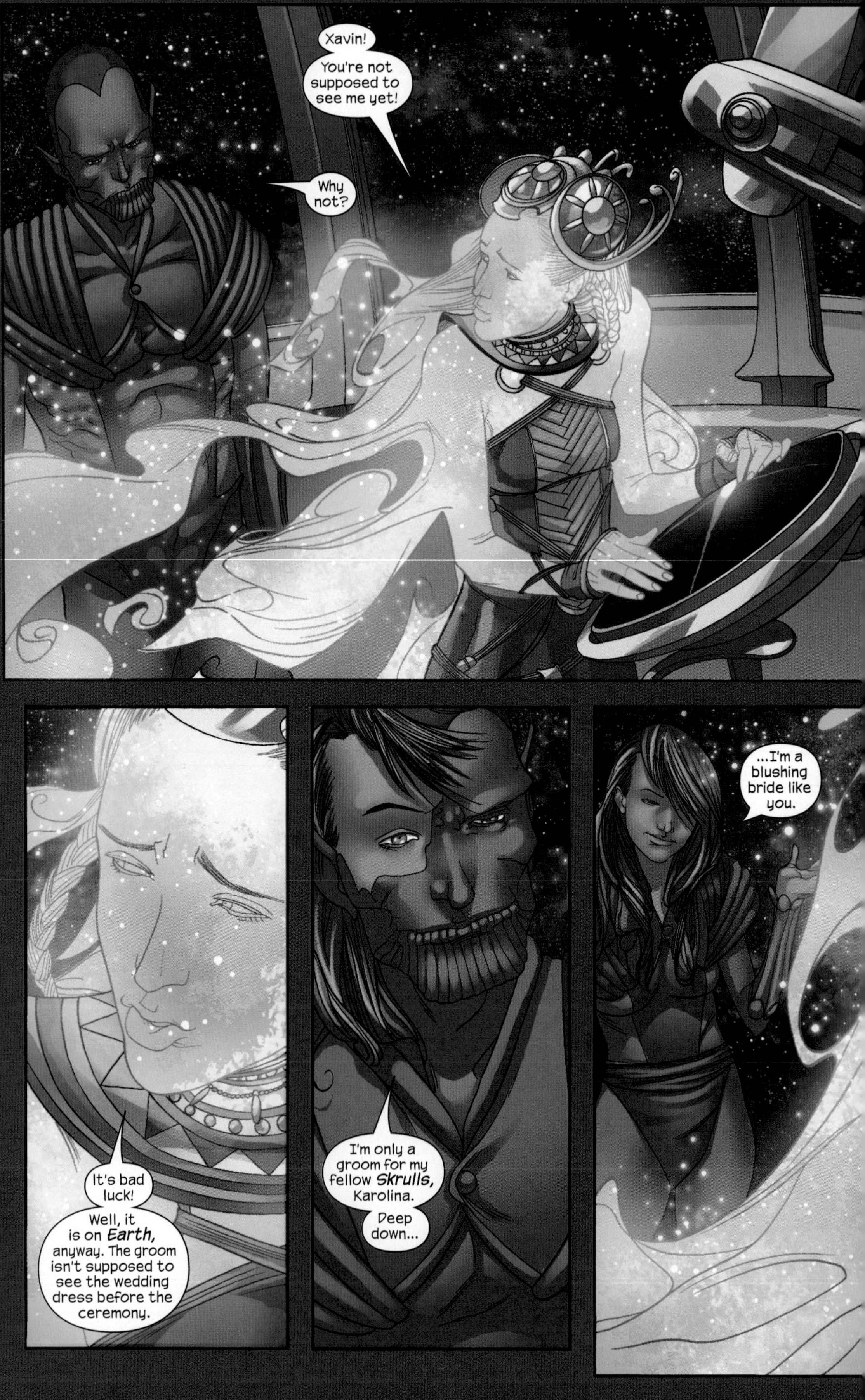

Xavin!
You're not supposed to see me yet!
Why not?
It's bad luck!
Well, it is on *Earth*, anyway. The groom isn't supposed to see the wedding dress before the ceremony.
I'm only a groom for my fellow *Skrulls*, Karolina.
Deep down...
...I'm a blushing bride like you.

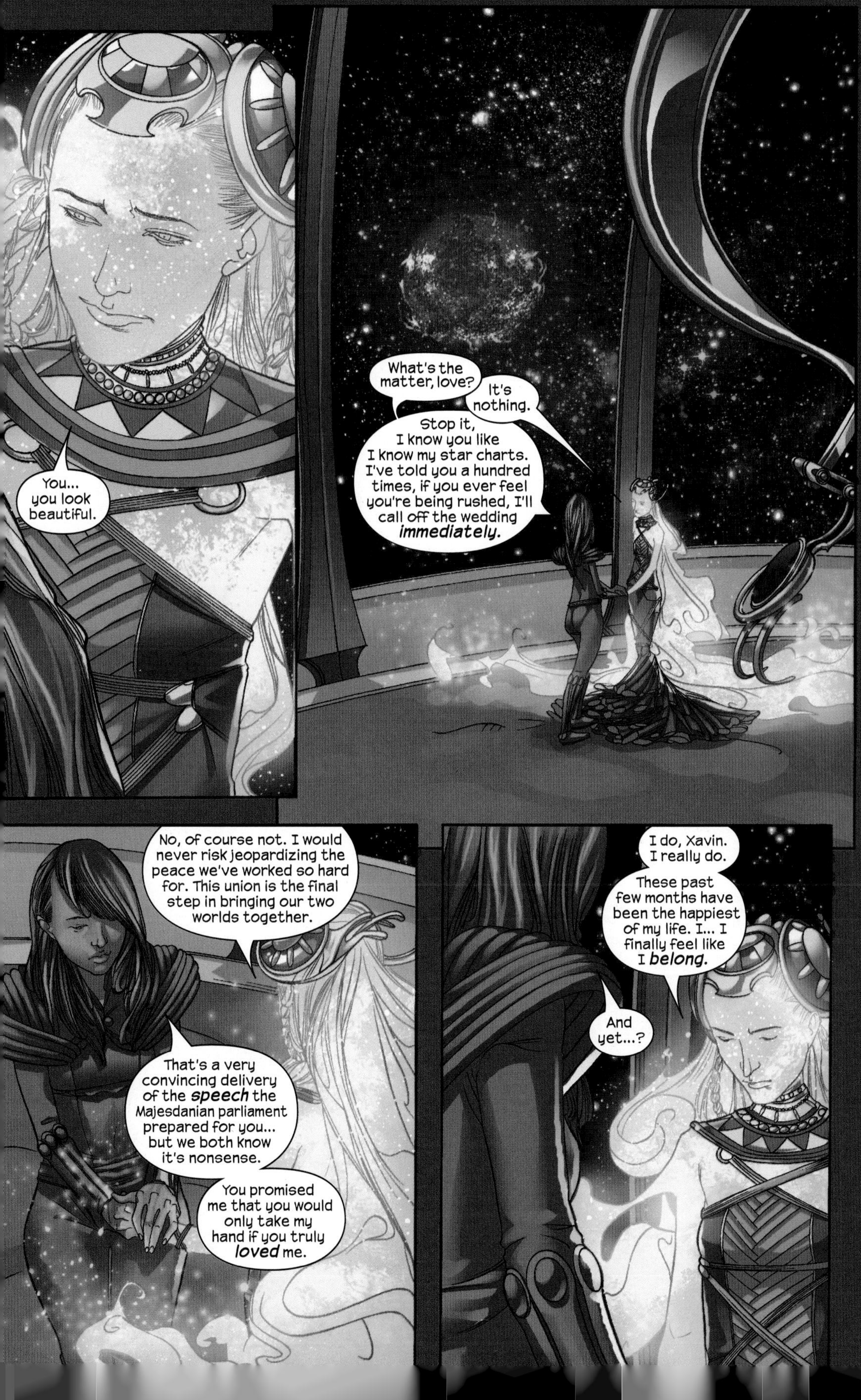
You... you look beautiful.
What's the matter, love?
It's nothing.
Stop it, I know you like I know my star charts. I've told you a hundred times, if you ever feel you're being rushed, I'll call off the wedding *immediately*.
No, of course not. I would never risk jeopardizing the peace we've worked so hard for. This union is the final step in bringing our two worlds together.
That's a very convincing delivery of the *speech* the Majesdanian parliament prepared for you... but we both know it's nonsense.
You promised me that you would only take my hand if you truly *loved* me.
I do, Xavin. I really do.
These past few months have been the happiest of my life. I... I finally feel like I *belong*.
And yet...?

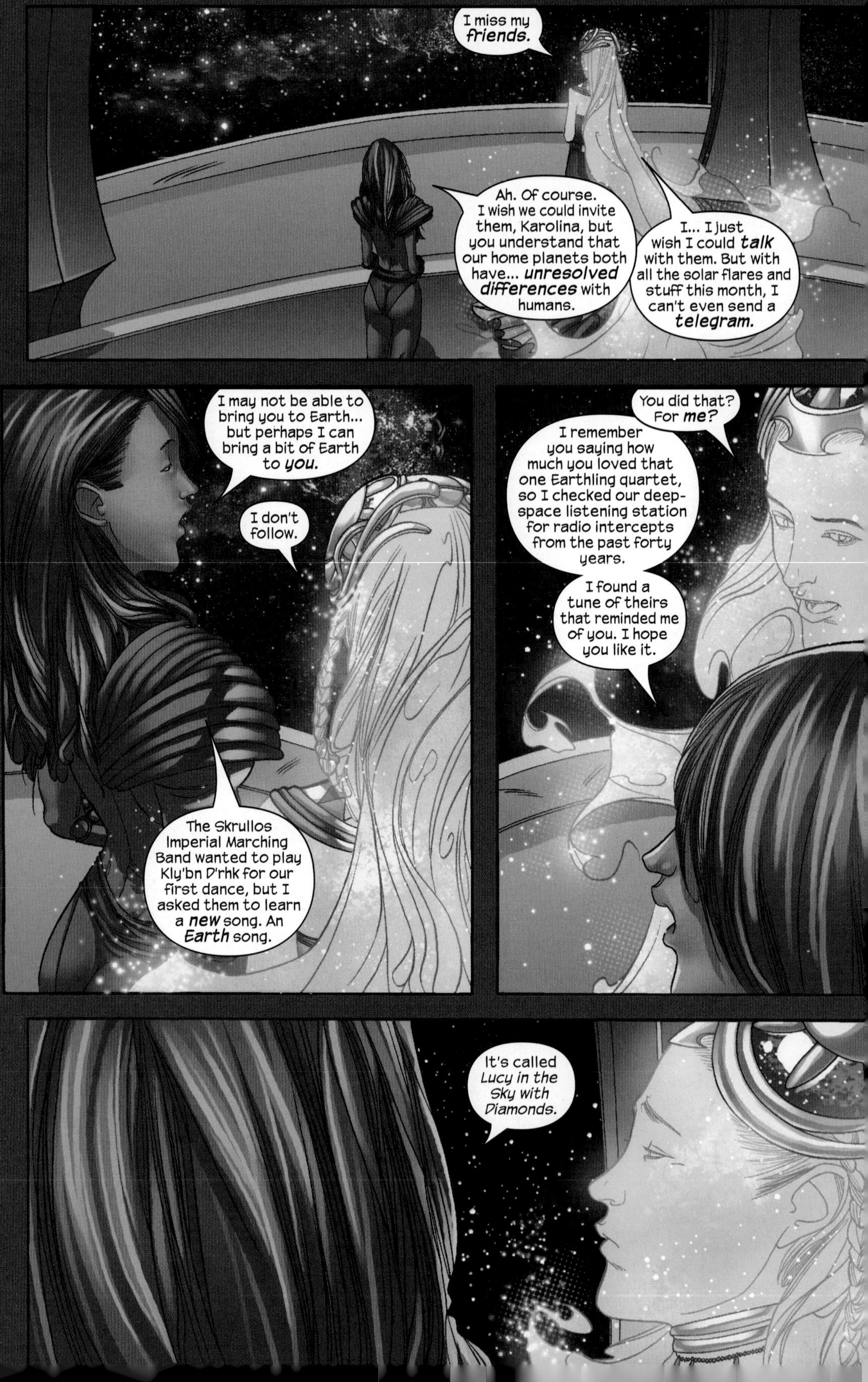
I miss my friends.
Ah. Of course. I wish we could invite them, Karolina, but you understand that our home planets both have... unresolved differences with humans.
I... I just wish I could talk with them. But with all the solar flares and stuff this month, I can't even send a telegram.
I may not be able to bring you to Earth... but perhaps I can bring a bit of Earth to you.
I don't follow.
The Skrullos Imperial Marching Band wanted to play Kly'bn D'rhk for our first dance, but I asked them to learn a new song. An Earth song.
You did that? For me?
I remember you saying how much you loved that one Earthling quartet, so I checked our deep-space listening station for radio intercepts from the past forty years.
I found a tune of theirs that reminded me of you. I hope you like it.
It's called Lucy in the Sky with Diamonds.

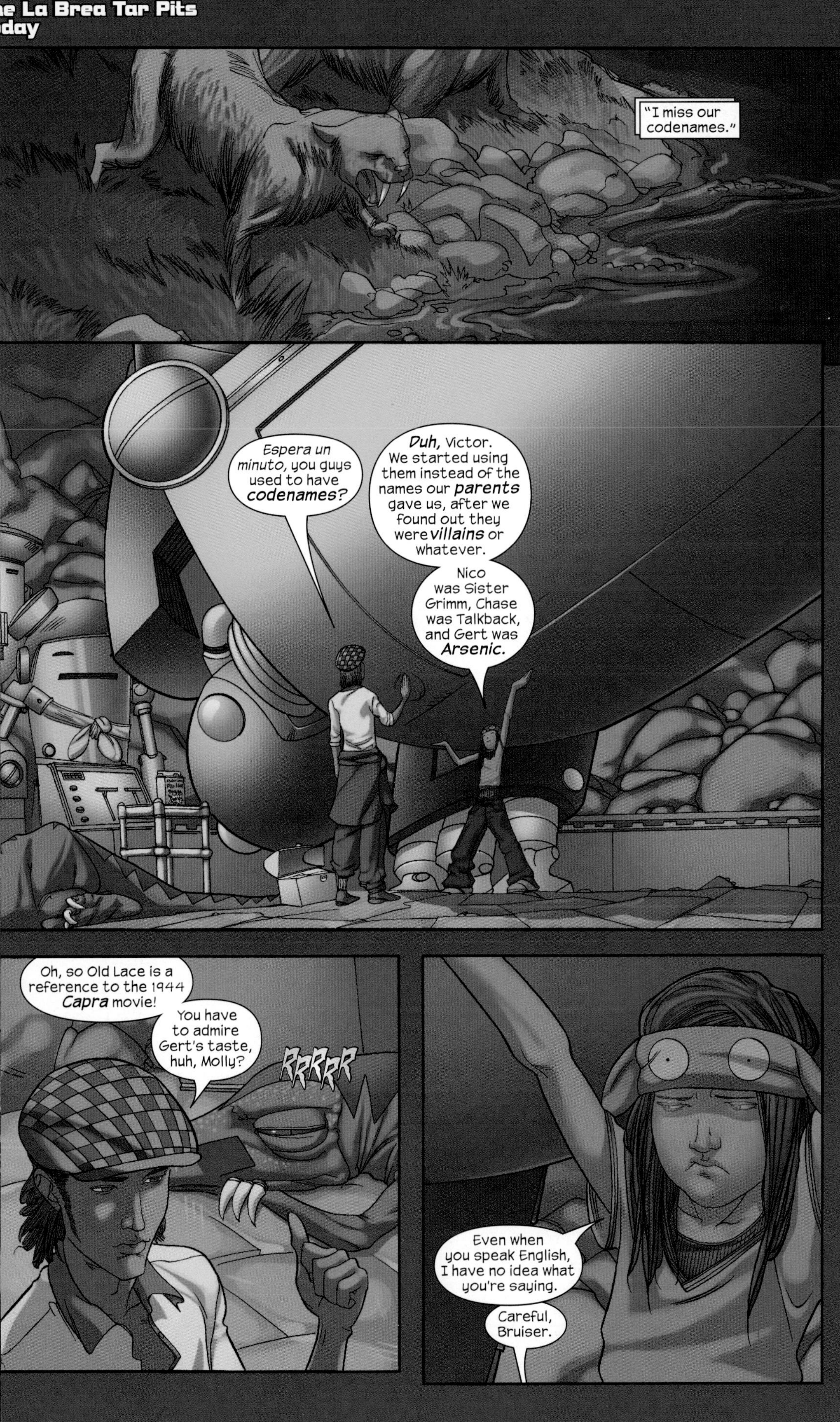

e La Brea Tar Pits
day
"I miss our codenames."
Espera un minuto, you guys used to have codenames?
Duh, Victor. We started using them instead of the names our parents gave us, after we found out they were villains or whatever.
Nico was Sister Grimm, Chase was Talkback, and Gert was Arsenic.
Oh, so Old Lace is a reference to the 1944 Capra movie!
You have to admire Gert's taste, huh, Molly?
RRRRR
Even when you speak English, I have no idea what you're saying.
Careful, Bruiser.

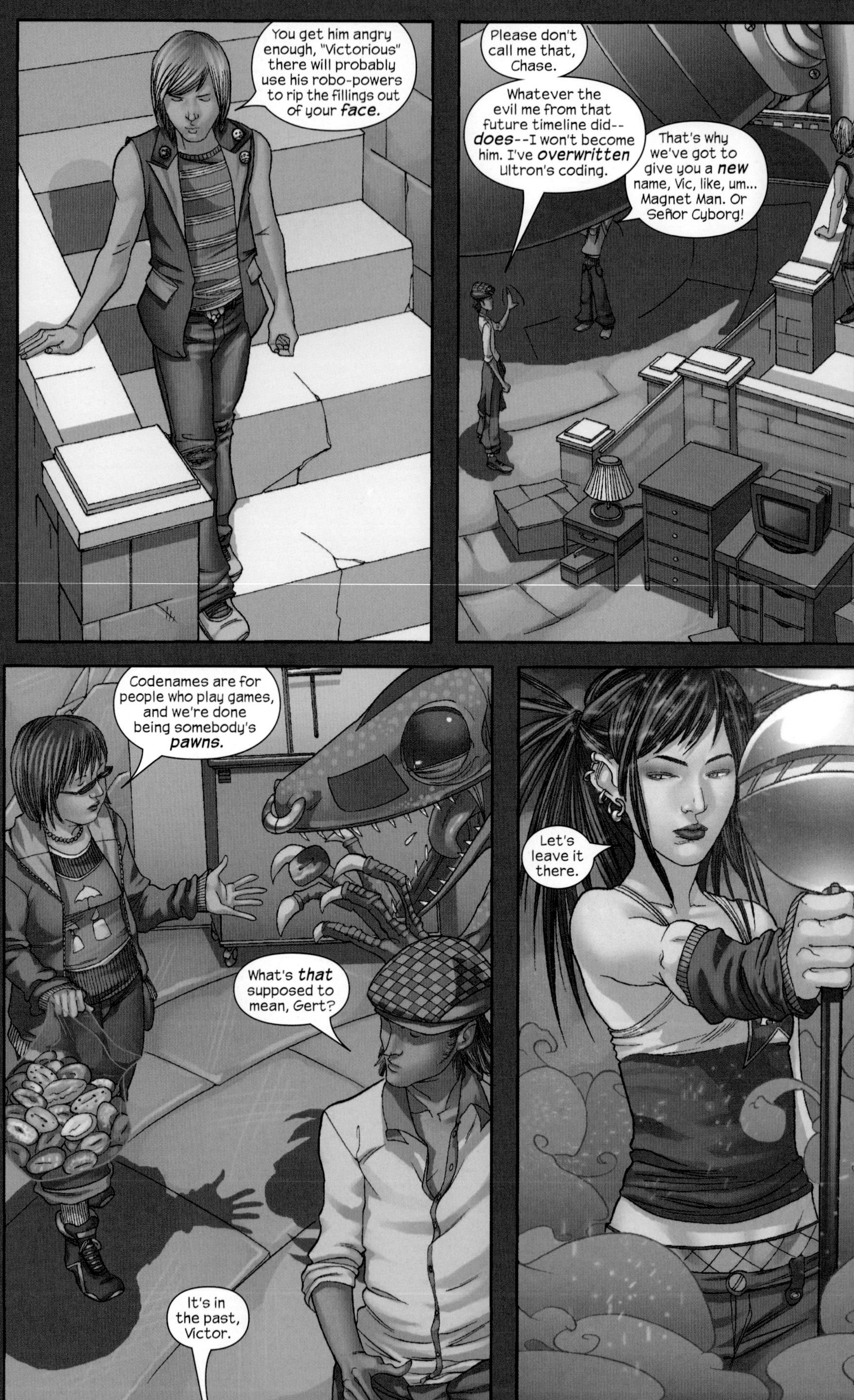

You get him angry enough, "Victorious" there will probably use his robo-powers to rip the fillings out of your *face.*
Please don't call me that, Chase.
Whatever the evil me from that future timeline did-- *does*--I won't become him. I've *overwritten* Ultron's coding.
That's why we've got to give you a *new* name, Vic, like, um... Magnet Man. Or Señor Cyborg!
Codenames are for people who play games, and we're done being somebody's *pawns.*
What's *that* supposed to mean, Gert?
It's in the past, Victor.
Let's leave it there.

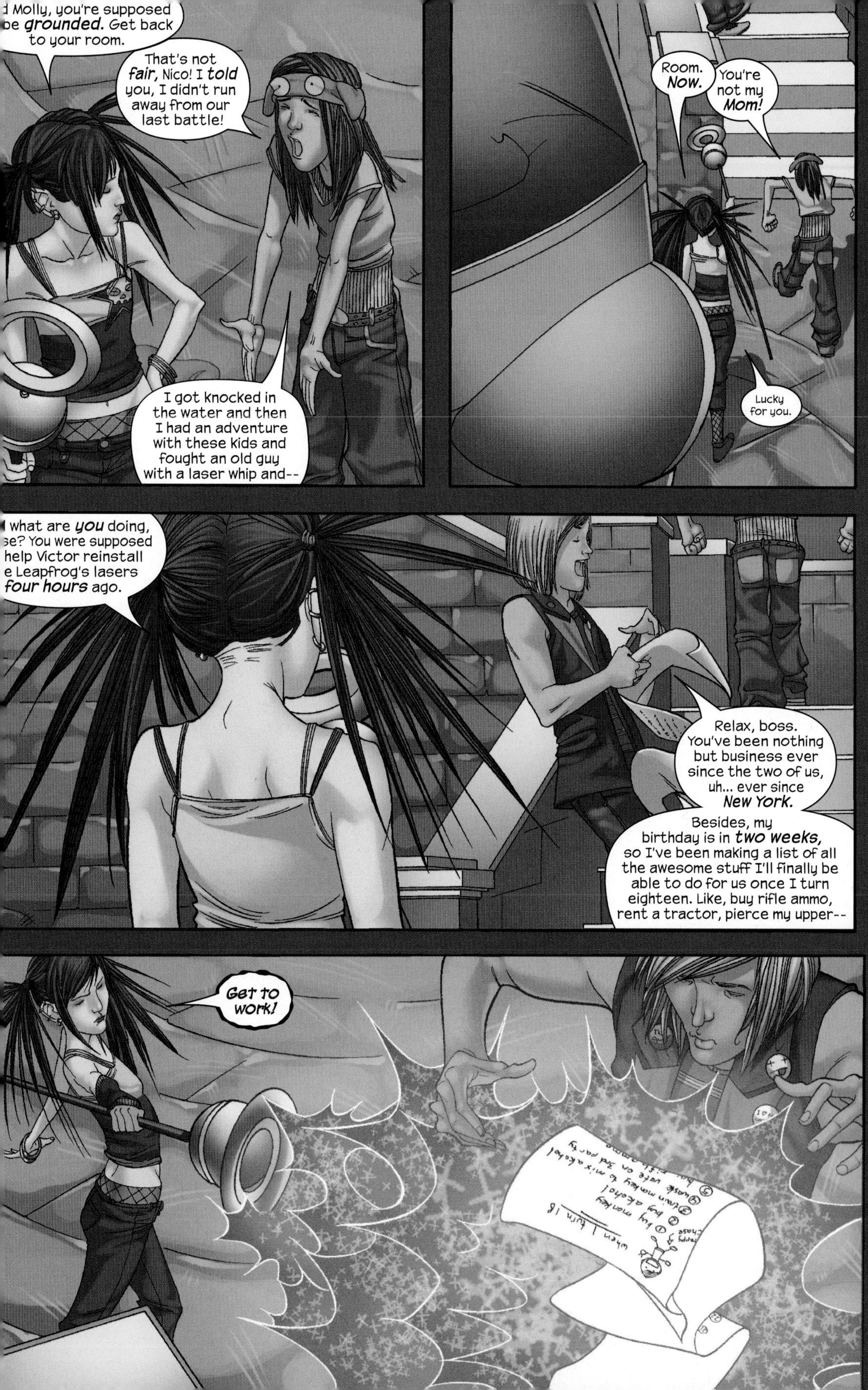

d Molly, you're supposed be grounded. Get back to your room.
That's not fair, Nico! I told you, I didn't run away from our last battle!
I got knocked in the water and then I had an adventure with these kids and fought an old guy with a laser whip and--
Room. Now.
You're not my Mom!
Lucky for you.
what are you doing, se? You were supposed help Victor reinstall e Leapfrog's lasers four hours ago.
Relax, boss. You've been nothing but business ever since the two of us, uh... ever since New York.
Besides, my birthday is in two weeks, so I've been making a list of all the awesome stuff I'll finally be able to do for us once I turn eighteen. Like, buy rifle ammo, rent a tractor, pierce my upper--
Get to work!

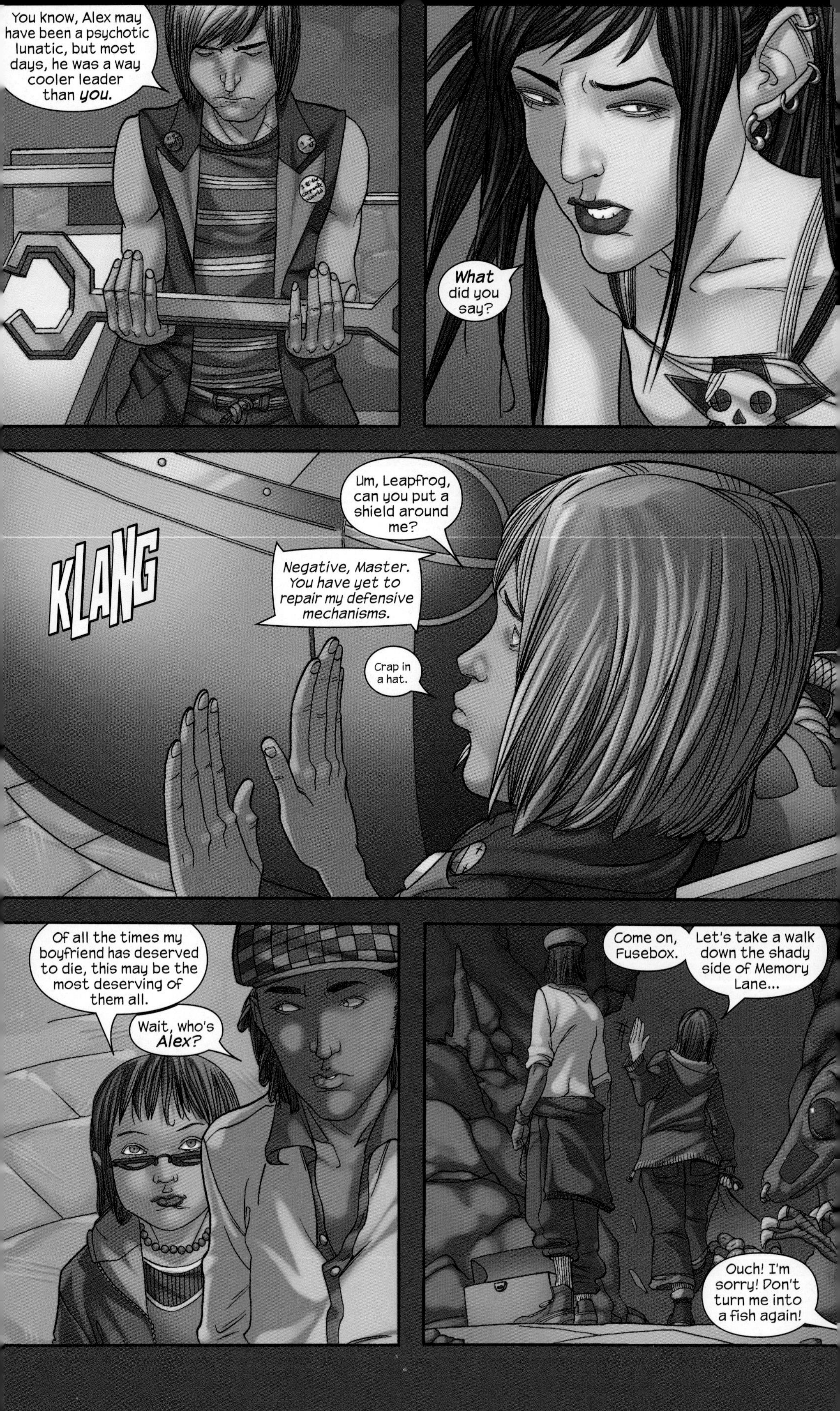
You know, Alex may have been a psychotic lunatic, but most days, he was a way cooler leader than *you.*
What did you say?
KLANG
Um, Leapfrog, can you put a shield around me?
Negative, Master. You have yet to repair my defensive mechanisms.
Crap in a hat.
Of all the times my boyfriend has deserved to die, this may be the most deserving of them all.
Wait, who's *Alex?*
Come on, Fusebox.
Let's take a walk down the shady side of Memory Lane...
Ouch! I'm sorry! Don't turn me into a fish again!

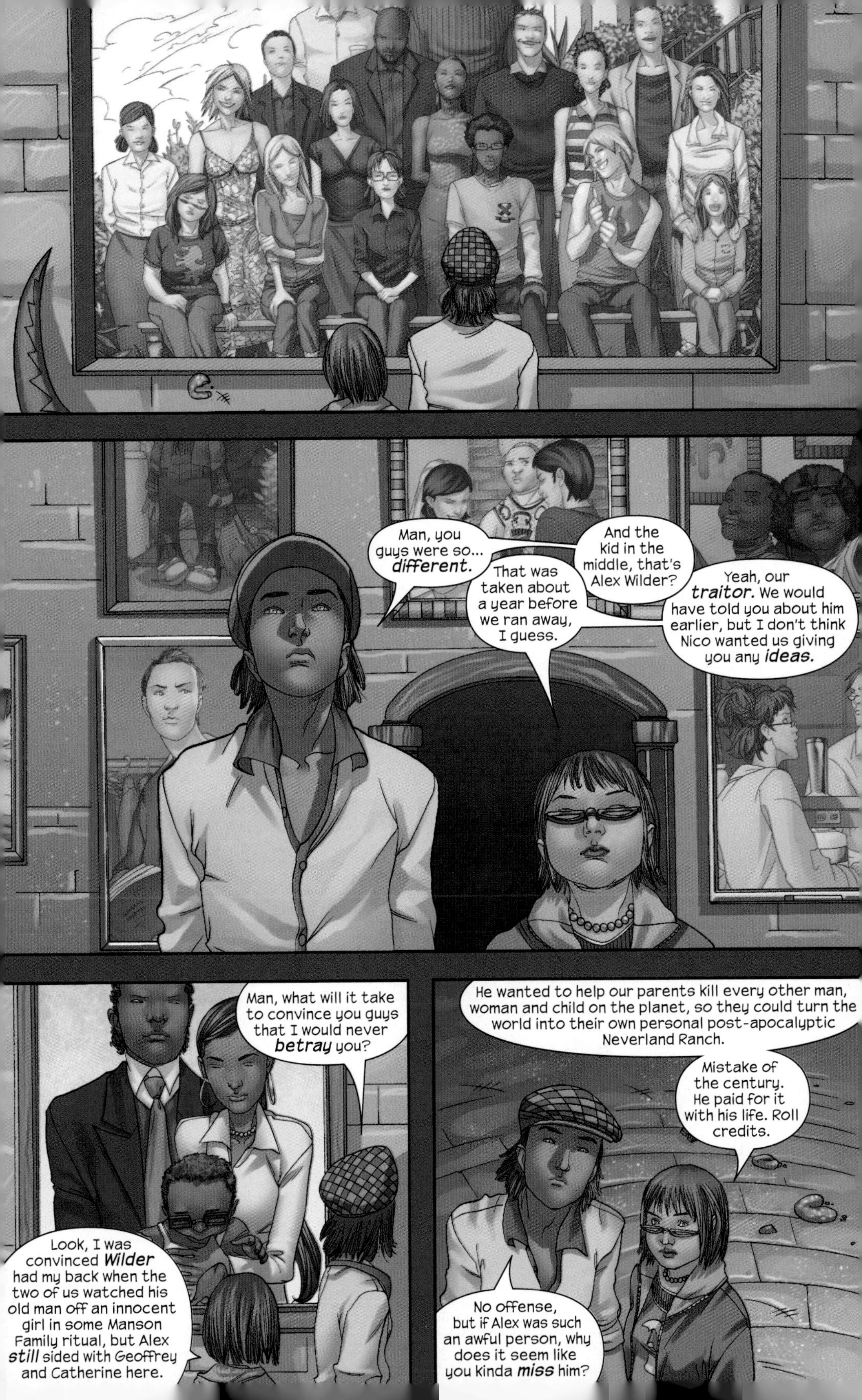
Man, you guys were so... different.
And the kid in the middle, that's Alex Wilder?
That was taken about a year before we ran away, I guess.
Yeah, our traitor. We would have told you about him earlier, but I don't think Nico wanted us giving you any ideas.
Man, what will it take to convince you guys that I would never betray you?
Look, I was convinced Wilder had my back when the two of us watched his old man off an innocent girl in some Manson Family ritual, but Alex still sided with Geoffrey and Catherine here.
He wanted to help our parents kill every other man, woman and child on the planet, so they could turn the world into their own personal post-apocalyptic Neverland Ranch.
Mistake of the century. He paid for it with his life. Roll credits.
No offense, but if Alex was such an awful person, why does it seem like you kinda miss him?

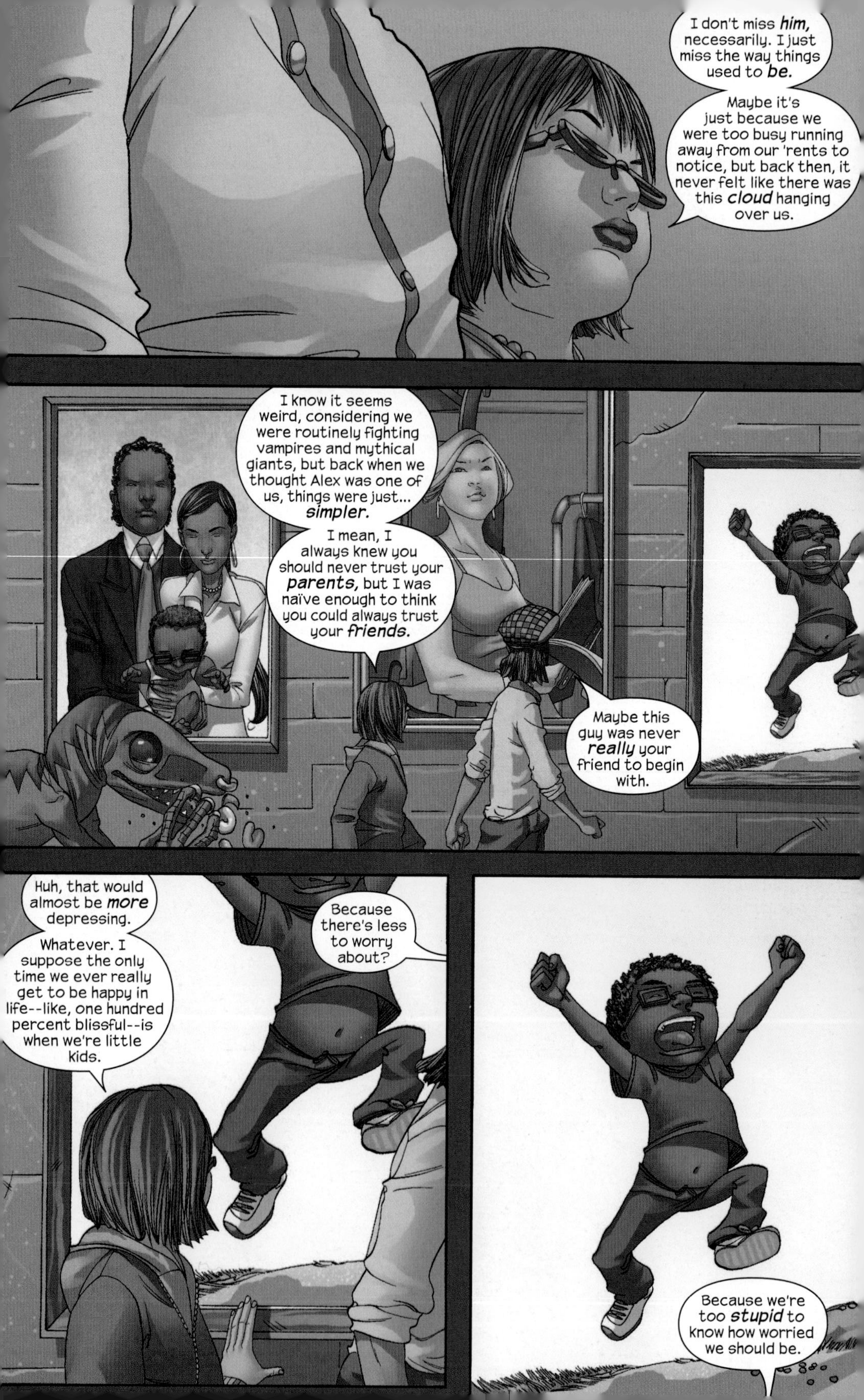
I don't miss him, necessarily. I just miss the way things used to be.
Maybe it's just because we were too busy running away from our 'rents to notice, but back then, it never felt like there was this cloud hanging over us.
I know it seems weird, considering we were routinely fighting vampires and mythical giants, but back when we thought Alex was one of us, things were just... simpler.
I mean, I always knew you should never trust your parents, but I was naïve enough to think you could always trust your friends.
Maybe this guy was never really your friend to begin with.
Huh, that would almost be more depressing.
Whatever. I suppose the only time we ever really get to be happy in life--like, one hundred percent blissful--is when we're little kids.
Because there's less to worry about?
Because we're too stupid to know how worried we should be.

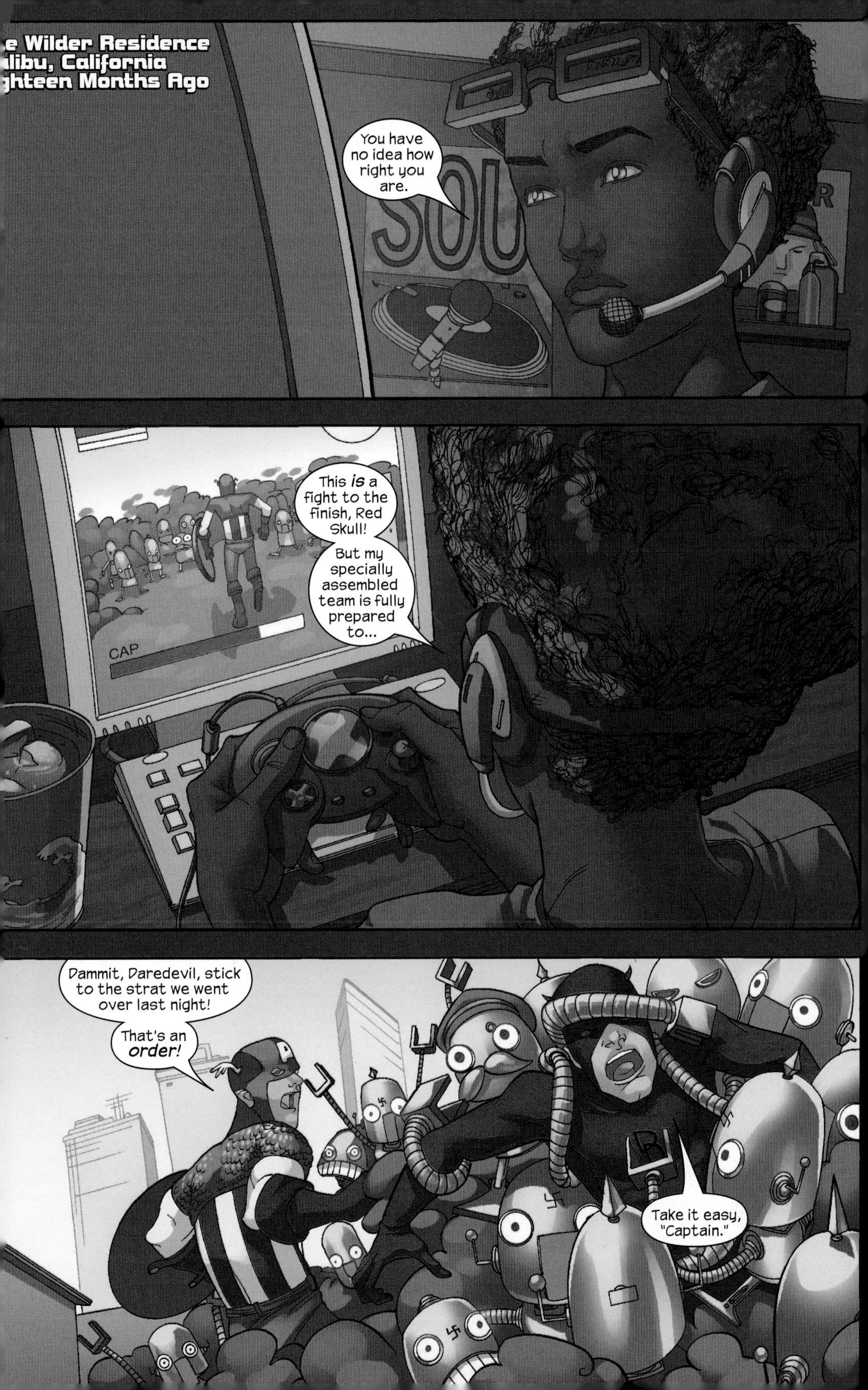
e Wilder Residence
alibu, California
ghteen Months Ago
You have no idea how right you are.
This *is* a fight to the finish, Red Skull!
But my specially assembled team is fully prepared to...
CAP
Dammit, Daredevil, stick to the strat we went over last night!
That's an *order!*
Take it easy, "Captain."

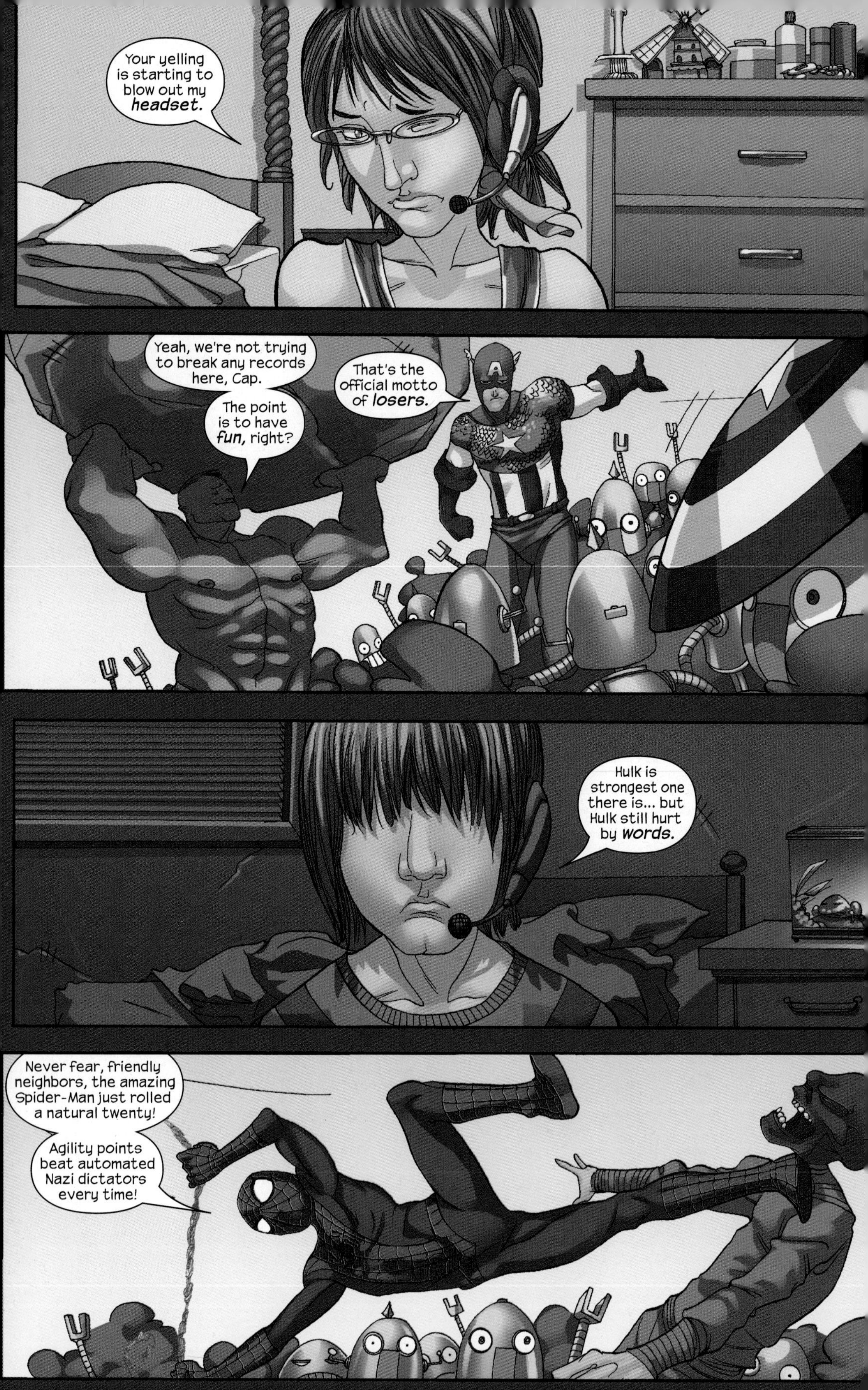
Your yelling is starting to blow out my *headset.*
Yeah, we're not trying to break any records here, Cap.
The point is to have *fun,* right?
That's the official motto of *losers.*
Hulk is strongest one there is... but Hulk still hurt by *words.*
Never fear, friendly neighbors, the amazing Spider-Man just rolled a natural twenty!
Agility points beat automated Nazi dictators every time!

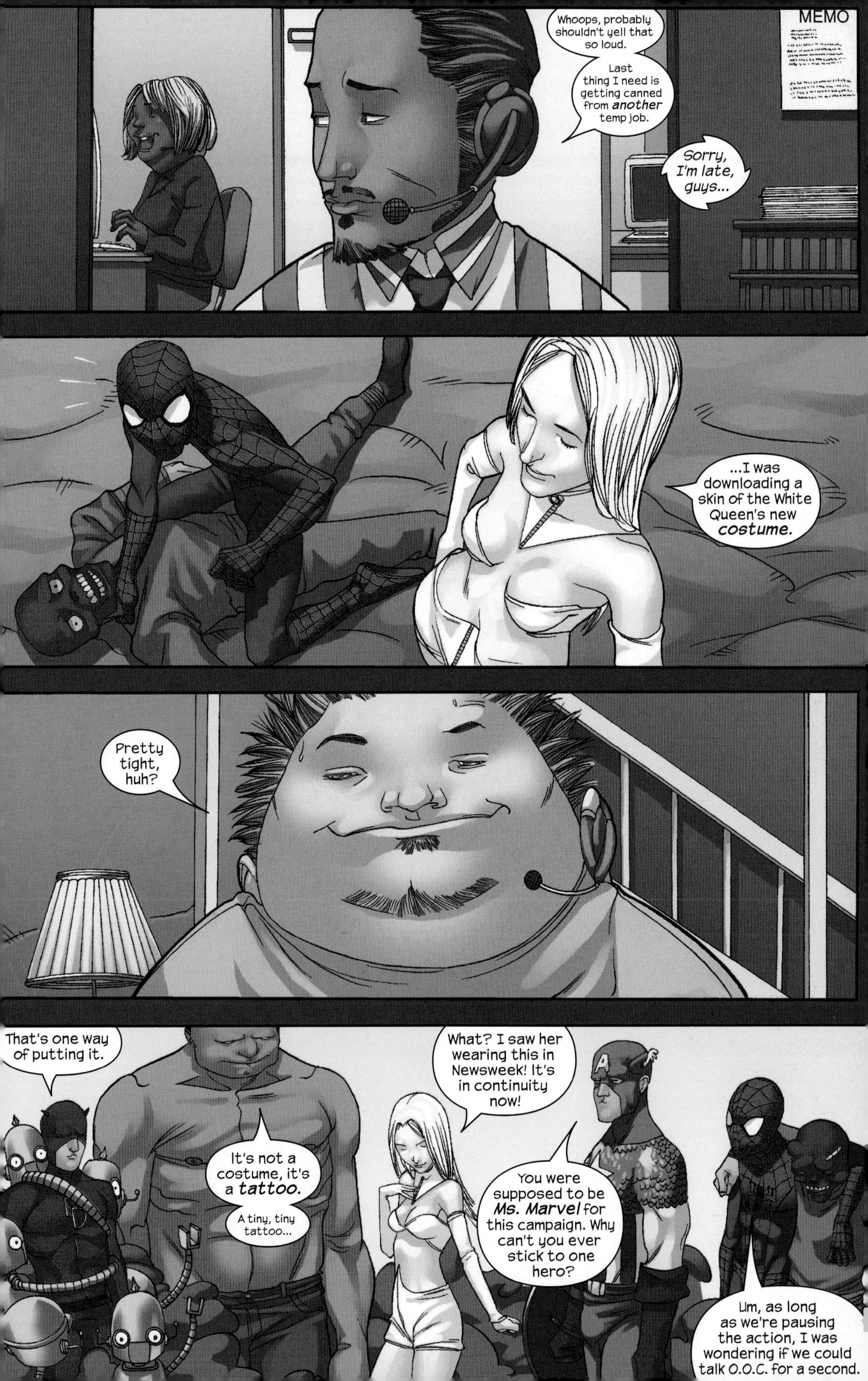

Whoops, probably shouldn't yell that so loud.
Last thing I need is getting canned from *another* temp job.
Sorry, I'm late, guys...
MEMO
...I was downloading a skin of the White Queen's new *costume.*
Pretty tight, huh?
That's one way of putting it.
What? I saw her wearing this in Newsweek! It's in continuity now!
It's not a costume, it's a *tattoo.*
A tiny, tiny tattoo...
You were supposed to be *Ms. Marvel* for this campaign. Why can't you ever stick to one hero?
Um, as long as we're pausing the action, I was wondering if we could talk O.O.C. for a second.

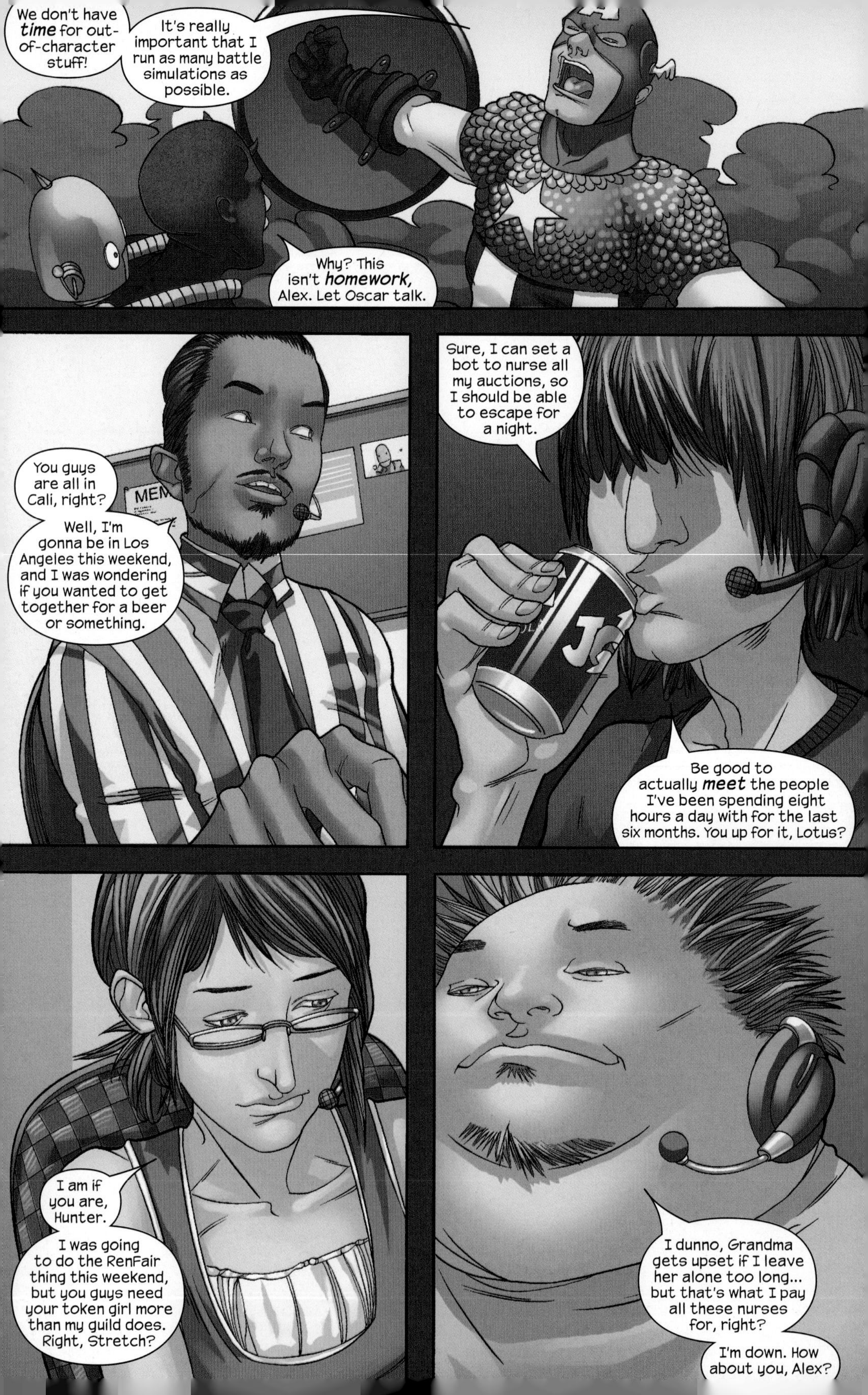
We don't have *time* for out-of-character stuff!
It's really important that I run as many battle simulations as possible.
Why? This isn't ***homework,*** Alex. Let Oscar talk.
You guys are all in Cali, right?
Well, I'm gonna be in Los Angeles this weekend, and I was wondering if you wanted to get together for a beer or something.
Sure, I can set a bot to nurse all my auctions, so I should be able to escape for a night.
Be good to actually ***meet*** the people I've been spending eight hours a day with for the last six months. You up for it, Lotus?
I am if you are, Hunter.
I was going to do the RenFair thing this weekend, but you guys need your token girl more than my guild does. Right, Stretch?
I dunno, Grandma gets upset if I leave her alone too long... but that's what I pay all these nurses for, right?
I'm down. How about you, Alex?

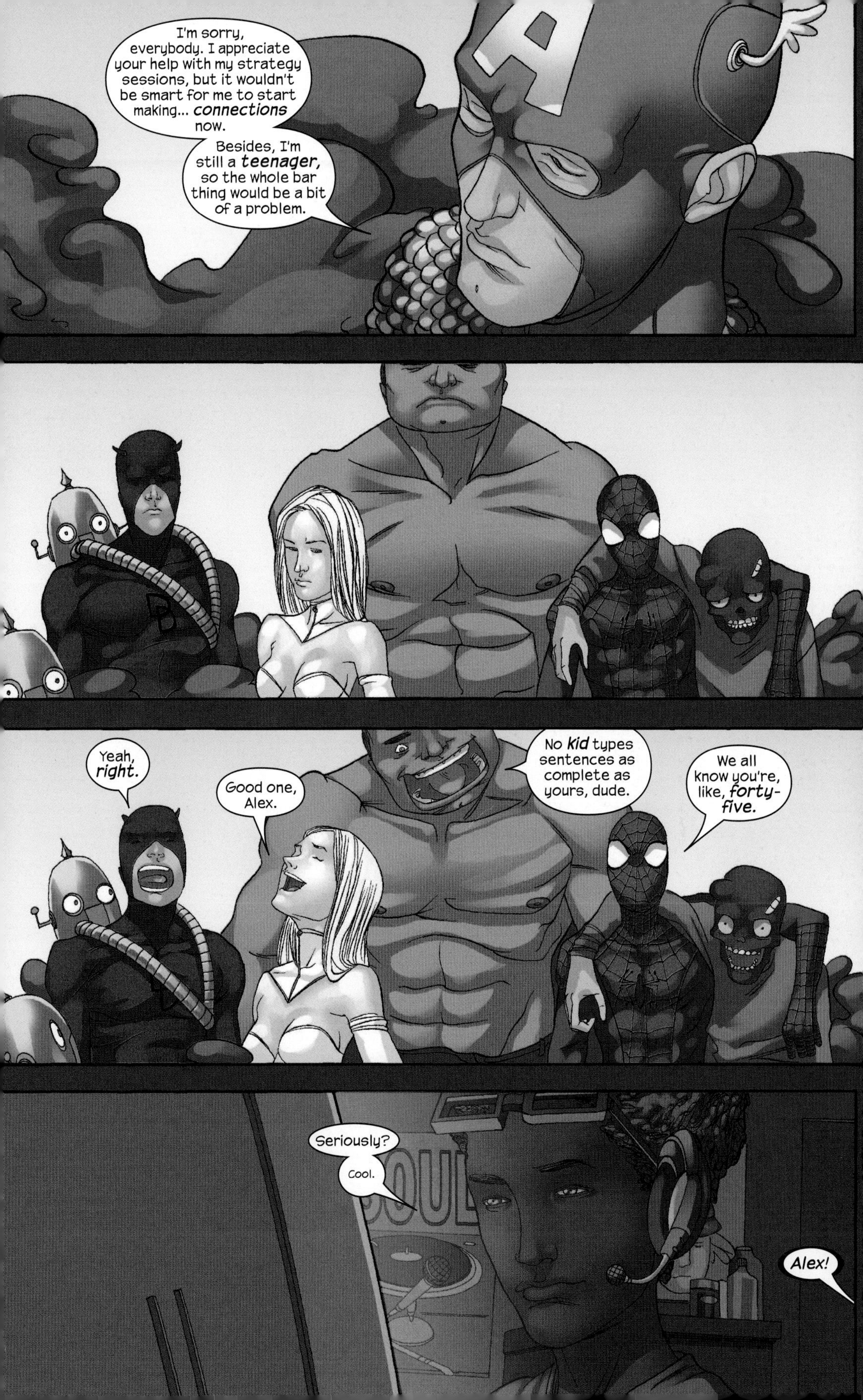
I'm sorry, everybody. I appreciate your help with my strategy sessions, but it wouldn't be smart for me to start making... *connections* now.
Besides, I'm still a *teenager,* so the whole bar thing would be a bit of a problem.
Yeah, *right.*
Good one, Alex.
No *kid* types sentences as complete as yours, dude.
We all know you're, like, *forty-five.*
Seriously?
Cool.
Alex!

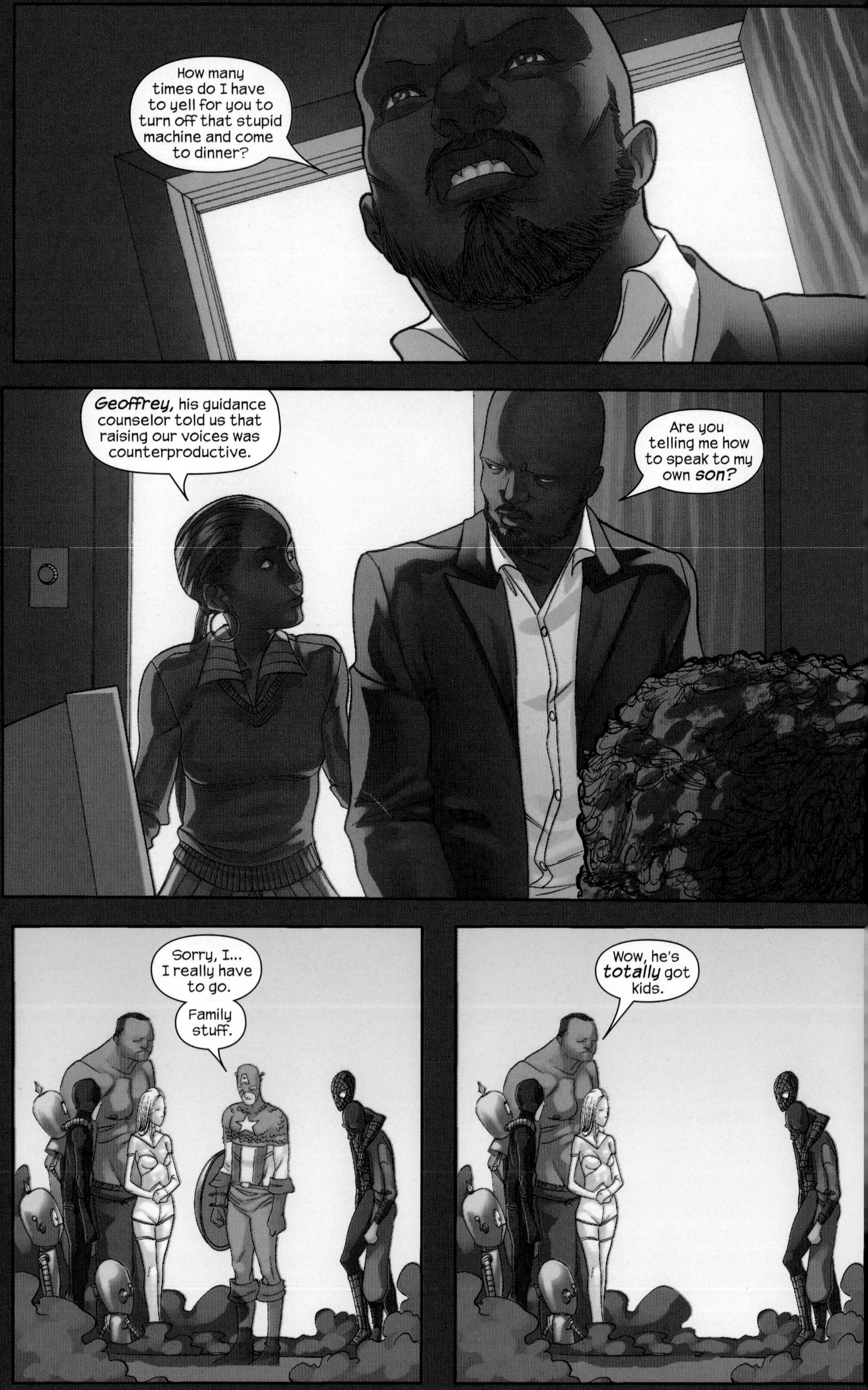
How many times do I have to yell for you to turn off that stupid machine and come to dinner?
Geoffrey, his guidance counselor told us that raising our voices was counterproductive.
Are you telling me how to speak to my own *son?*
Sorry, I... I really have to go.
Family stuff.
Wow, he's *totally* got kids.

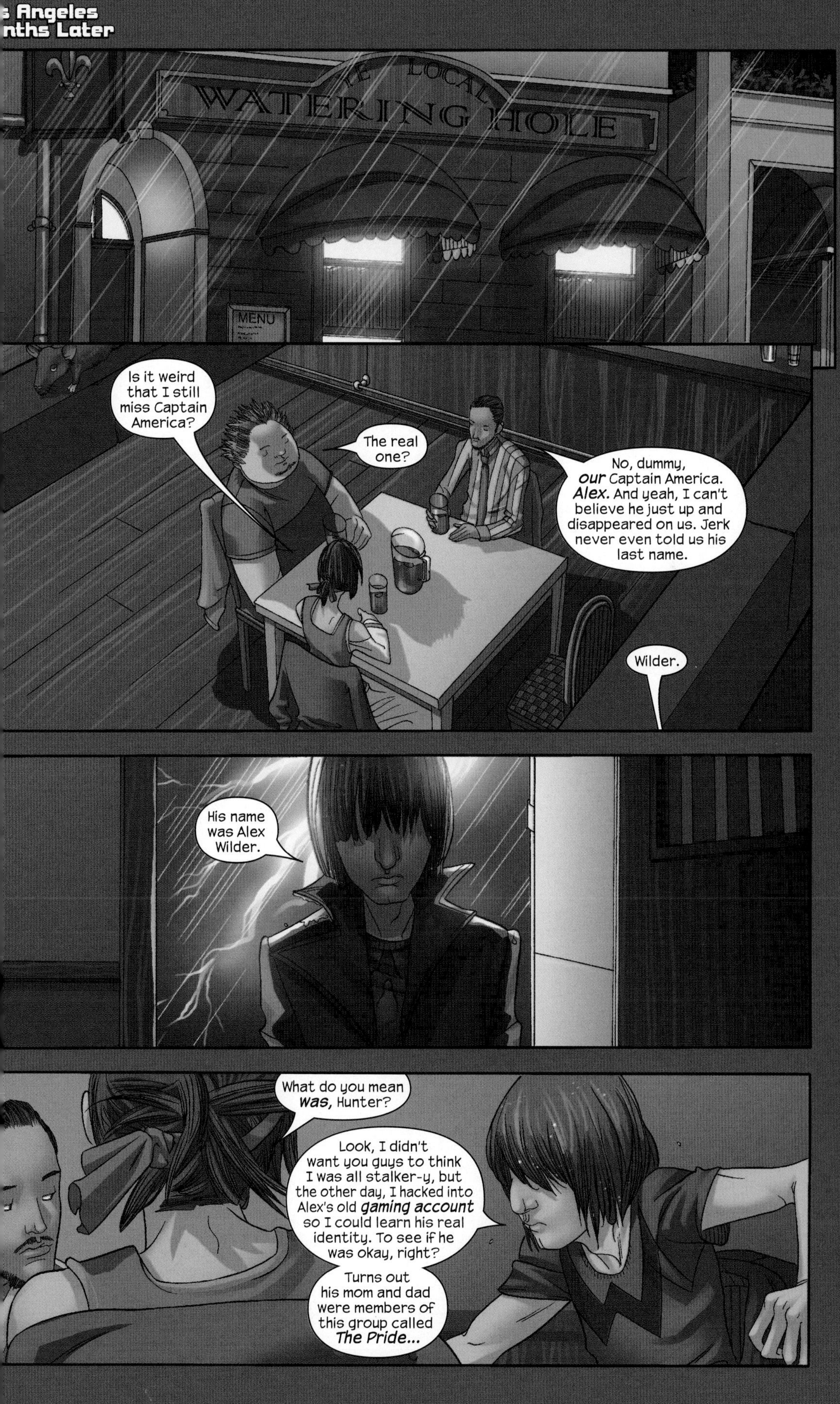

s Angeles
nths Later
THE LOCAL
WATERING HOLE
MENU
Is it weird that I still miss Captain America?
The real one?
No, dummy, *our* Captain America. *Alex.* And yeah, I can't believe he just up and disappeared on us. Jerk never even told us his last name.
Wilder.
His name was Alex Wilder.
What do you mean *was,* Hunter?
Look, I didn't want you guys to think I was all stalker-y, but the other day, I hacked into Alex's old *gaming account* so I could learn his real identity. To see if he was okay, right?
Turns out his mom and dad were members of this group called *The Pride...*

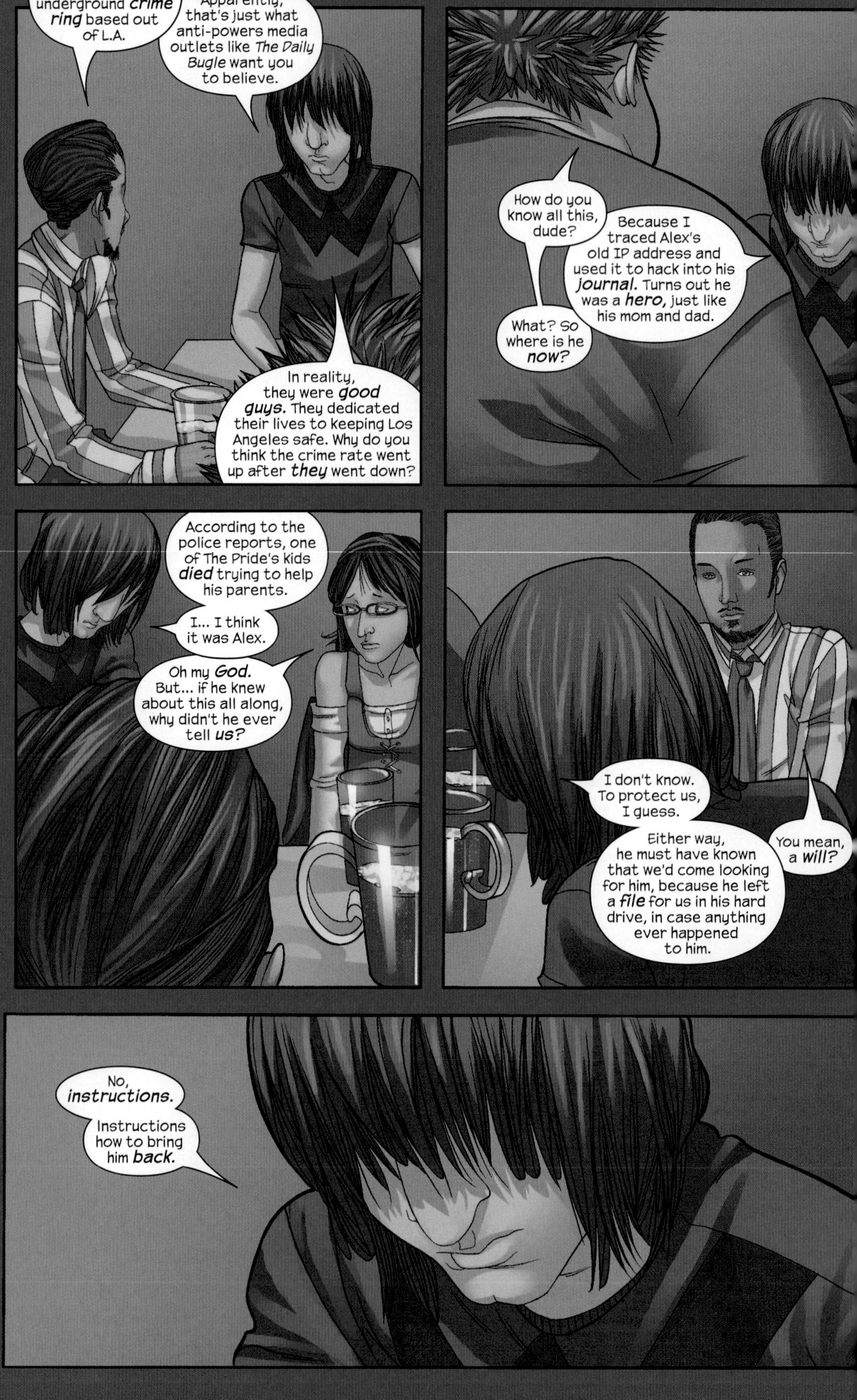
Wait, I read about them. They were some underground *crime ring* based out of L.A.
Apparently, that's just what anti-powers media outlets like *The Daily Bugle* want you to believe.
In reality, they were *good guys.* They dedicated their lives to keeping Los Angeles safe. Why do you think the crime rate went up after *they* went down?
How do you know all this, dude?
Because I traced Alex's old IP address and used it to hack into his *journal.* Turns out he was a *hero,* just like his mom and dad.
What? So where is he *now?*
According to the police reports, one of The Pride's kids *died* trying to help his parents.
I... I think it was Alex.
Oh my *God.* But... if he knew about this all along, why didn't he ever tell *us?*
I don't know. To protect us, I guess.
Either way, he must have known that we'd come looking for him, because he left a *file* for us in his hard drive, in case anything ever happened to him.
You mean, a *will?*
No, *instructions.*
Instructions how to bring him *back.*

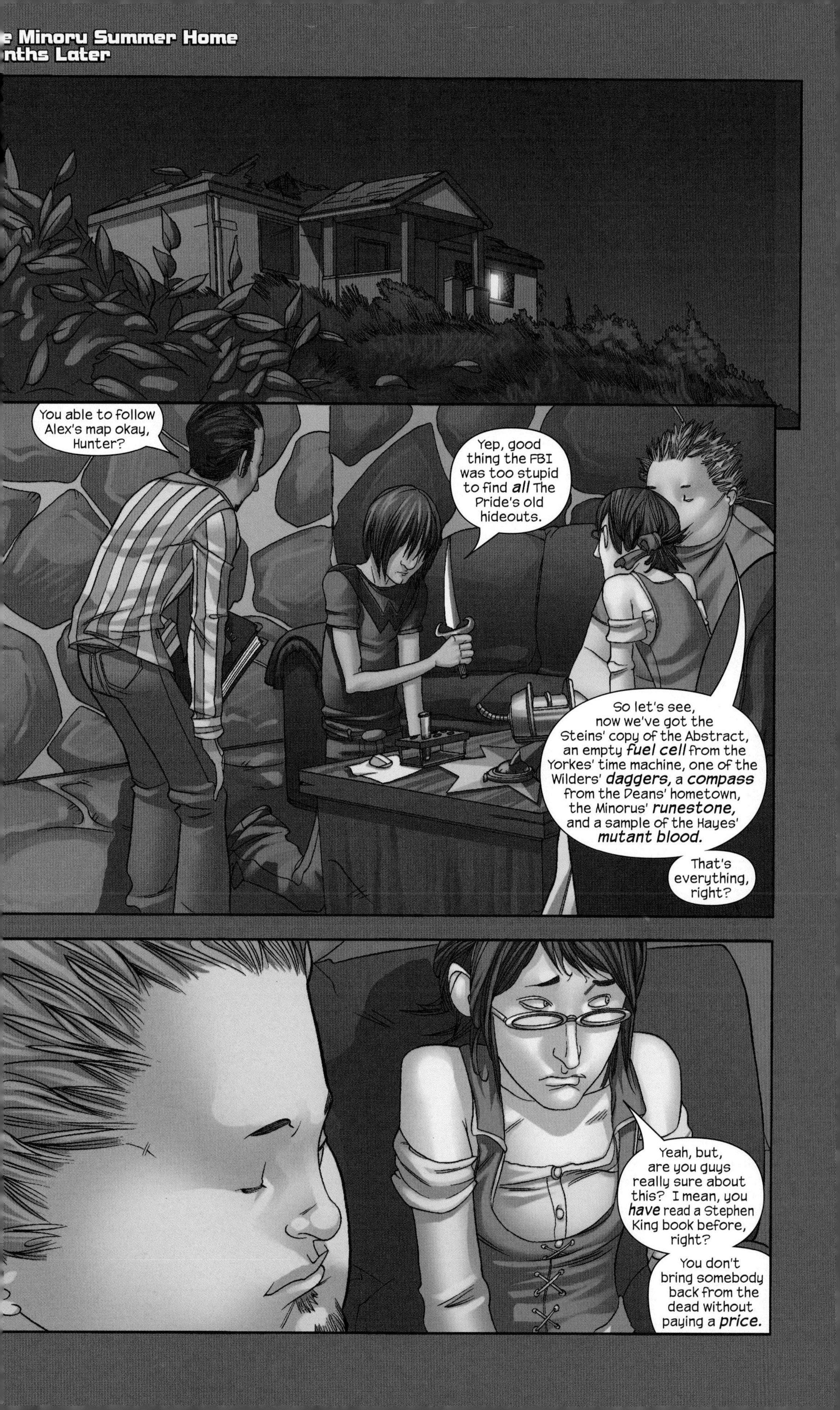
e Minoru Summer Home
nths Later
You able to follow Alex's map okay, Hunter?
Yep, good thing the FBI was too stupid to find *all* The Pride's old hideouts.
So let's see, now we've got the Steins' copy of the Abstract, an empty *fuel cell* from the Yorkes' time machine, one of the Wilders' *daggers,* a *compass* from the Deans' hometown, the Minorus' *runestone,* and a sample of the Hayes' *mutant blood.*
That's everything, right?
Yeah, but, are you guys really sure about this? I mean, you *have* read a Stephen King book before, right?
You don't bring somebody back from the dead without paying a *price.*

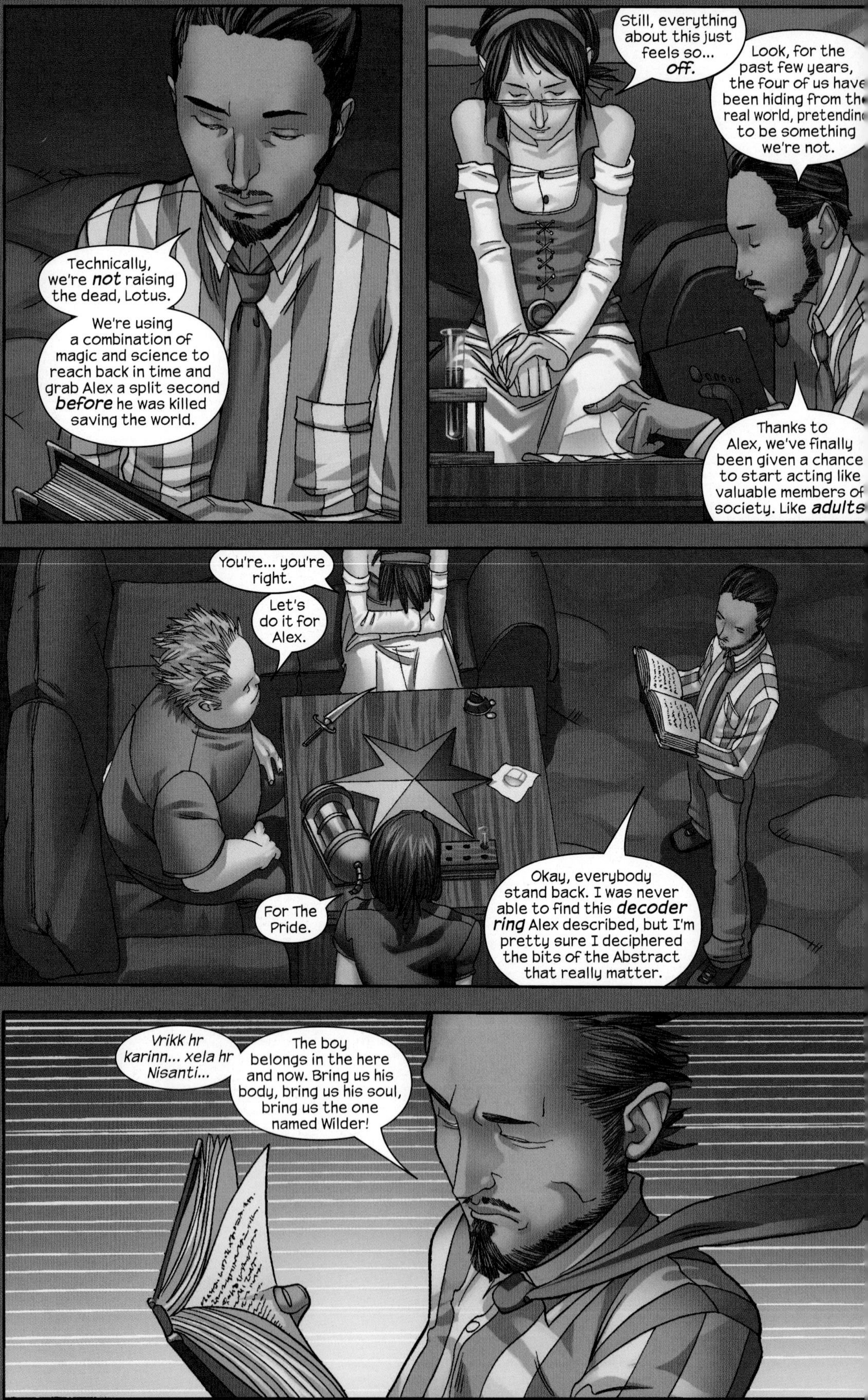

Technically, we're *not* raising the dead, Lotus.
We're using a combination of magic and science to reach back in time and grab Alex a split second *before* he was killed saving the world.
Still, everything about this just feels so... *off.*
Look, for the past few years, the four of us have been hiding from the real world, pretending to be something we're not.
Thanks to Alex, we've finally been given a chance to start acting like valuable members of society. Like *adults*
You're... you're right.
Let's do it for Alex.
For The Pride.
Okay, everybody stand back. I was never able to find this *decoder ring* Alex described, but I'm pretty sure I deciphered the bits of the Abstract that really matter.
Vrikk hr karinn... xela hr Nisanti...
The boy belongs in the here and now. Bring us his body, bring us his soul, bring us the one named Wilder!

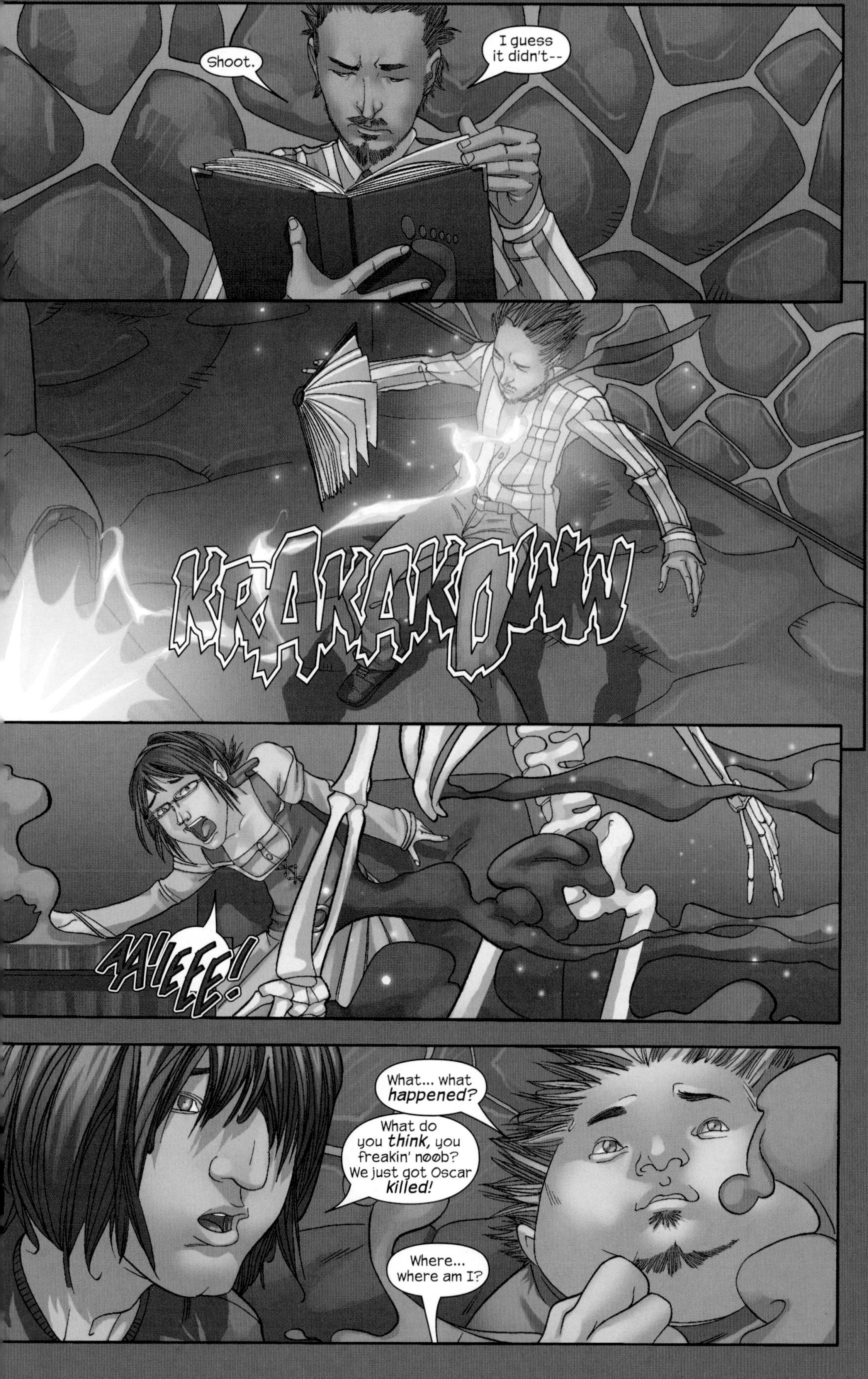
Shoot.
I guess it didn't--
KRAKAKOWW
AAIEEE!
What... what *happened*?
What do you *think*, you freakin' noob? We just got Oscar *killed*!
Where... where am I?

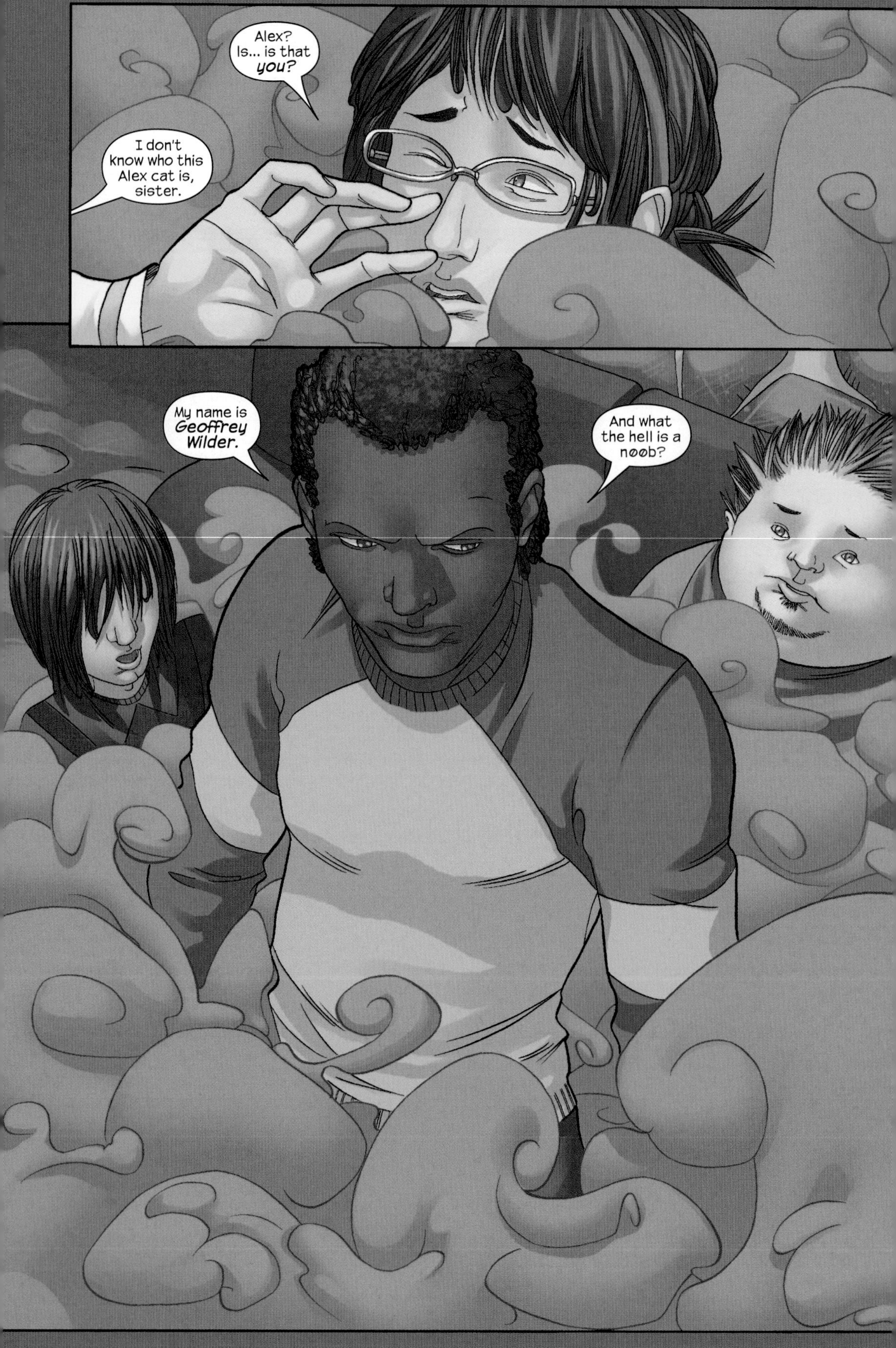

Alex? Is... is that *you?*
I don't know who this Alex cat is, sister.
My name is *Geoffrey Wilder.*
And what the hell is a n00b?

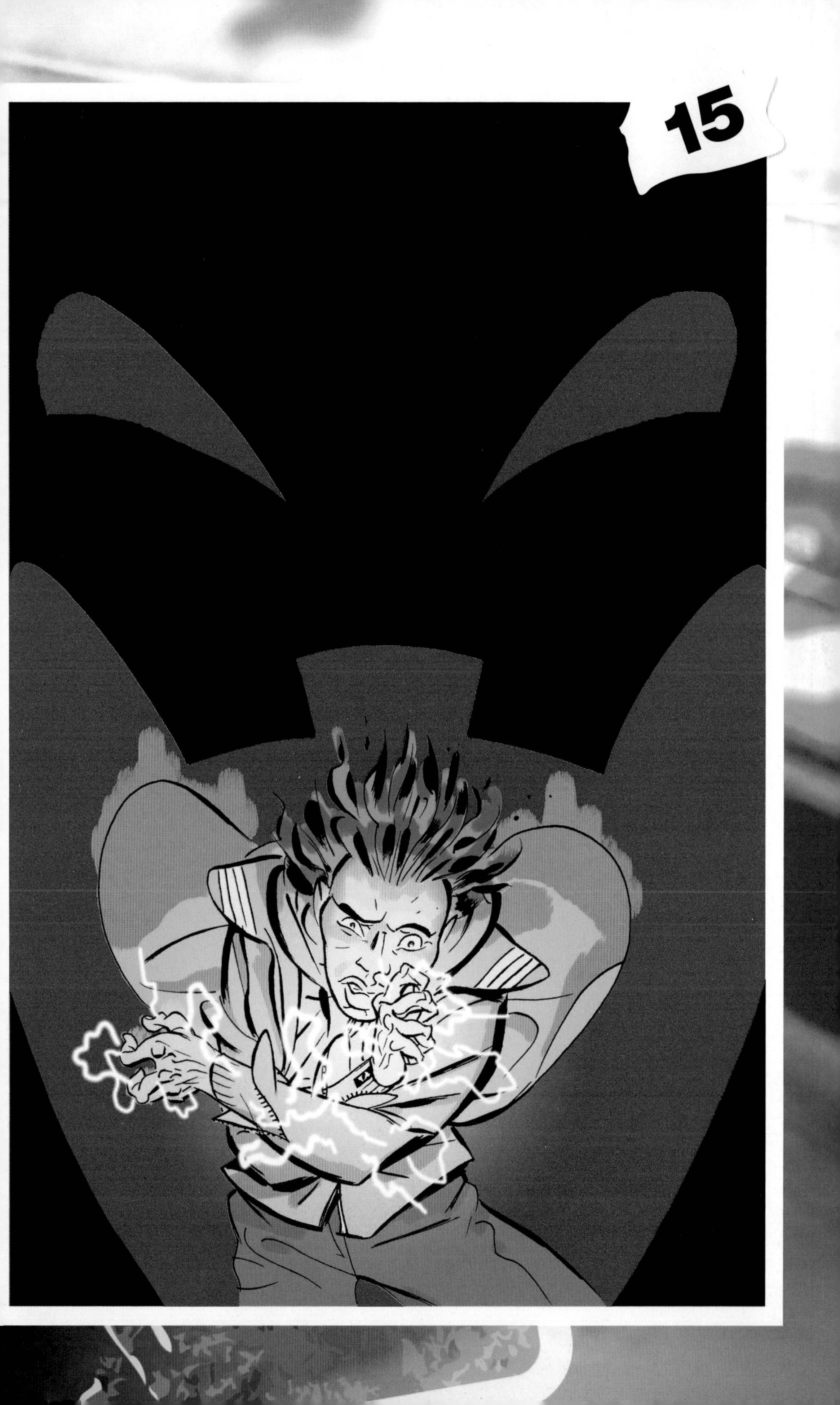
15

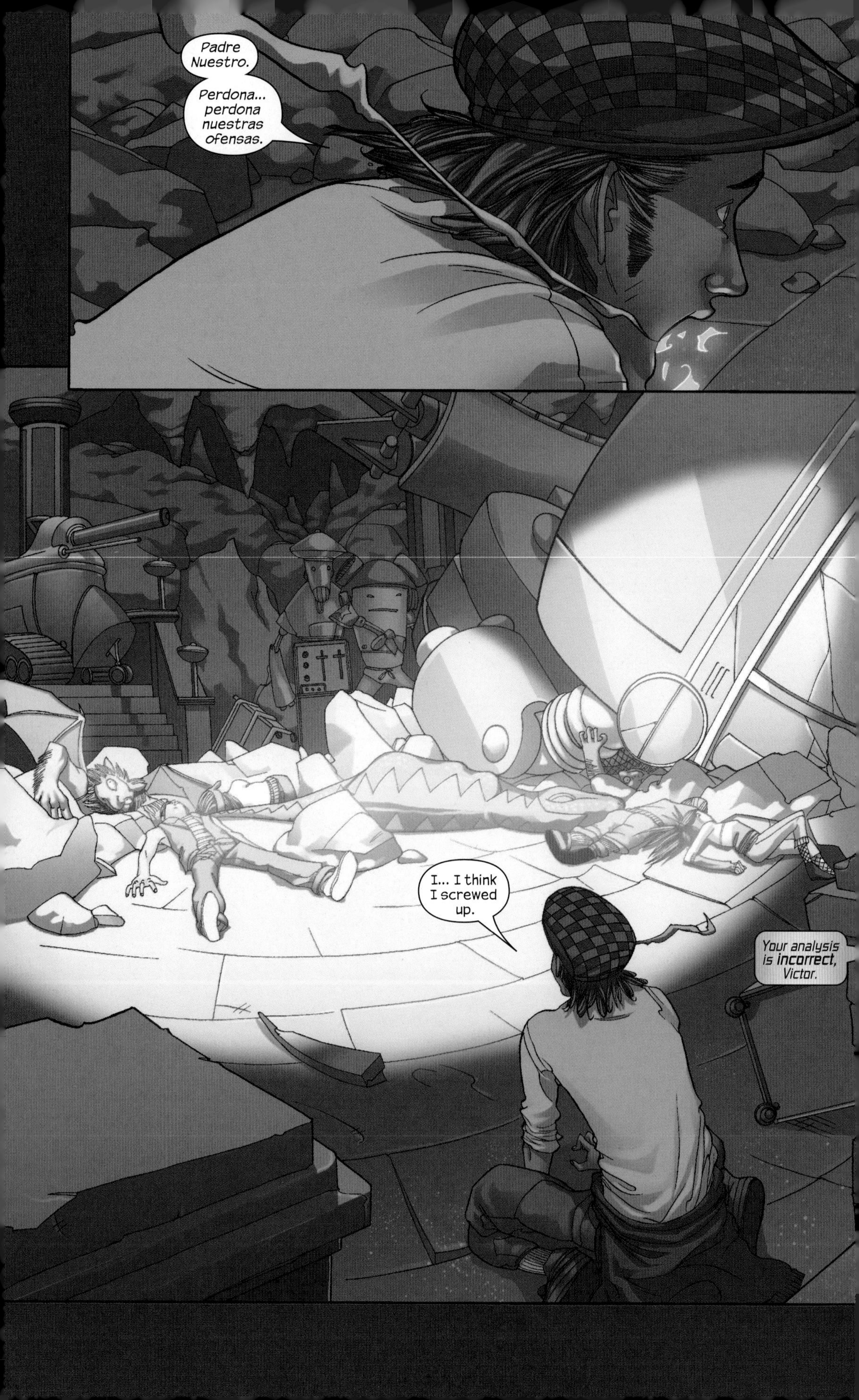
Padre Nuestro.
Perdona... perdona nuestras ofensas.
I... I think I screwed up.
Your analysis is **incorrect,** Victor.

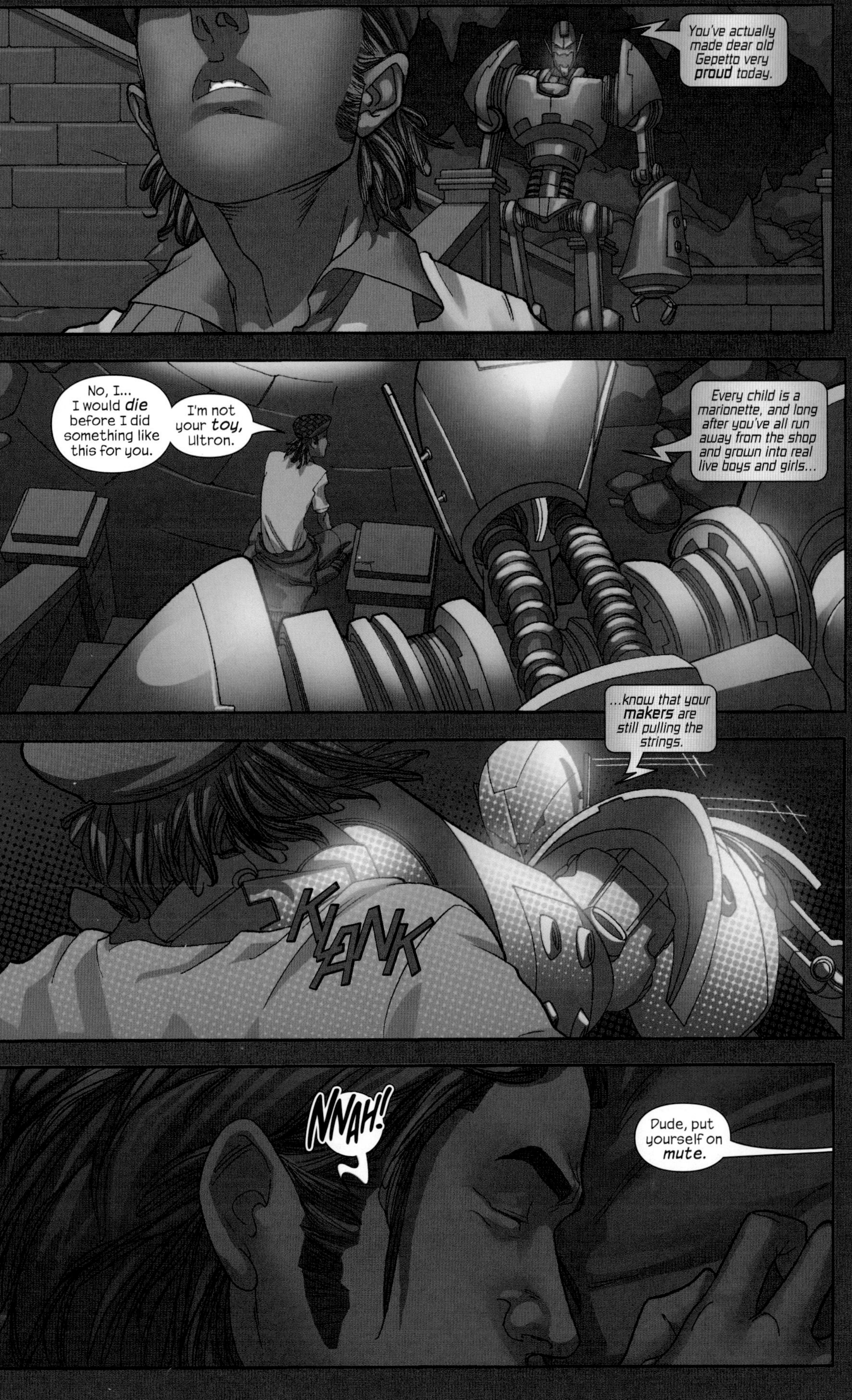
You've actually made dear old Gepetto very proud today.
No, I... I would die before I did something like this for you.
I'm not your toy, Ultron.
Every child is a marionette, and long after you've all run away from the shop and grown into real live boys and girls...
...know that your makers are still pulling the strings.
KLANK
NNAH!
Dude, put yourself on mute.

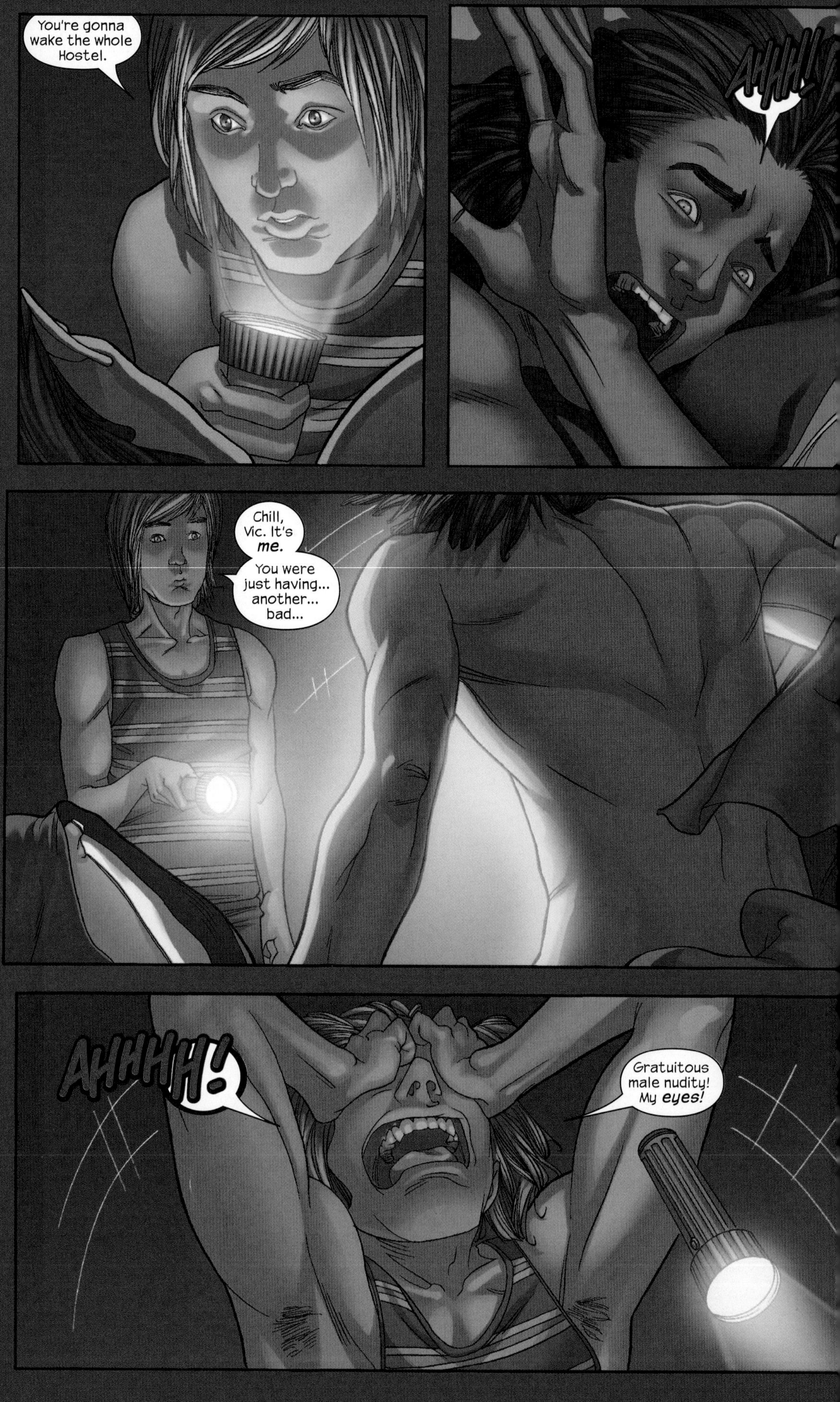
You're gonna wake the whole Hostel.
AHHH!
Chill, Vic. It's *me.*
You were just having... another... bad...
AHHHH!
Gratuitous male nudity! My *eyes!*

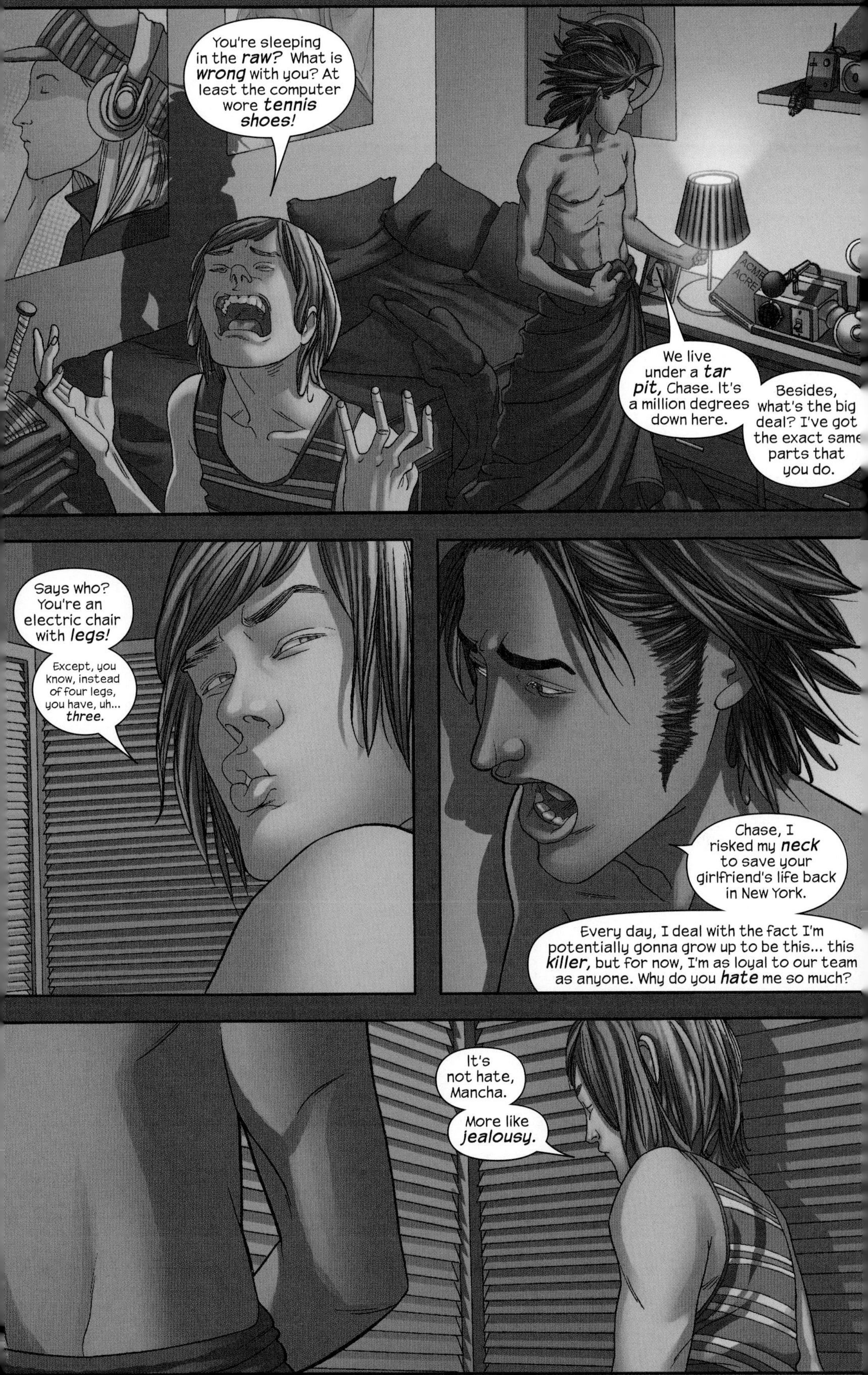
You're sleeping in the *raw?* What is *wrong* with you? At least the computer wore *tennis shoes!*
ACME
We live under a *tar pit,* Chase. It's a million degrees down here.
Besides, what's the big deal? I've got the exact same parts that you do.
Says who? You're an electric chair with *legs!*
Except, you know, instead of four legs, you have, uh... *three.*
Chase, I risked my *neck* to save your girlfriend's life back in New York.
Every day, I deal with the fact I'm potentially gonna grow up to be this... this *killer,* but for now, I'm as loyal to our team as anyone. Why do you *hate* me so much?
It's not hate, Mancha.
More like *jealousy.*

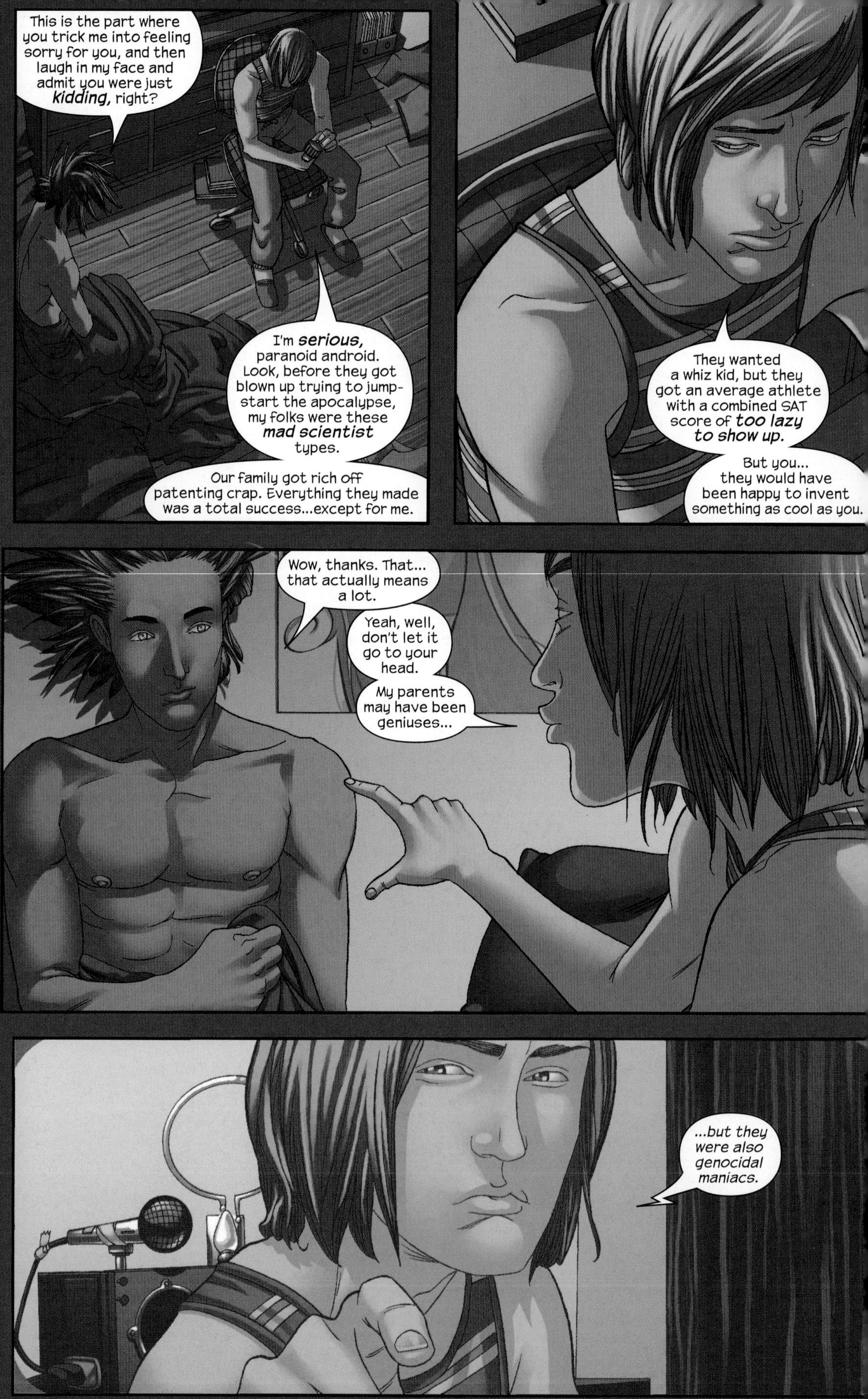
This is the part where you trick me into feeling sorry for you, and then laugh in my face and admit you were just *kidding,* right?
I'm *serious,* paranoid android. Look, before they got blown up trying to jump-start the apocalypse, my folks were these *mad scientist* types.
Our family got rich off patenting crap. Everything they made was a total success...except for me.
They wanted a whiz kid, but they got an average athlete with a combined SAT score of *too lazy to show up.*
But you... they would have been happy to invent something as cool as you.
Wow, thanks. That... that actually means a lot.
Yeah, well, don't let it go to your head.
My parents may have been geniuses...
...but they were also genocidal maniacs.

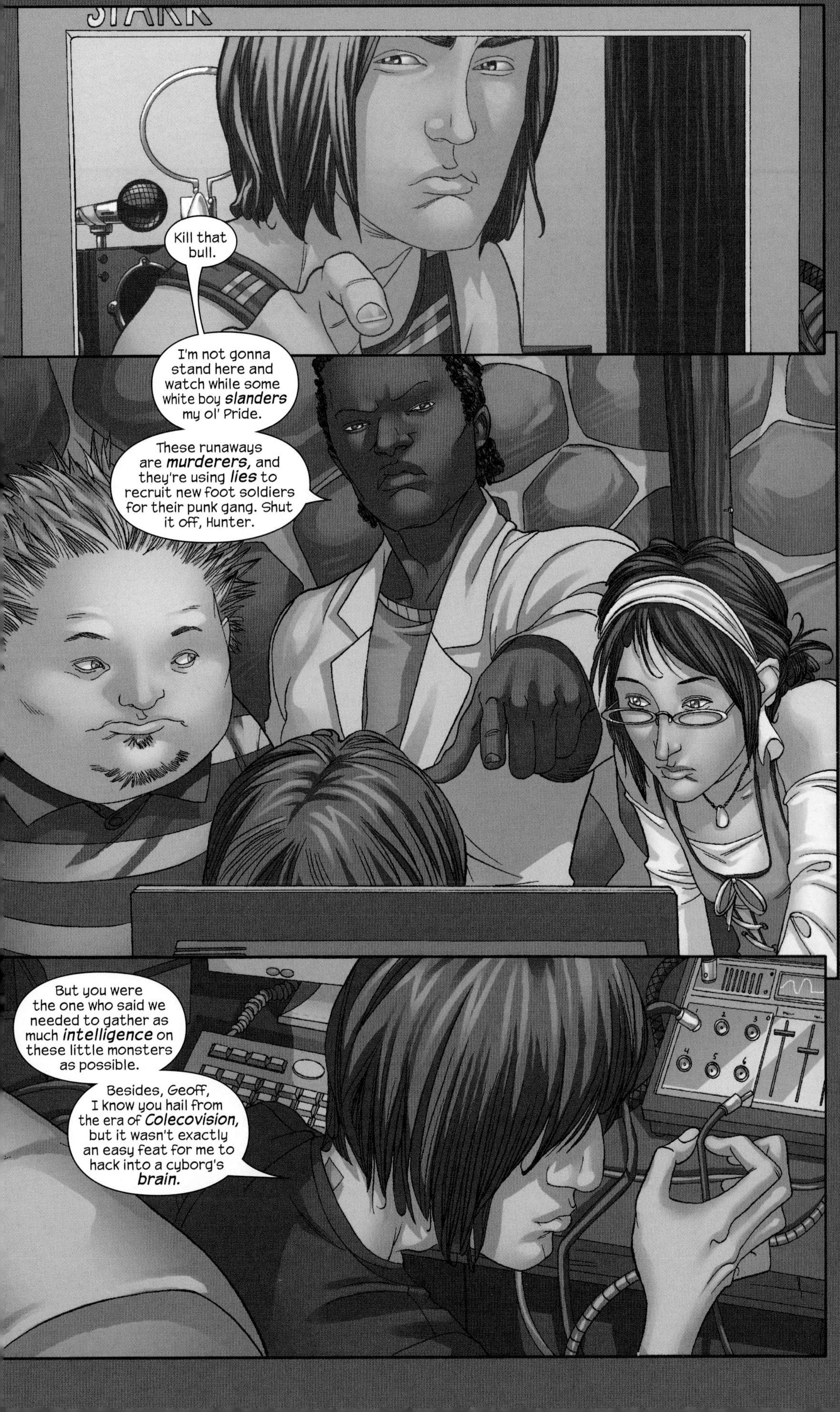
STARK
Kill that bull.
I'm not gonna stand here and watch while some white boy *slanders* my ol' Pride.
These runaways are ***murderers,*** and they're using ***lies*** to recruit new foot soldiers for their punk gang. Shut it off, Hunter.
But you were the one who said we needed to gather as much ***intelligence*** on these little monsters as possible.
Besides, Geoff, I know you hail from the era of *Colecovision,* but it wasn't exactly an easy feat for me to hack into a cyborg's ***brain.***

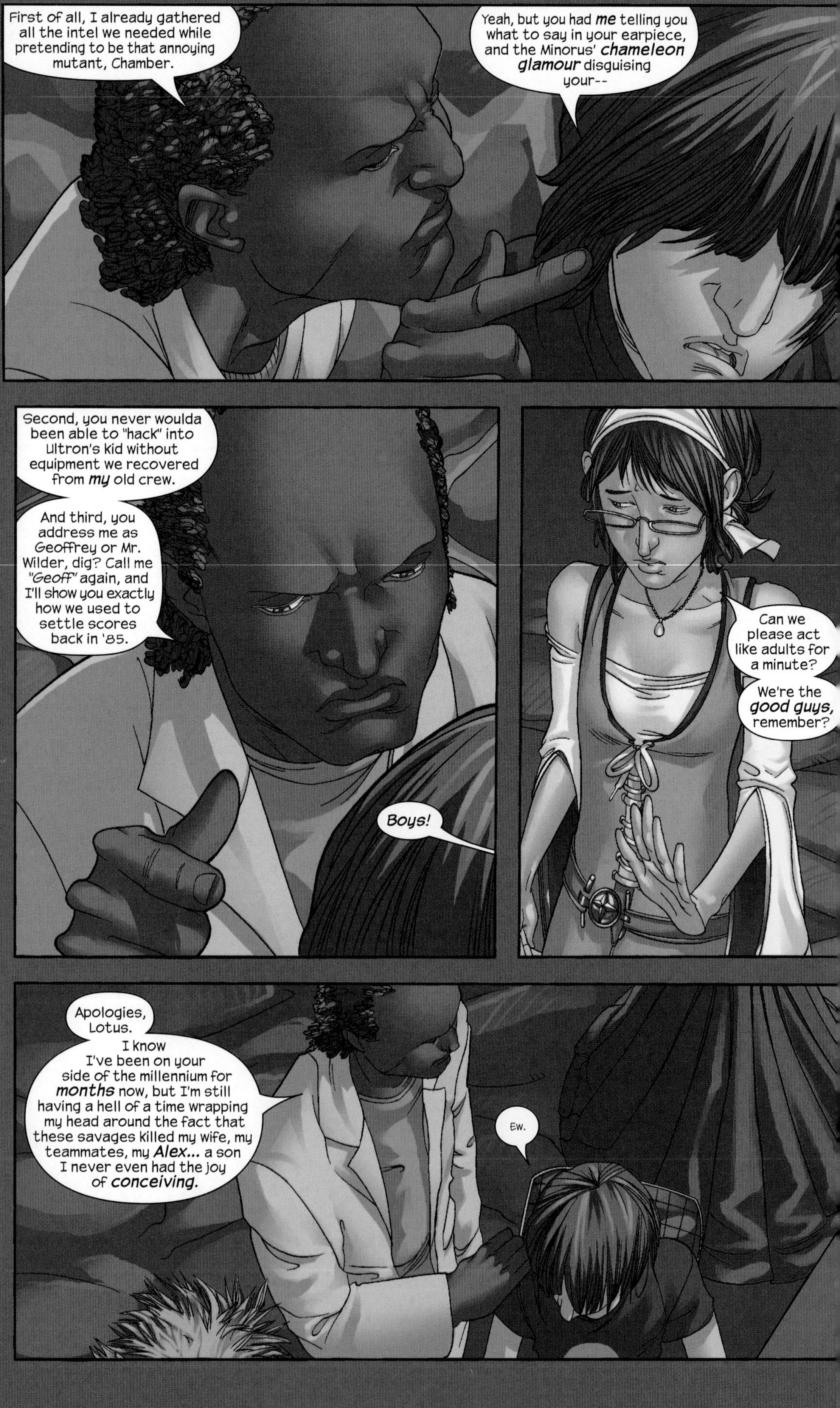

First of all, I already gathered all the intel we needed while pretending to be that annoying mutant, Chamber.
Yeah, but you had *me* telling you what to say in your earpiece, and the Minorus' ***chameleon glamour*** disguising your--
Second, you never woulda been able to "hack" into Ultron's kid without equipment we recovered from *my* old crew.
And third, you address me as Geoffrey or Mr. Wilder, dig? Call me *"Geoff"* again, and I'll show you exactly how we used to settle scores back in '85.
Boys!
Can we please act like adults for a minute?
We're the ***good guys,*** remember?
Apologies, Lotus.
I know I've been on your side of the millennium for ***months*** now, but I'm still having a hell of a time wrapping my head around the fact that these savages killed my wife, my teammates, my ***Alex...*** a son I never even had the joy of ***conceiving.***
Ew.

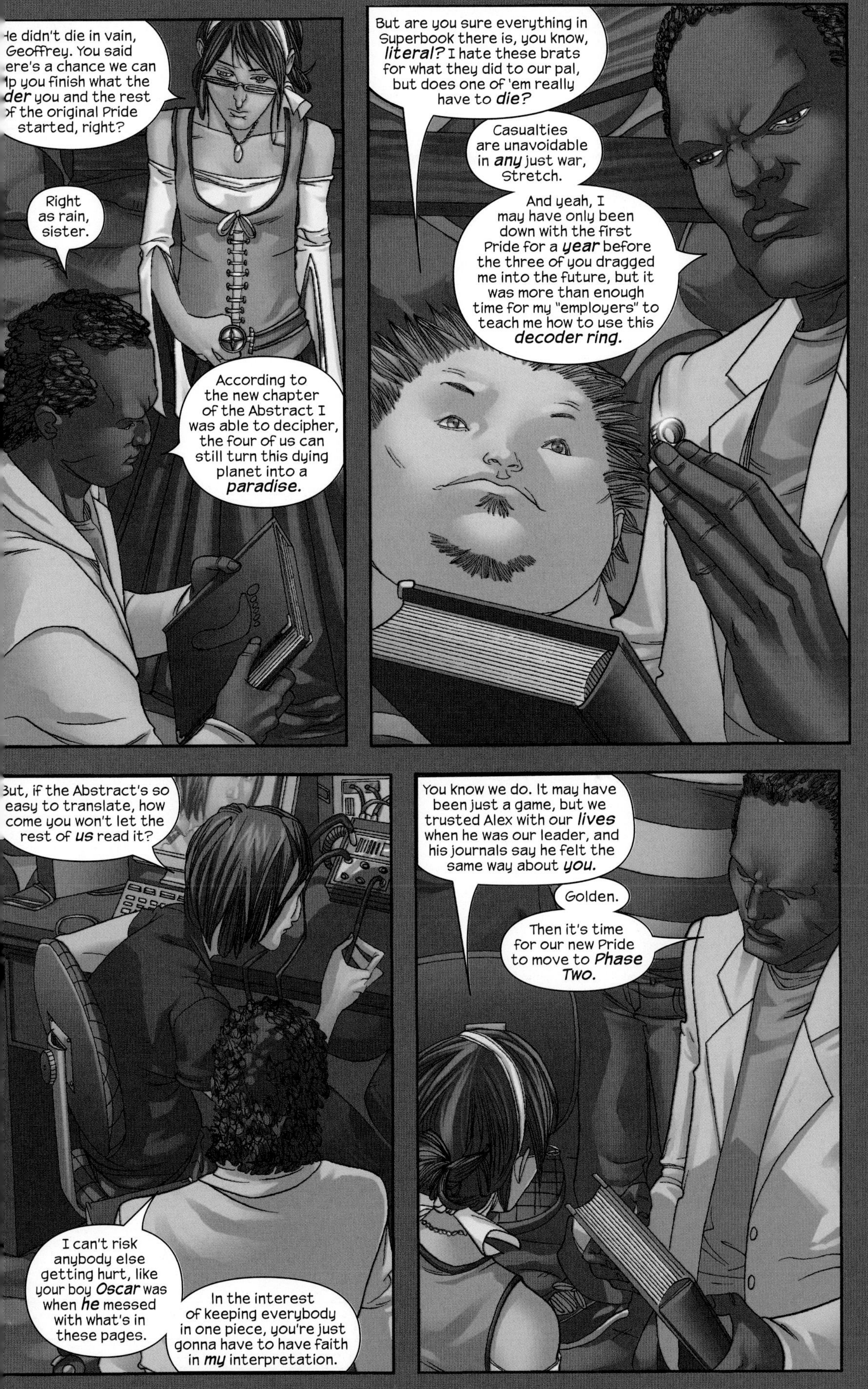
He didn't die in vain, Geoffrey. You said ere's a chance we can lp you finish what the der you and the rest of the original Pride started, right?
Right as rain, sister.
According to the new chapter of the Abstract I was able to decipher, the four of us can still turn this dying planet into a paradise.
But are you sure everything in Superbook there is, you know, literal? I hate these brats for what they did to our pal, but does one of 'em really have to die?
Casualties are unavoidable in any just war, Stretch.
And yeah, I may have only been down with the first Pride for a year before the three of you dragged me into the future, but it was more than enough time for my "employers" to teach me how to use this decoder ring.
But, if the Abstract's so easy to translate, how come you won't let the rest of us read it?
I can't risk anybody else getting hurt, like your boy Oscar was when he messed with what's in these pages.
In the interest of keeping everybody in one piece, you're just gonna have to have faith in my interpretation.
You know we do. It may have been just a game, but we trusted Alex with our lives when he was our leader, and his journals say he felt the same way about you.
Golden.
Then it's time for our new Pride to move to Phase Two.

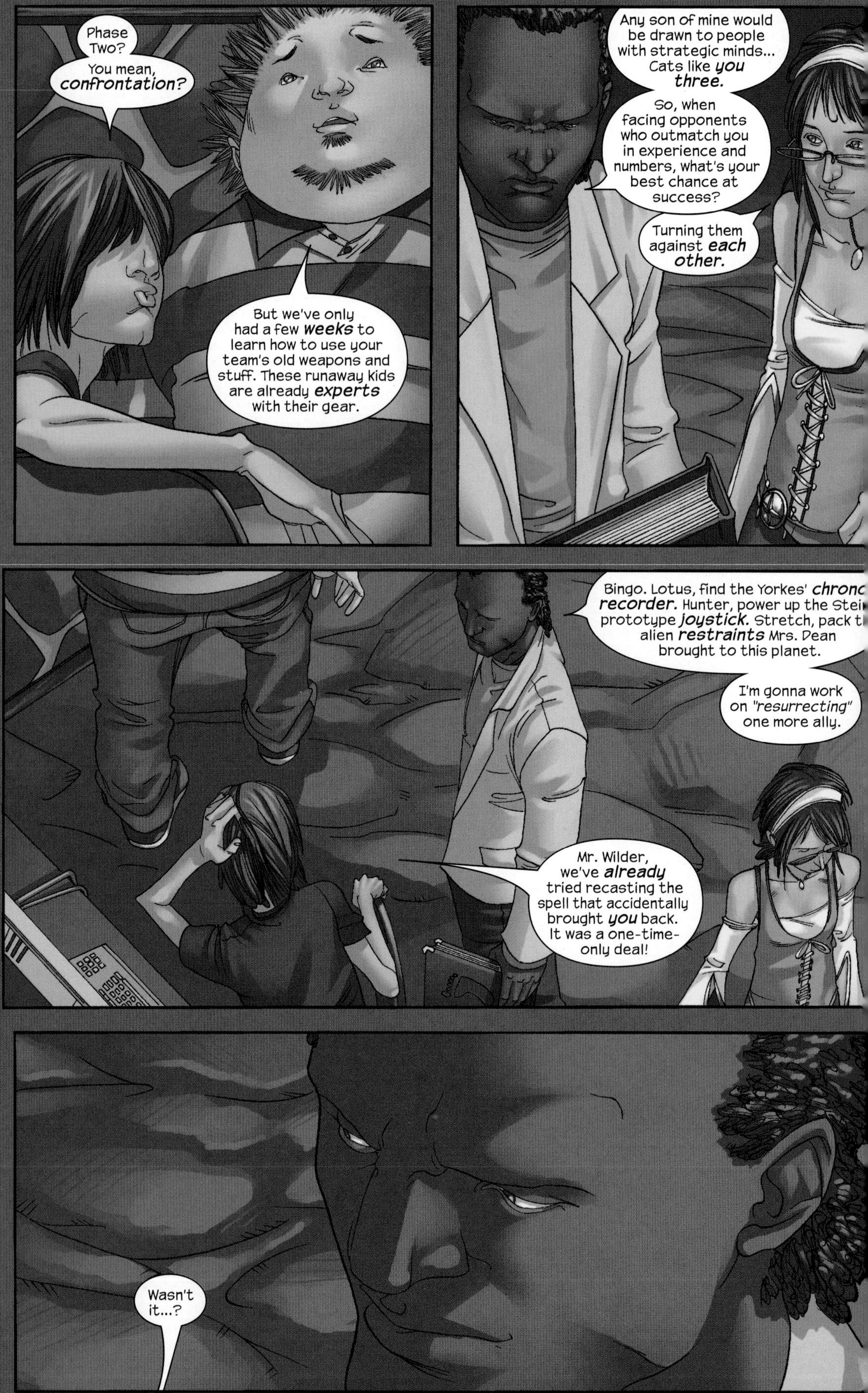

Phase Two? You mean, confrontation?
But we've only had a few weeks to learn how to use your team's old weapons and stuff. These runaway kids are already experts with their gear.
Any son of mine would be drawn to people with strategic minds... Cats like you three.
So, when facing opponents who outmatch you in experience and numbers, what's your best chance at success?
Turning them against each other.
Bingo. Lotus, find the Yorkes' chrono recorder. Hunter, power up the Stei prototype joystick. Stretch, pack t alien restraints Mrs. Dean brought to this planet.
I'm gonna work on "resurrecting" one more ally.
Mr. Wilder, we've already tried recasting the spell that accidentally brought you back. It was a one-time-only deal!
Wasn't it...?

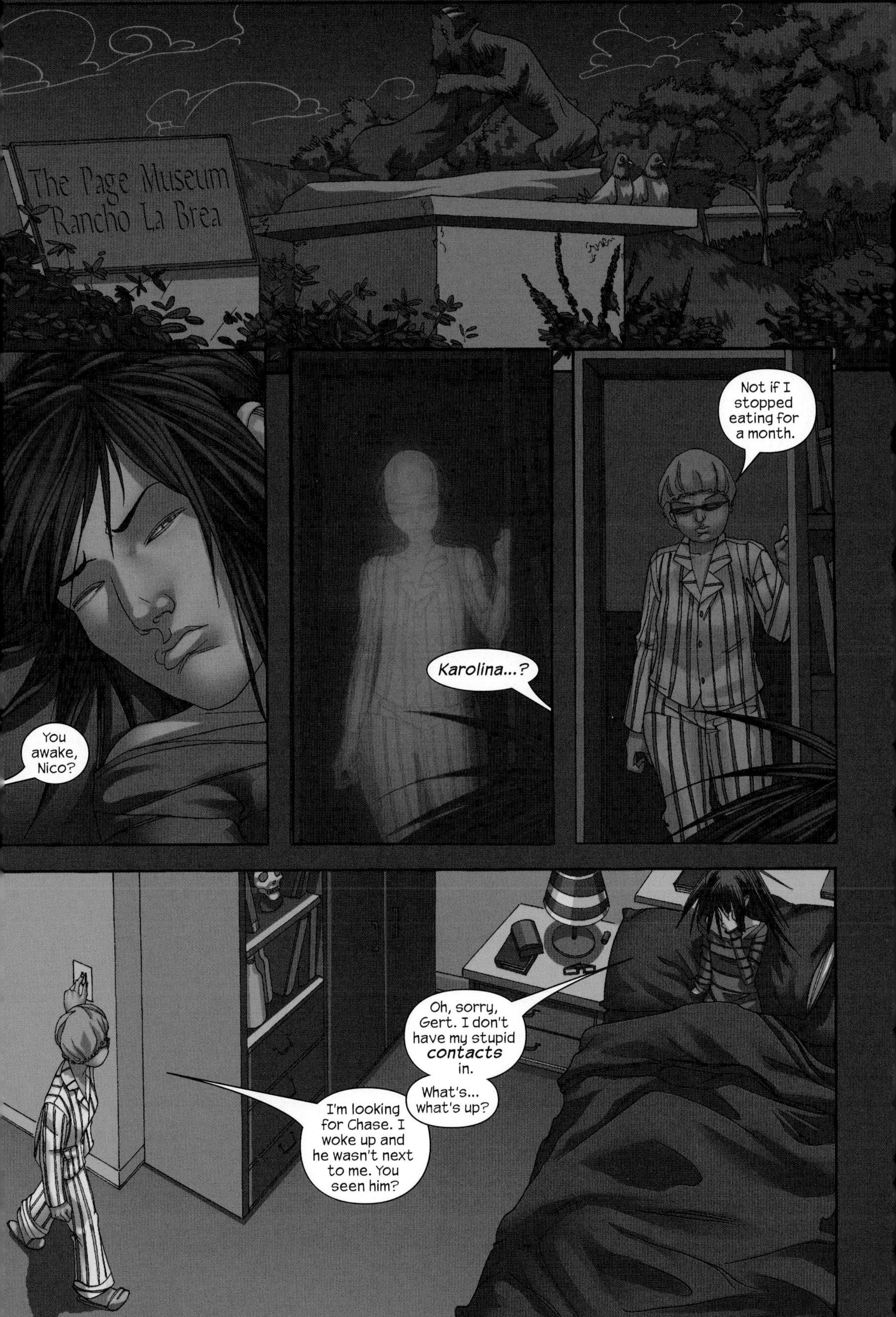

The Page Museum
Rancho La Brea
You awake, Nico?
Karolina...?
Not if I stopped eating for a month.
Oh, sorry, Gert. I don't have my stupid *contacts* in.
What's... what's up?
I'm looking for Chase. I woke up and he wasn't next to me. You seen him?

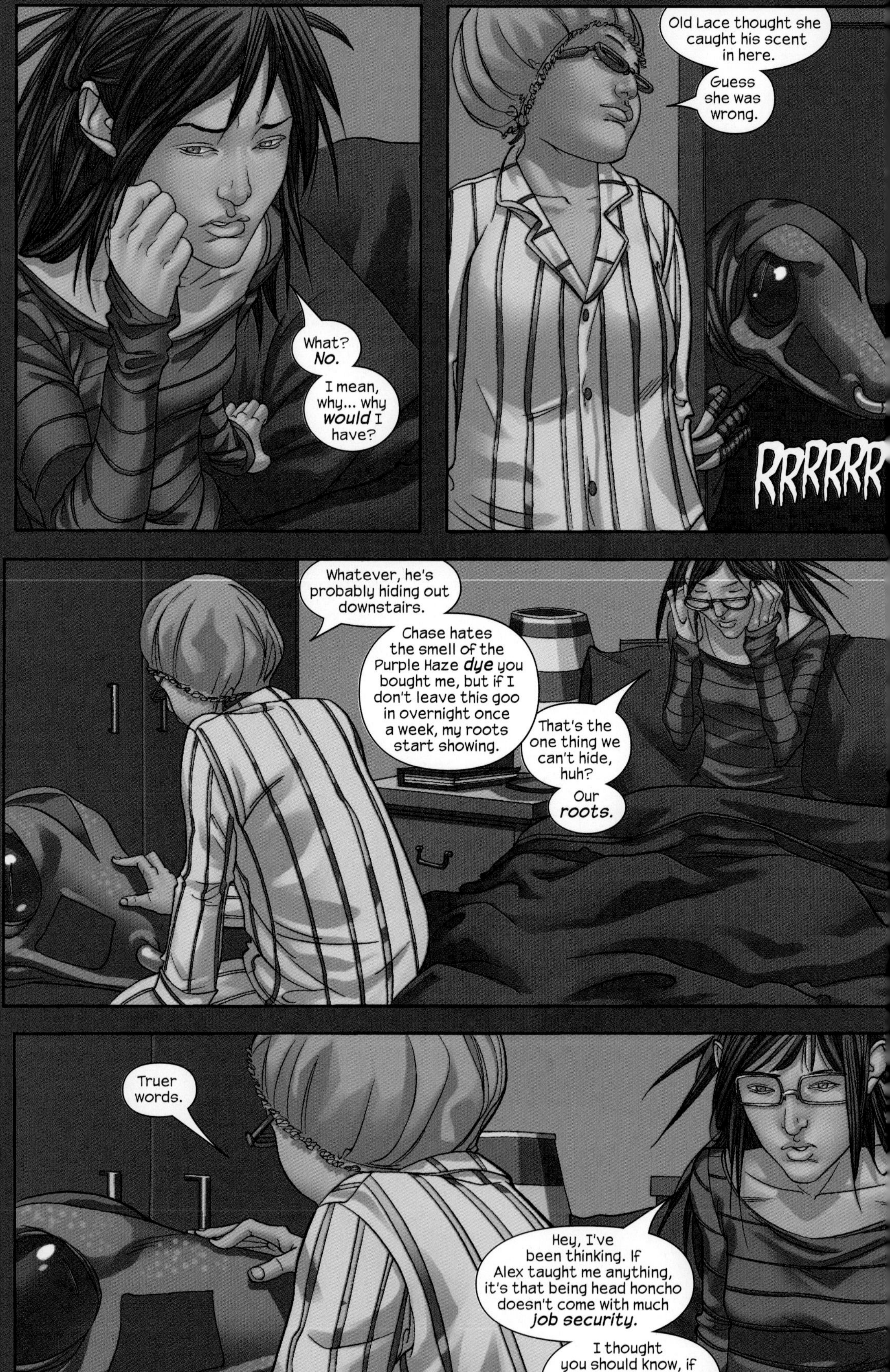

Old Lace thought she caught his scent in here.
Guess she was wrong.
What? *No.*
I mean, why... why *would* I have?
RRRRRR
Whatever, he's probably hiding out downstairs.
Chase hates the smell of the Purple Haze *dye* you bought me, but if I don't leave this goo in overnight once a week, my roots start showing.
That's the one thing we can't hide, huh?
Our *roots.*
Truer words.
Hey, I've been thinking. If Alex taught me anything, it's that being head honcho doesn't come with much *job security.*
I thought you should know, if anything ever happens to me... I want *you* to be team leader.

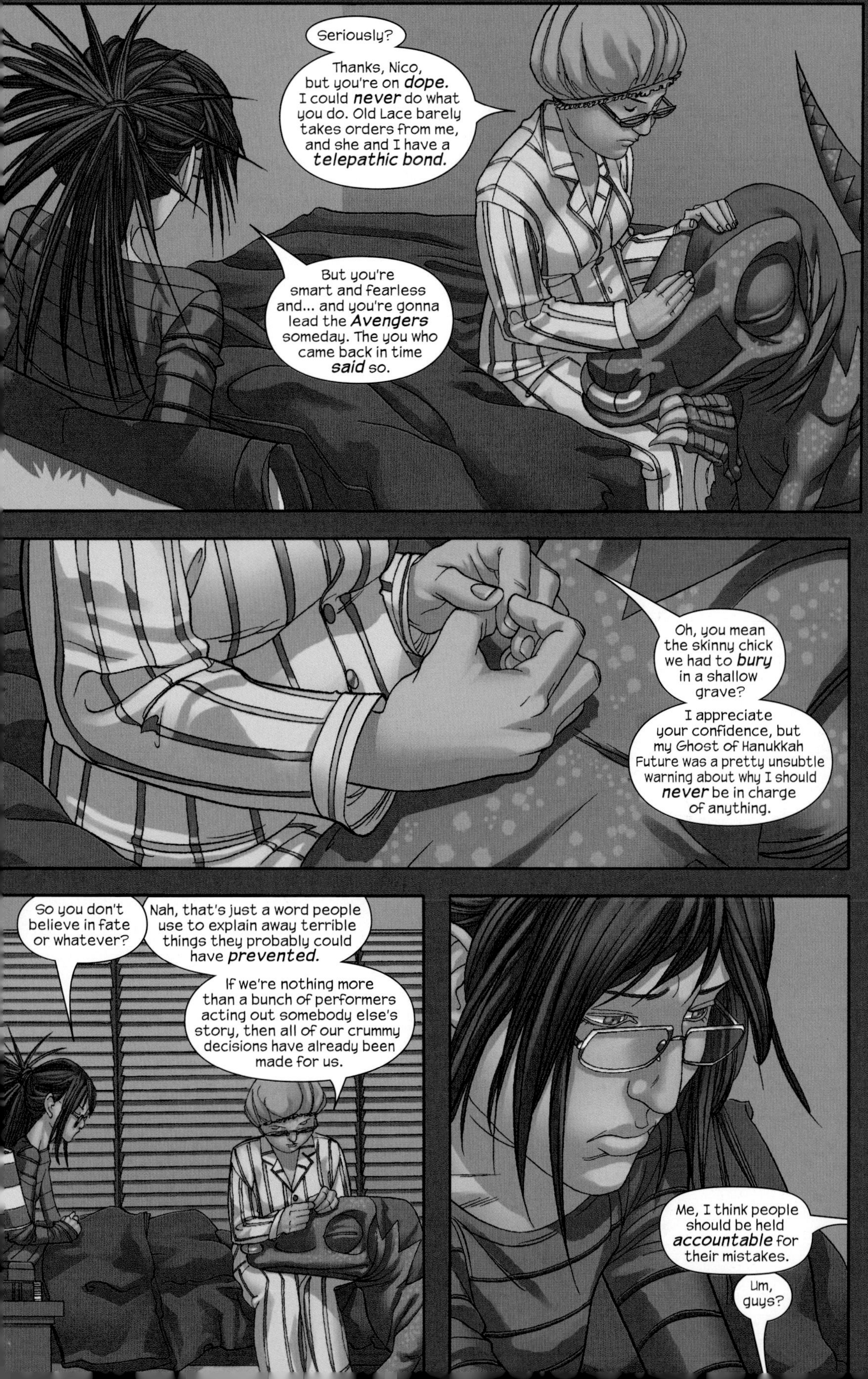

Seriously?
Thanks, Nico, but you're on dope. I could never do what you do. Old Lace barely takes orders from me, and she and I have a telepathic bond.
But you're smart and fearless and... and you're gonna lead the Avengers someday. The you who came back in time said so.
Oh, you mean the skinny chick we had to bury in a shallow grave?
I appreciate your confidence, but my Ghost of Hanukkah Future was a pretty unsubtle warning about why I should never be in charge of anything.
So you don't believe in fate or whatever?
Nah, that's just a word people use to explain away terrible things they probably could have prevented.
If we're nothing more than a bunch of performers acting out somebody else's story, then all of our crummy decisions have already been made for us.
Me, I think people should be held accountable for their mistakes.
Um, guys?

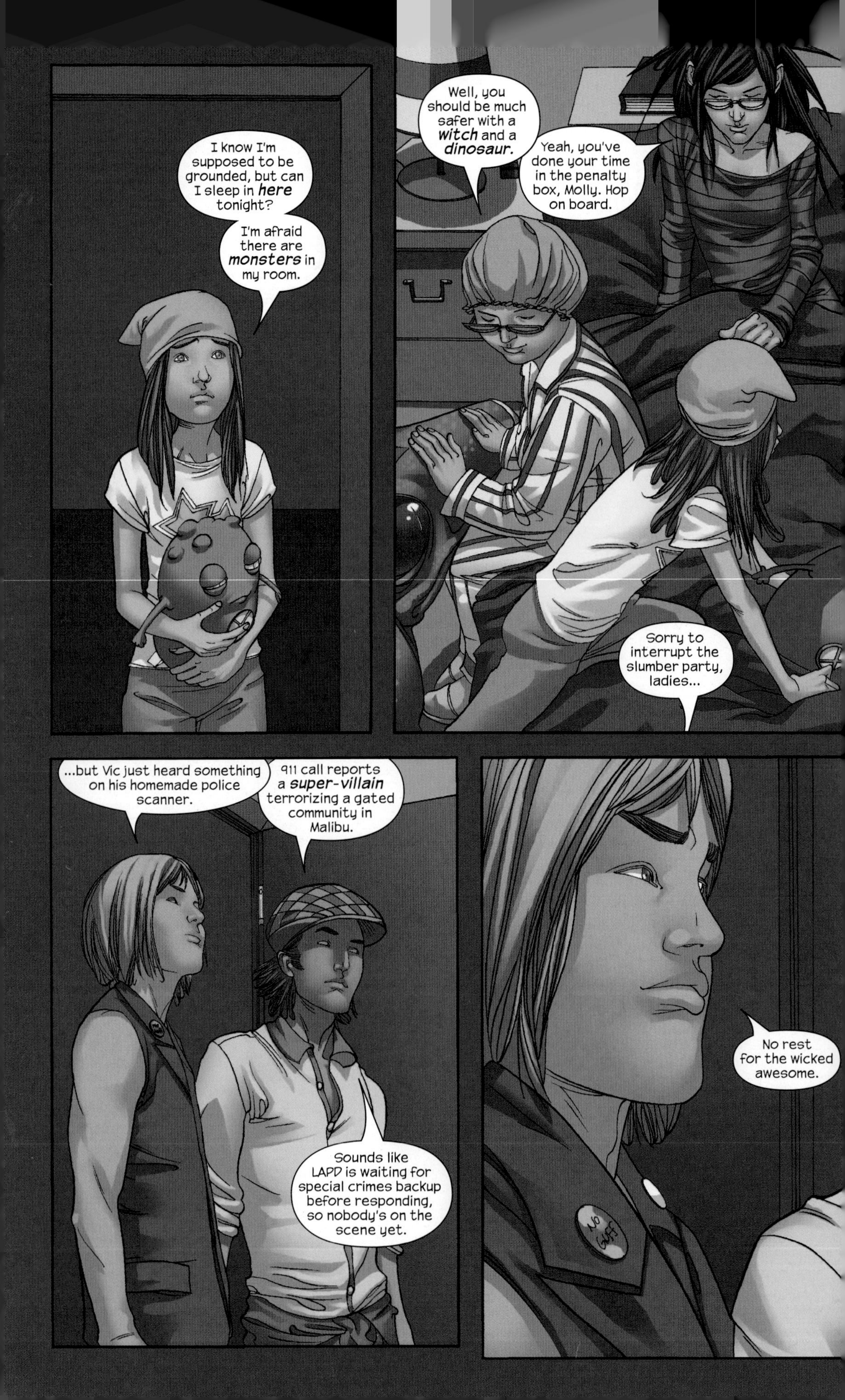

I know I'm supposed to be grounded, but can I sleep in here tonight?
I'm afraid there are monsters in my room.
Well, you should be much safer with a witch and a dinosaur.
Yeah, you've done your time in the penalty box, Molly. Hop on board.
Sorry to interrupt the slumber party, ladies...
...but Vic just heard something on his homemade police scanner.
911 call reports a super-villain terrorizing a gated community in Malibu.
Sounds like LAPD is waiting for special crimes backup before responding, so nobody's on the scene yet.
No rest for the wicked awesome.
NO GUFF

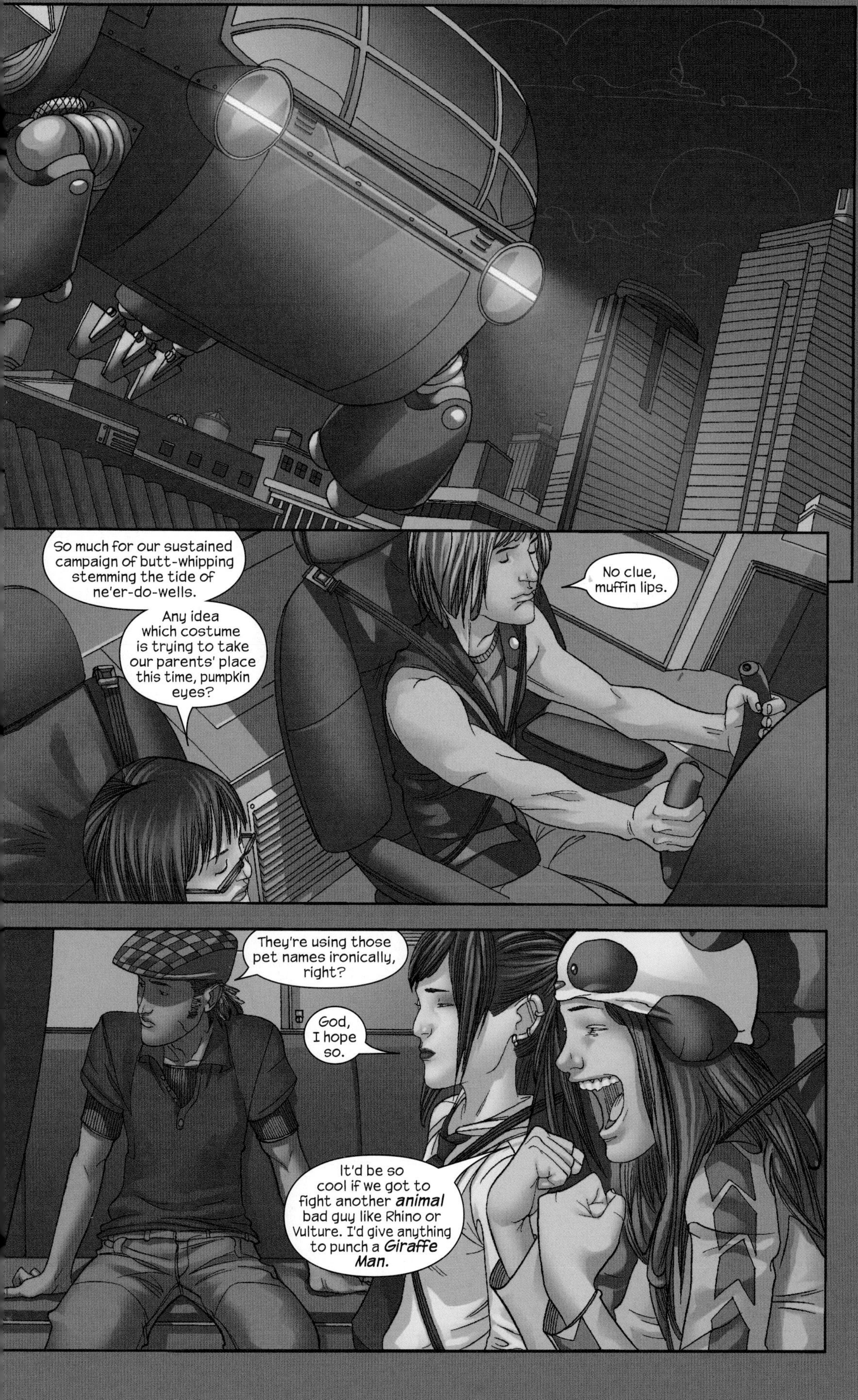
So much for our sustained campaign of butt-whipping stemming the tide of ne'er-do-wells.
Any idea which costume is trying to take our parents' place this time, pumpkin eyes?
No clue, muffin lips.
They're using those pet names ironically, right?
God, I hope so.
It'd be so cool if we got to fight another *animal* bad guy like Rhino or Vulture. I'd give anything to punch a *Giraffe Man.*

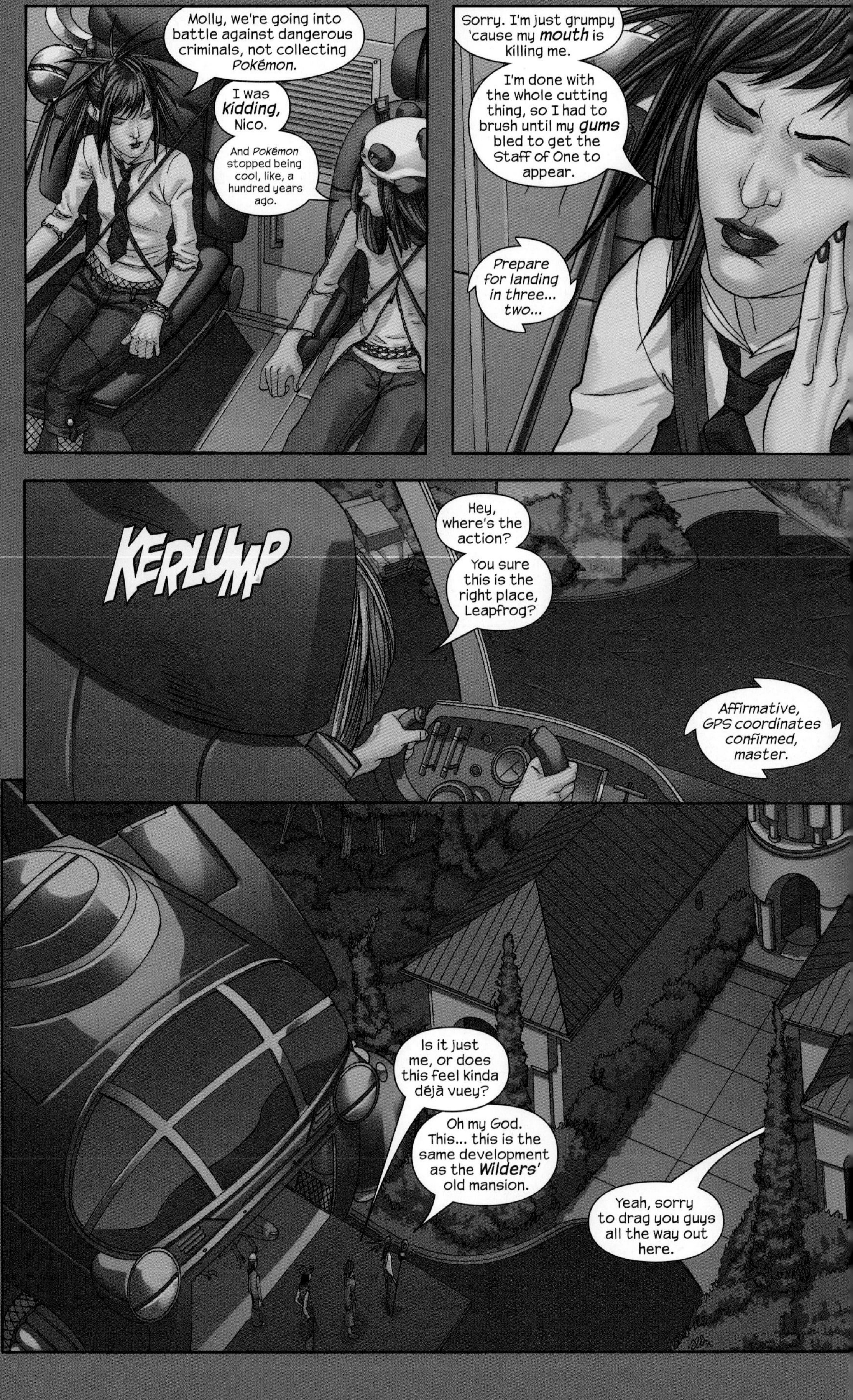
Molly, we're going into battle against dangerous criminals, not collecting Pokémon.
I was kidding, Nico.
And Pokémon stopped being cool, like, a hundred years ago.
Sorry. I'm just grumpy 'cause my mouth is killing me.
I'm done with the whole cutting thing, so I had to brush until my gums bled to get the Staff of One to appear.
Prepare for landing in three... two...
KERLUMP
Hey, where's the action?
You sure this is the right place, Leapfrog?
Affirmative, GPS coordinates confirmed, master.
Is it just me, or does this feel kinda déjà vuey?
Oh my God. This... this is the same development as the Wilders' old mansion.
Yeah, sorry to drag you guys all the way out here.

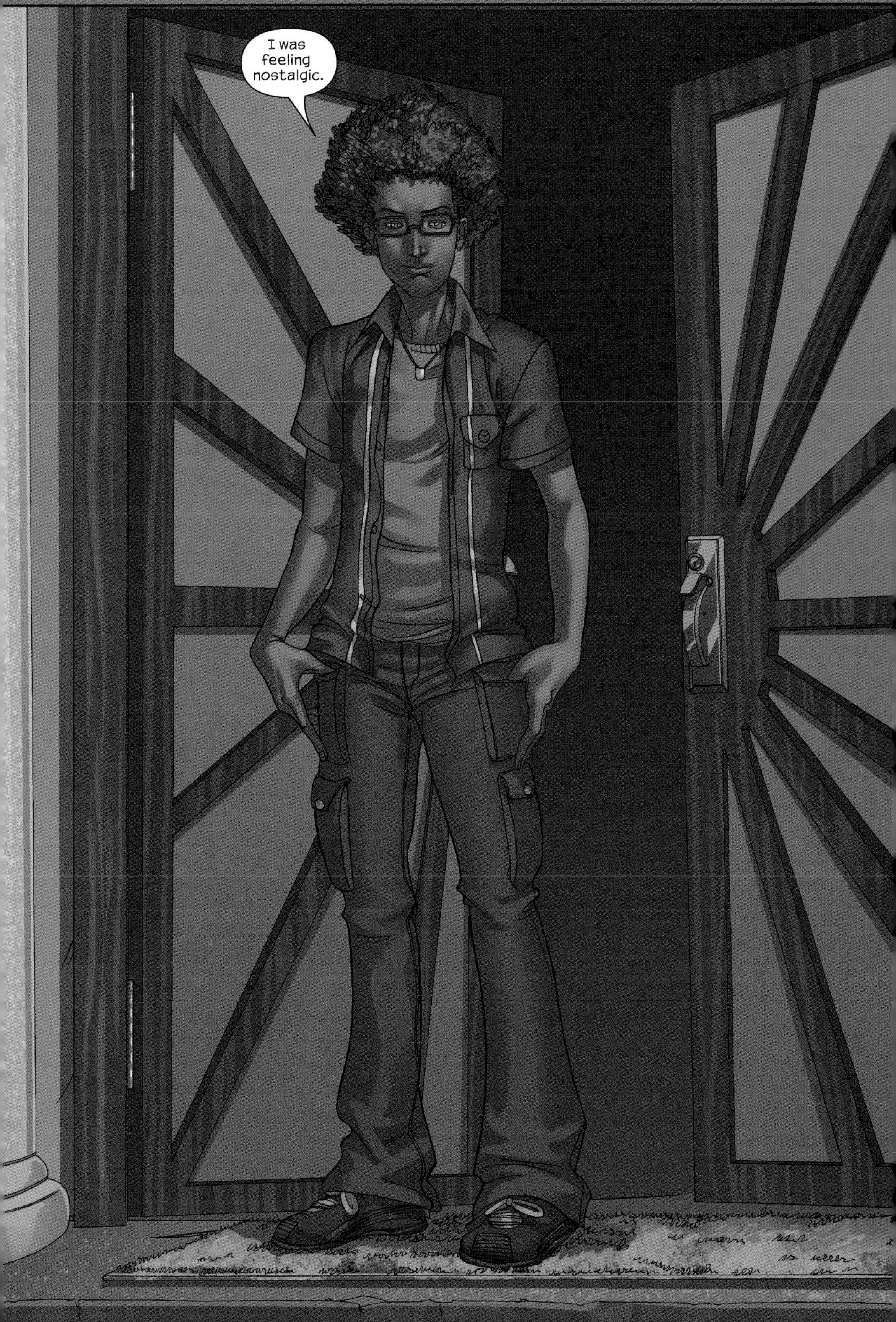
I was feeling nostalgic.

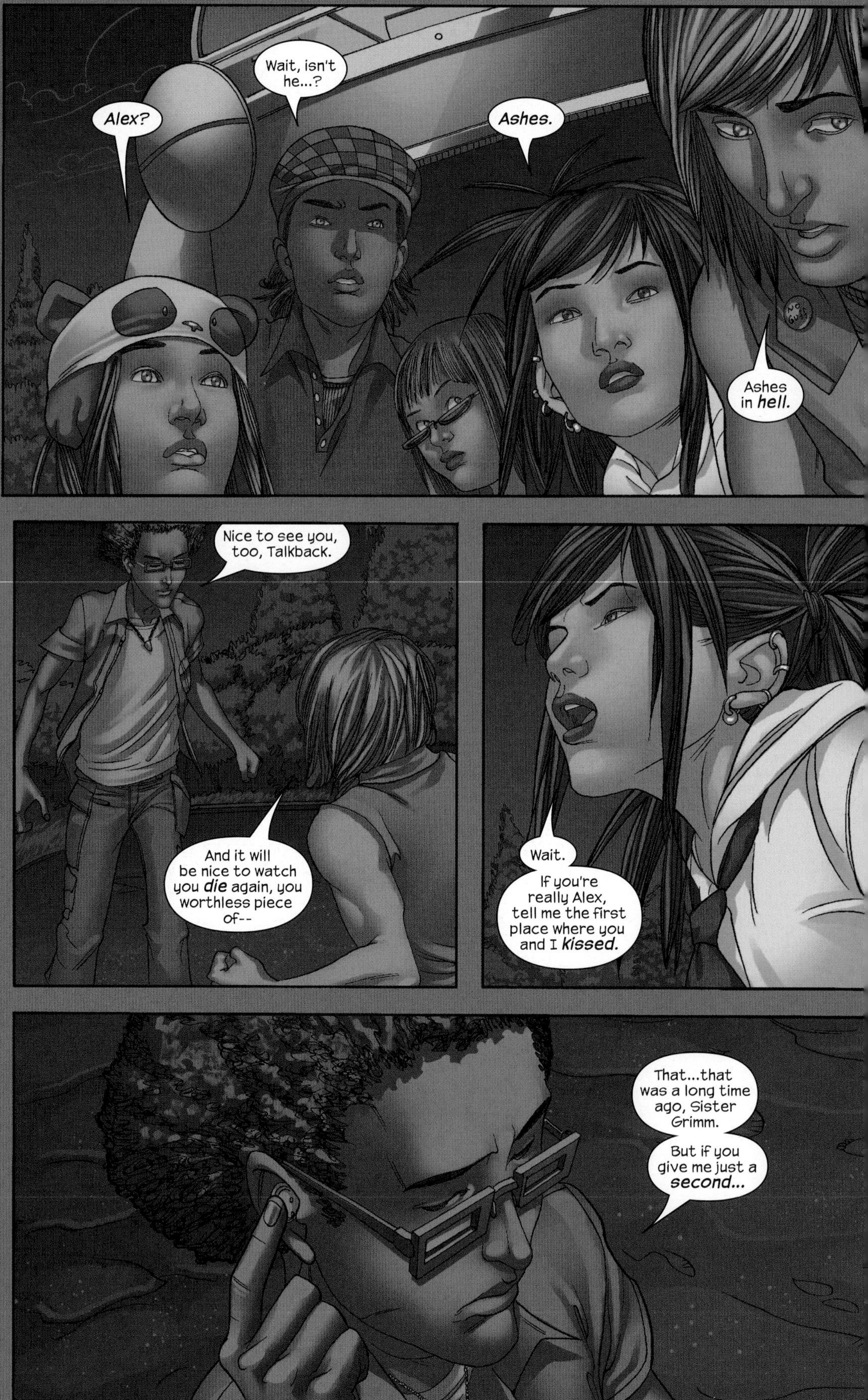
Alex?
Wait, isn't he...?
Ashes.
Ashes in hell.
Nice to see you, too, Talkback.
And it will be nice to watch you die again, you worthless piece of--
Wait.
If you're really Alex, tell me the first place where you and I kissed.
That...that was a long time ago, Sister Grimm.
But if you give me just a second...

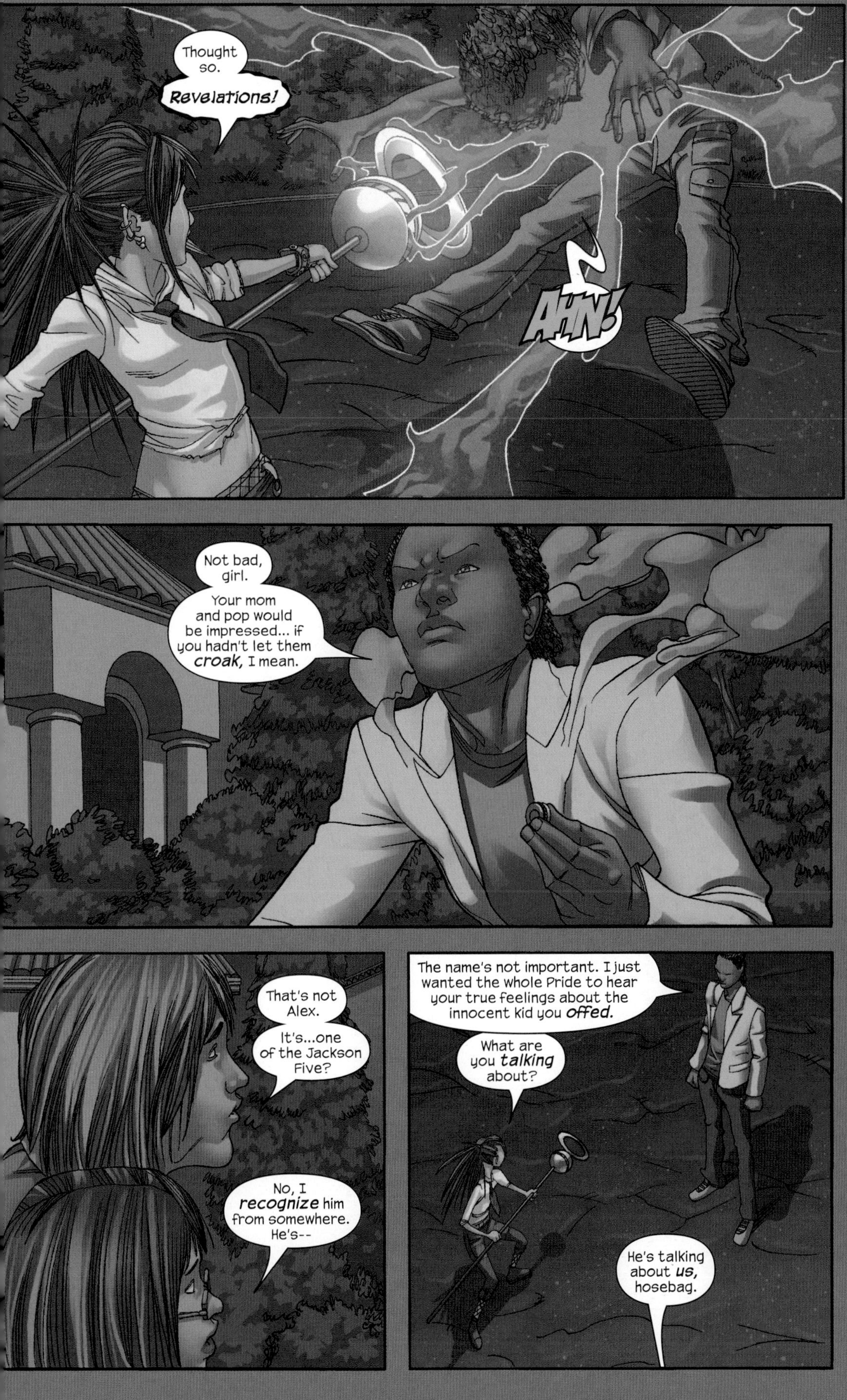

Thought so.
Revelations!
AHN!
Not bad, girl.
Your mom and pop would be impressed... if you hadn't let them croak, I mean.
That's not Alex.
It's...one of the Jackson Five?
No, I recognize him from somewhere. He's--
The name's not important. I just wanted the whole Pride to hear your true feelings about the innocent kid you offed.
What are you talking about?
He's talking about us, hosebag.

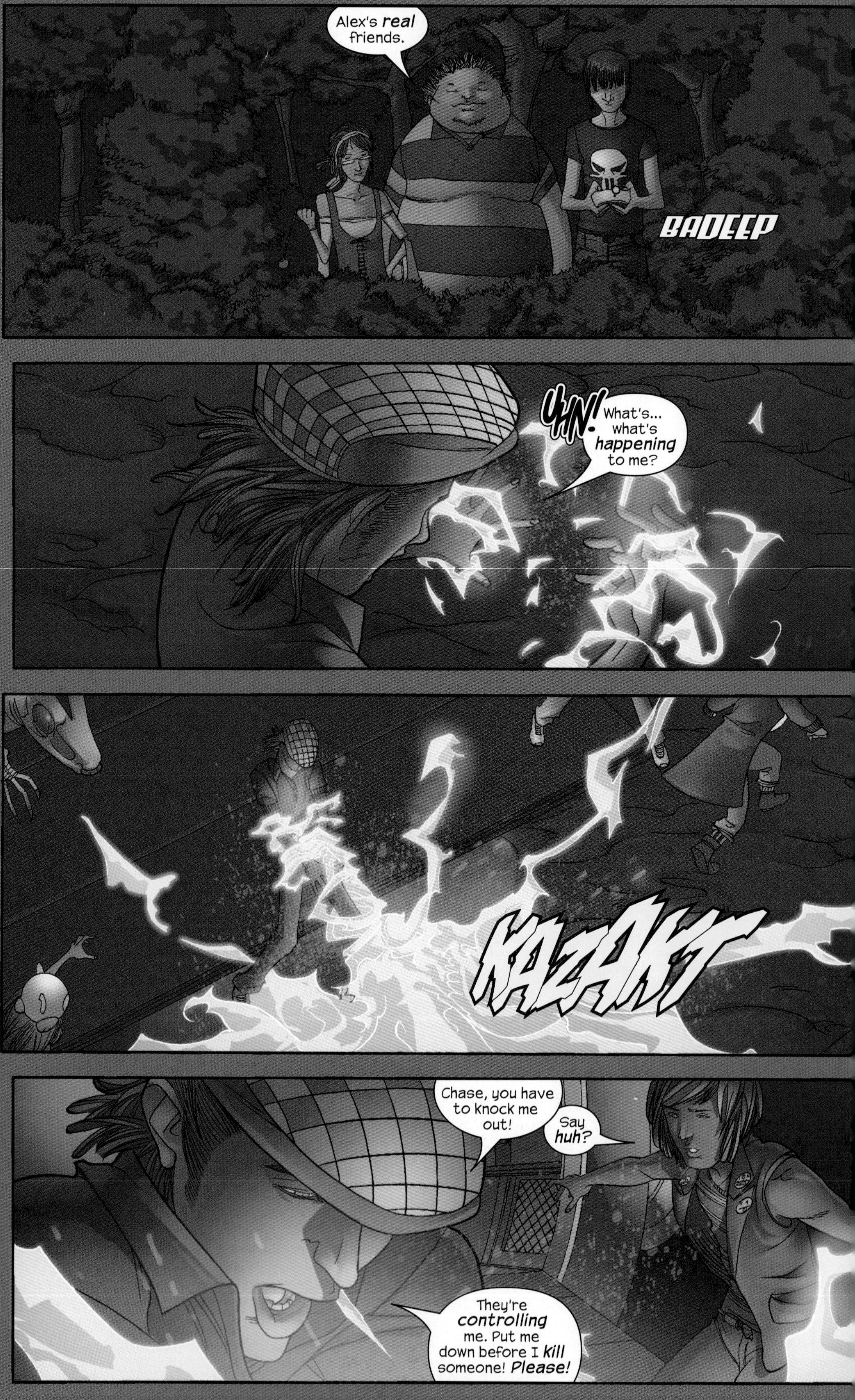

Alex's real friends.
BADEEP
UHN! What's... what's happening to me?
KAZAKT
Chase, you have to knock me out!
Say huh?
They're controlling me. Put me down before I kill someone! Please!

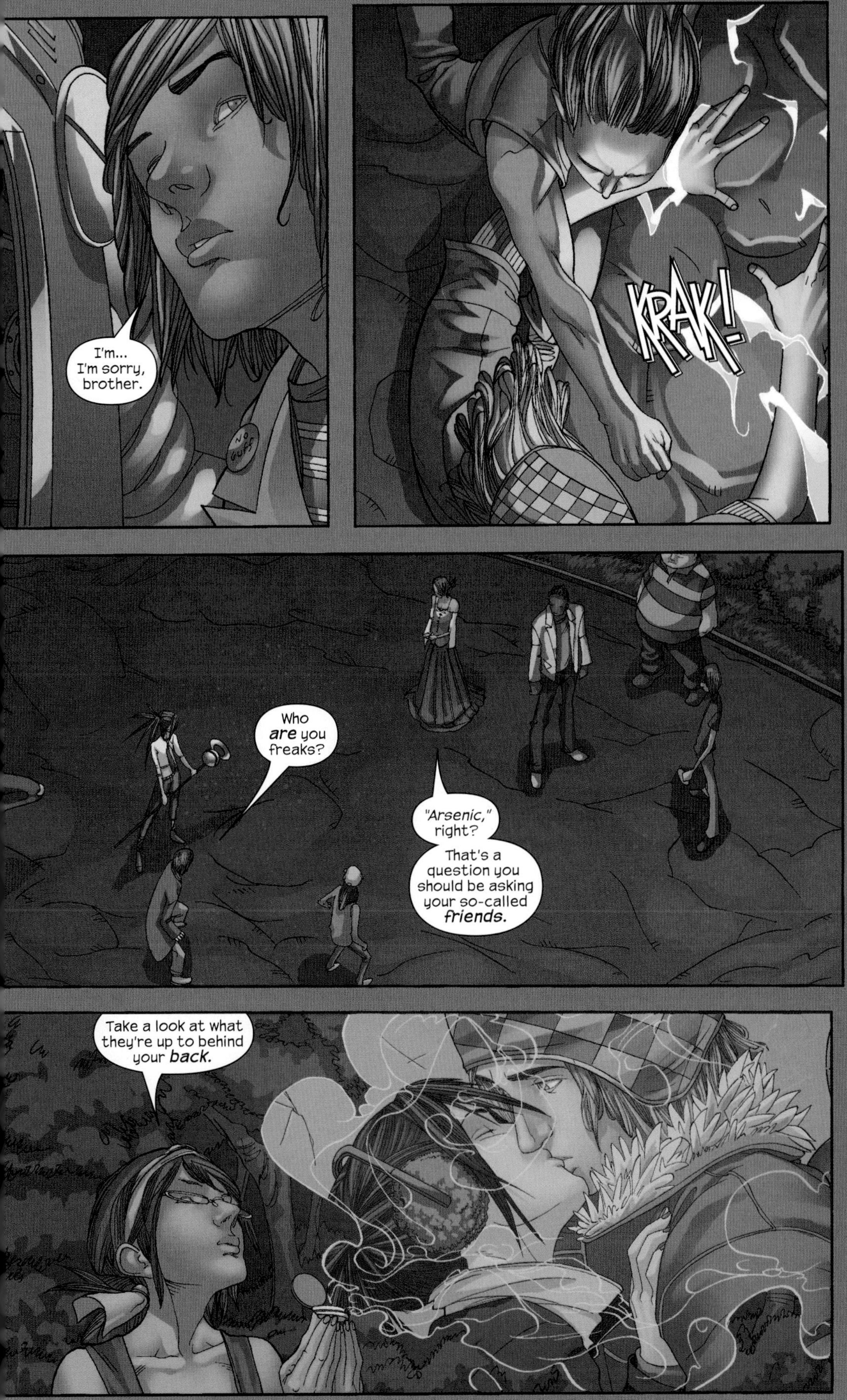
I'm... I'm sorry, brother.
KRAK!
Who *are* you freaks?
"Arsenic," right?
That's a question you should be asking your so-called *friends.*
Take a look at what they're up to behind your *back.*

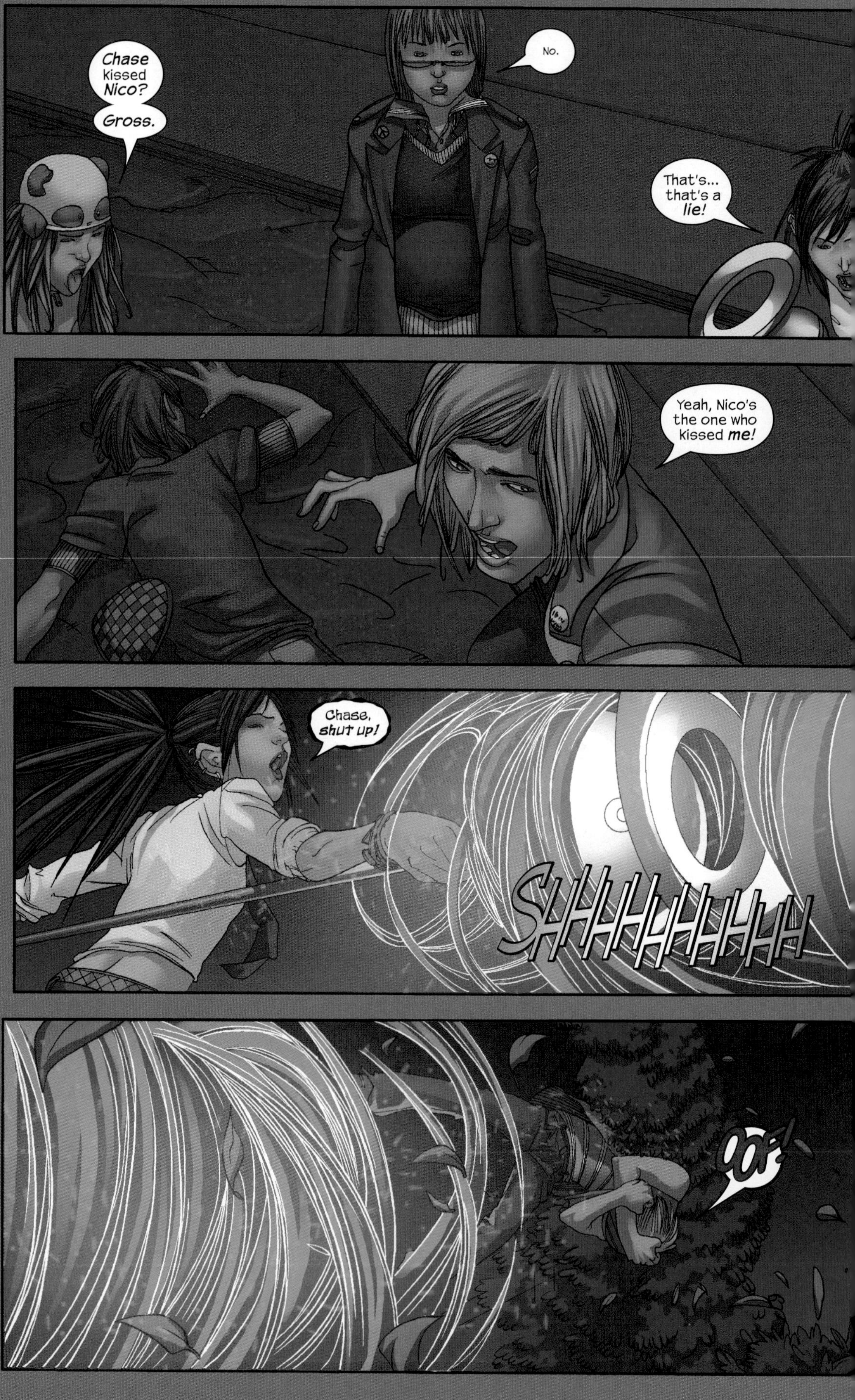
Chase kissed Nico?
Gross.
No.
That's... that's a lie!
Yeah, Nico's the one who kissed me!
Chase, shut up!
SHHHHHHHHHH
OOF!

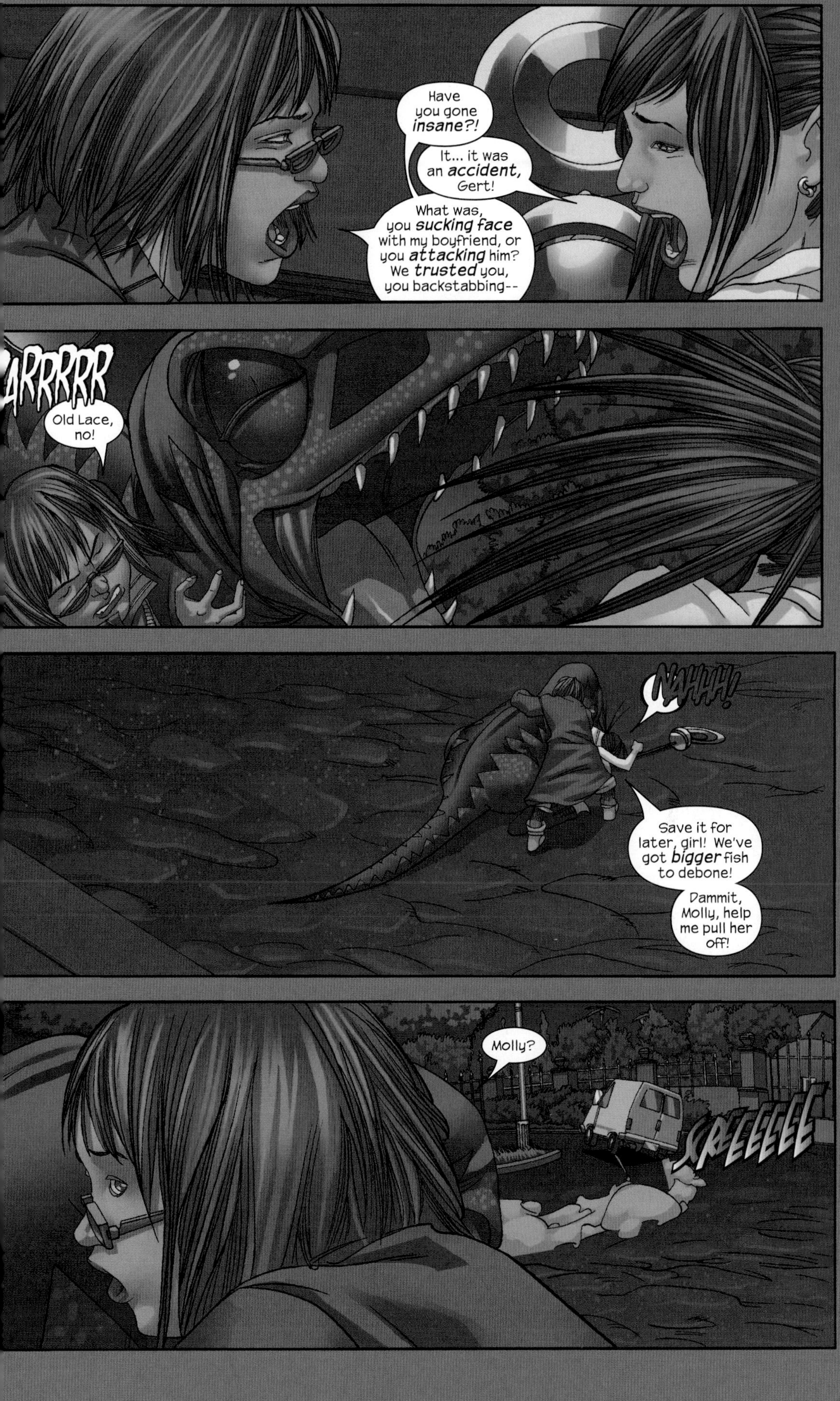
Have you gone *insane*?!
It... it was an *accident,* Gert!
What was, you ***sucking face*** with my boyfriend, or you ***attacking*** him? We ***trusted*** you, you backstabbing--
ARRRRR
Old Lace, no!
NAHHH!
Save it for later, girl! We've got ***bigger*** fish to debone!
Dammit, Molly, help me pull her off!
Molly?
SKREEEEEE

"Molly!"

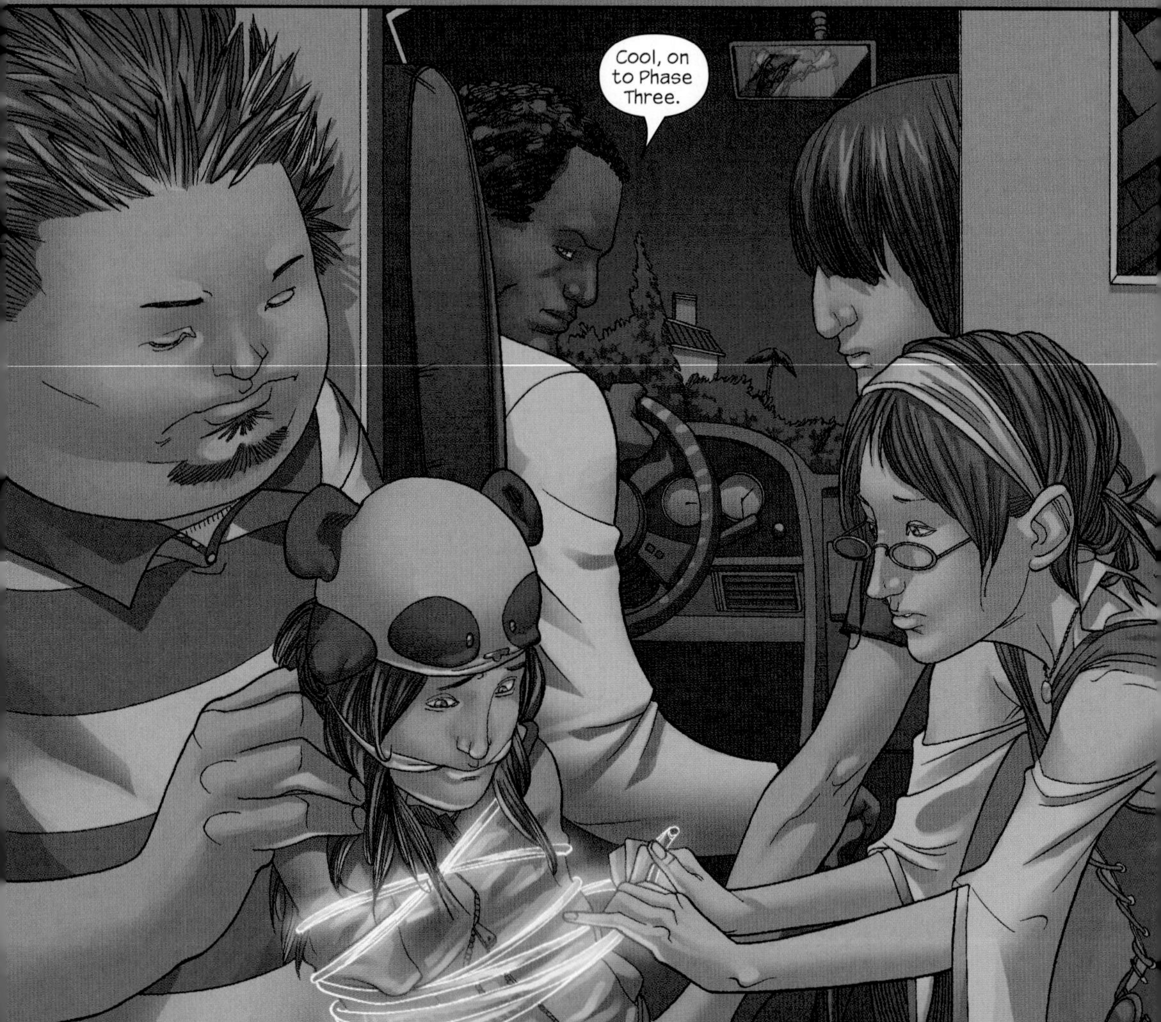
Cool, on to Phase Three.

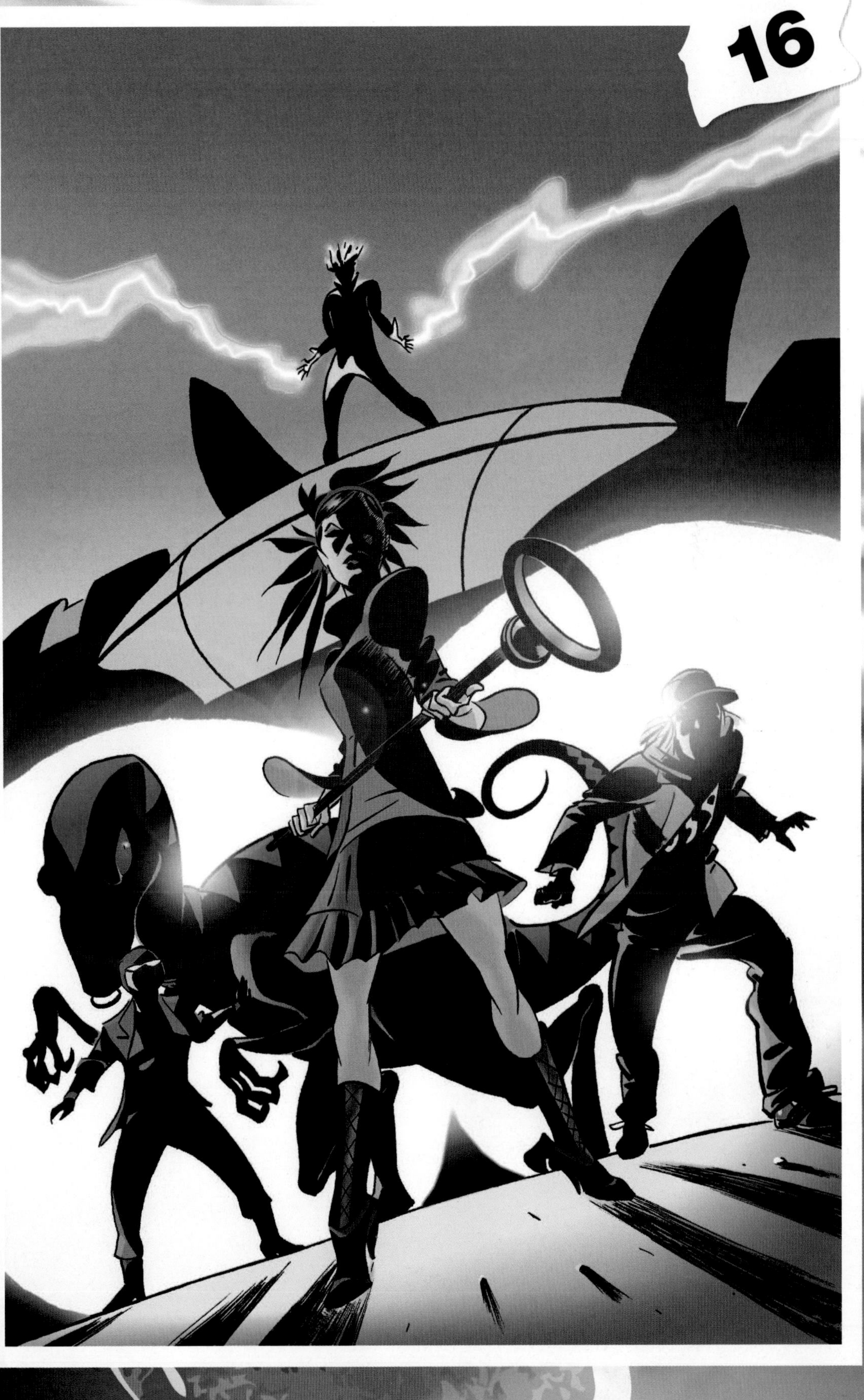
16

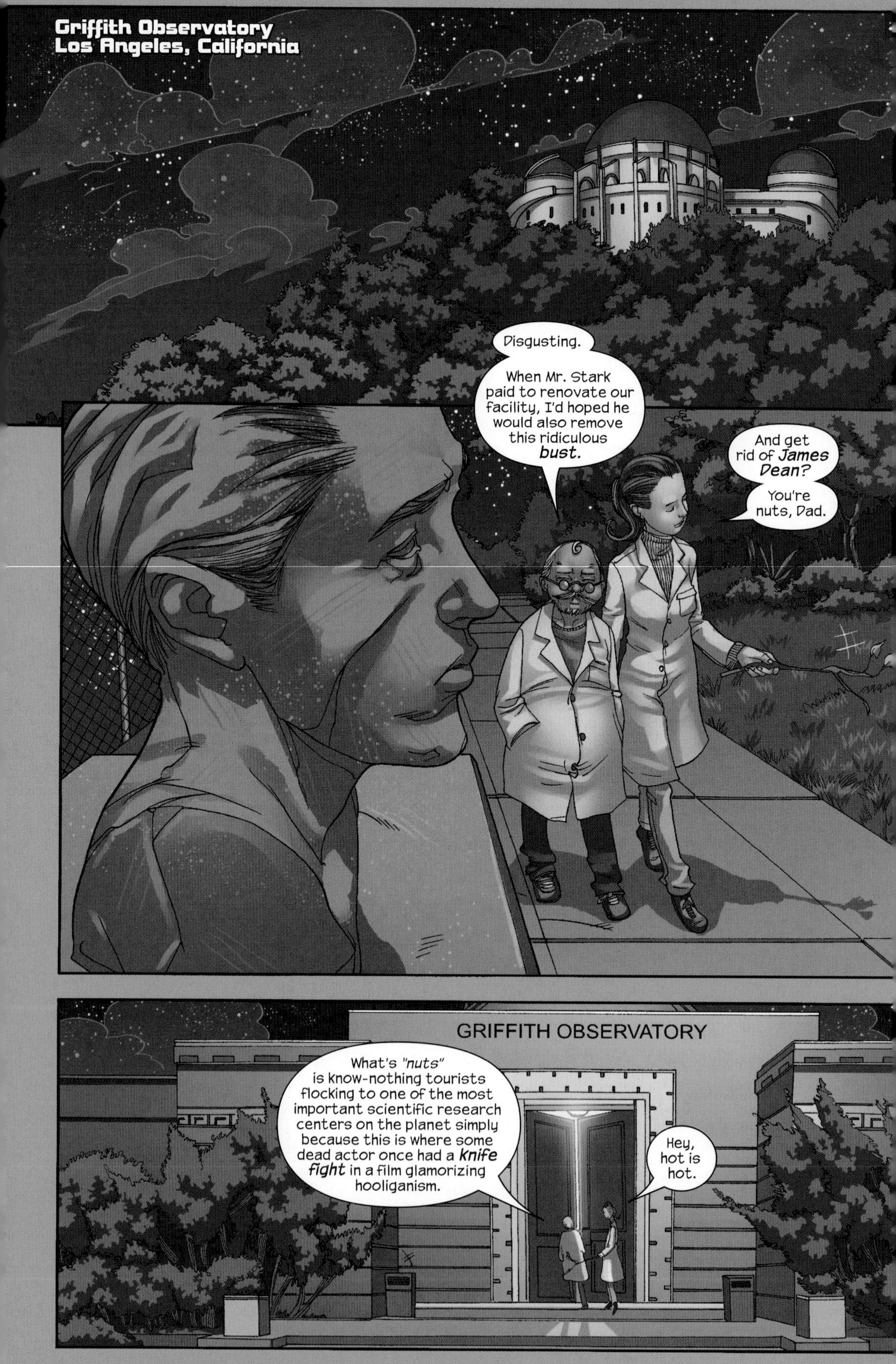
Griffith Observatory
Los Angeles, California
Disgusting.
When Mr. Stark paid to renovate our facility, I'd hoped he would also remove this ridiculous *bust.*
And get rid of *James Dean?*
You're nuts, Dad.
GRIFFITH OBSERVATORY
What's *"nuts"* is know-nothing tourists flocking to one of the most important scientific research centers on the planet simply because this is where some dead actor once had a *knife fight* in a film glamorizing hooliganism.
Hey, hot is hot.

I'm not sure Mr. [Ein]stein would agree [wit]h your assessment of *relativity,* Tatiana.

Now stop [d]awdling and [p]ower up the [t]elescope.

Yes, sir.

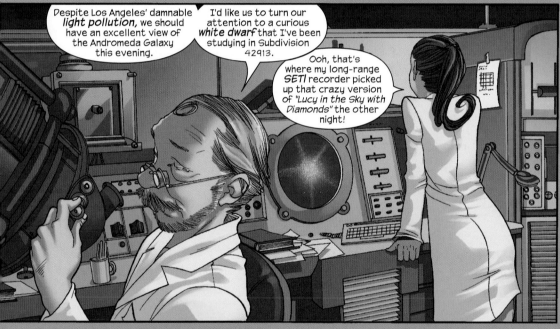

Despite Los Angeles' damnable *light pollution,* we should have an excellent view of the Andromeda Galaxy this evening.

I'd like us to turn our attention to a curious *white dwarf* that I've been studying in Subdivision 42913.

Ooh, that's where my long-range *SETI* recorder picked up that crazy version of *"Lucy in the Sky with Diamonds"* the other night!

Don't be ridiculous, [e]xtraterrestrials are [a] myth perpetuated by [sim]ply disturbed individuals. [I]t was probably just a [f]eedback loop from a satellite.

There's barely [i]ntelligent life on [th]*is* planet, much less [i]n other reaches of the--

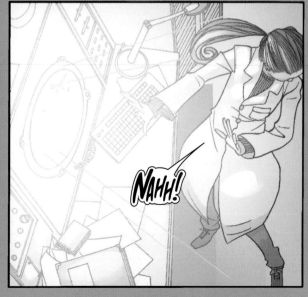

NAHH!

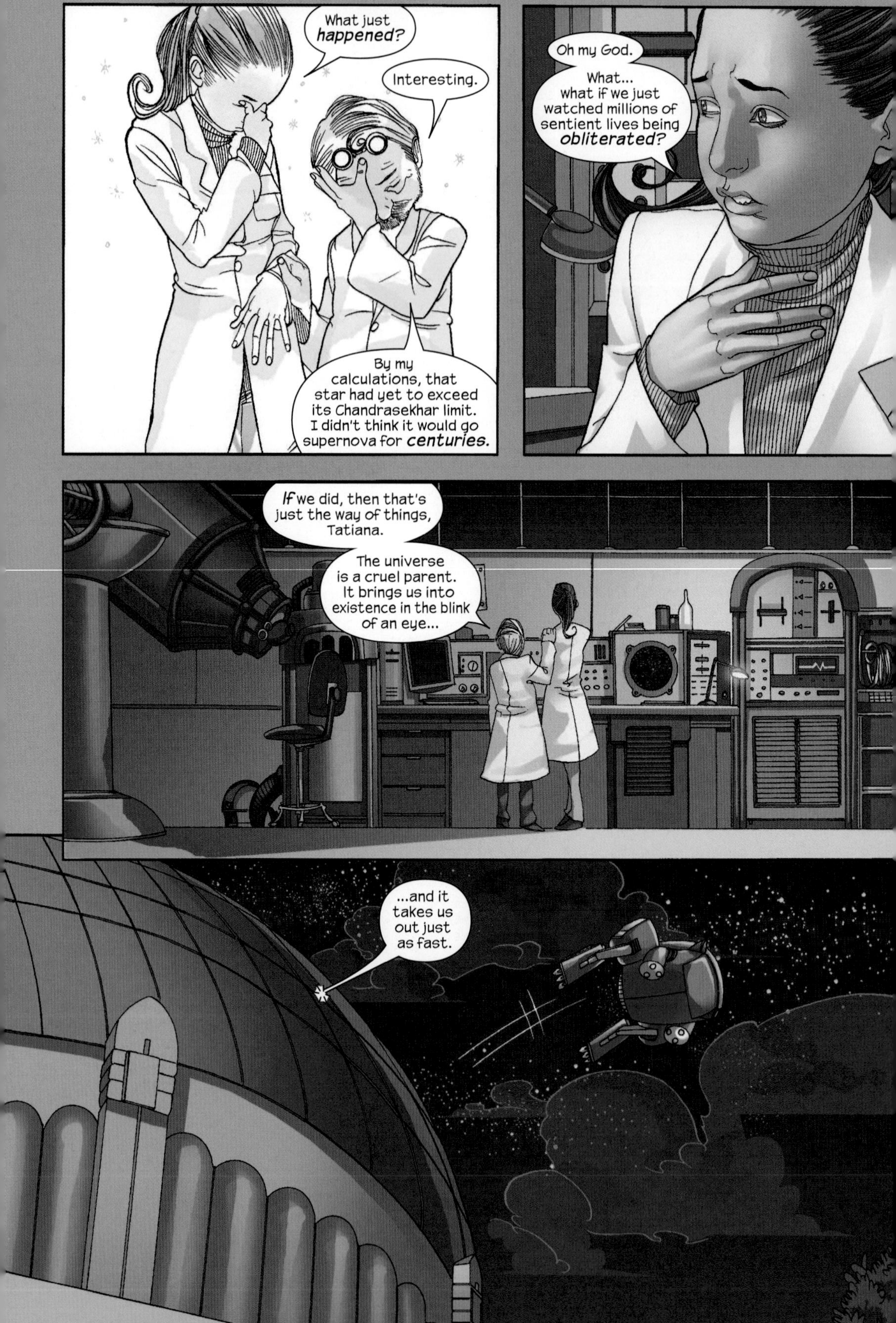
What just happened?
Interesting.
By my calculations, that star had yet to exceed its Chandrasekhar limit. I didn't think it would go supernova for centuries.
Oh my God.
What... what if we just watched millions of sentient lives being obliterated?
If we did, then that's just the way of things, Tatiana.
The universe is a cruel parent. It brings us into existence in the blink of an eye...
...and it takes us out just as fast.

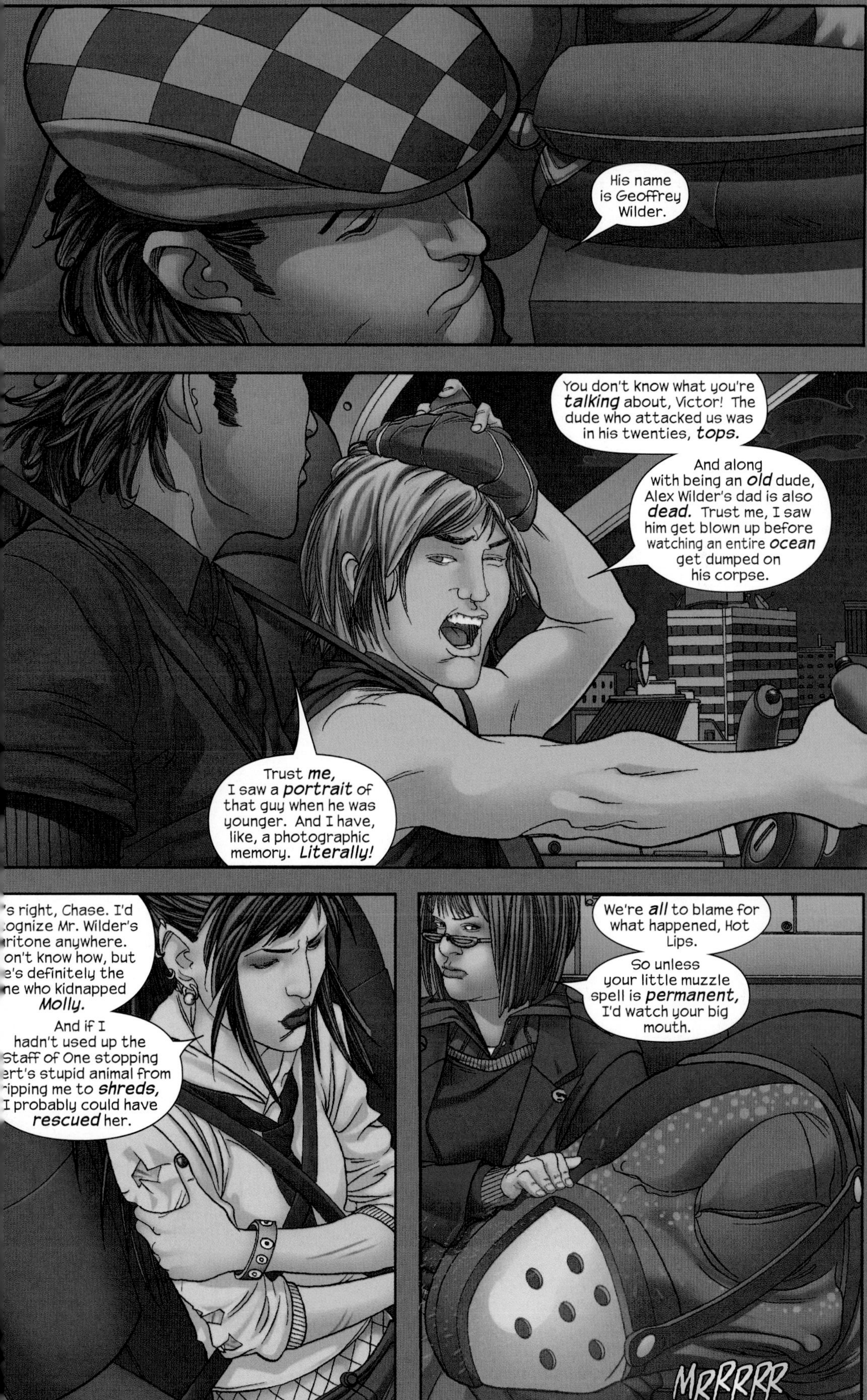

His name is Geoffrey Wilder.
You don't know what you're *talking* about, Victor! The dude who attacked us was in his twenties, *tops.*
And along with being an *old* dude, Alex Wilder's dad is also *dead.* Trust me, I saw him get blown up before watching an entire *ocean* get dumped on his corpse.
Trust *me,* I saw a *portrait* of that guy when he was younger. And I have, like, a photographic memory. *Literally!*
's right, Chase. I'd cognize Mr. Wilder's ritone anywhere. on't know how, but e's definitely the ne who kidnapped *Molly.*
And if I hadn't used up the Staff of One stopping ert's stupid animal from ripping me to *shreds,* I probably could have *rescued* her.
We're *all* to blame for what happened, Hot Lips.
So unless your little muzzle spell is *permanent,* I'd watch your big mouth.
MRRRRR

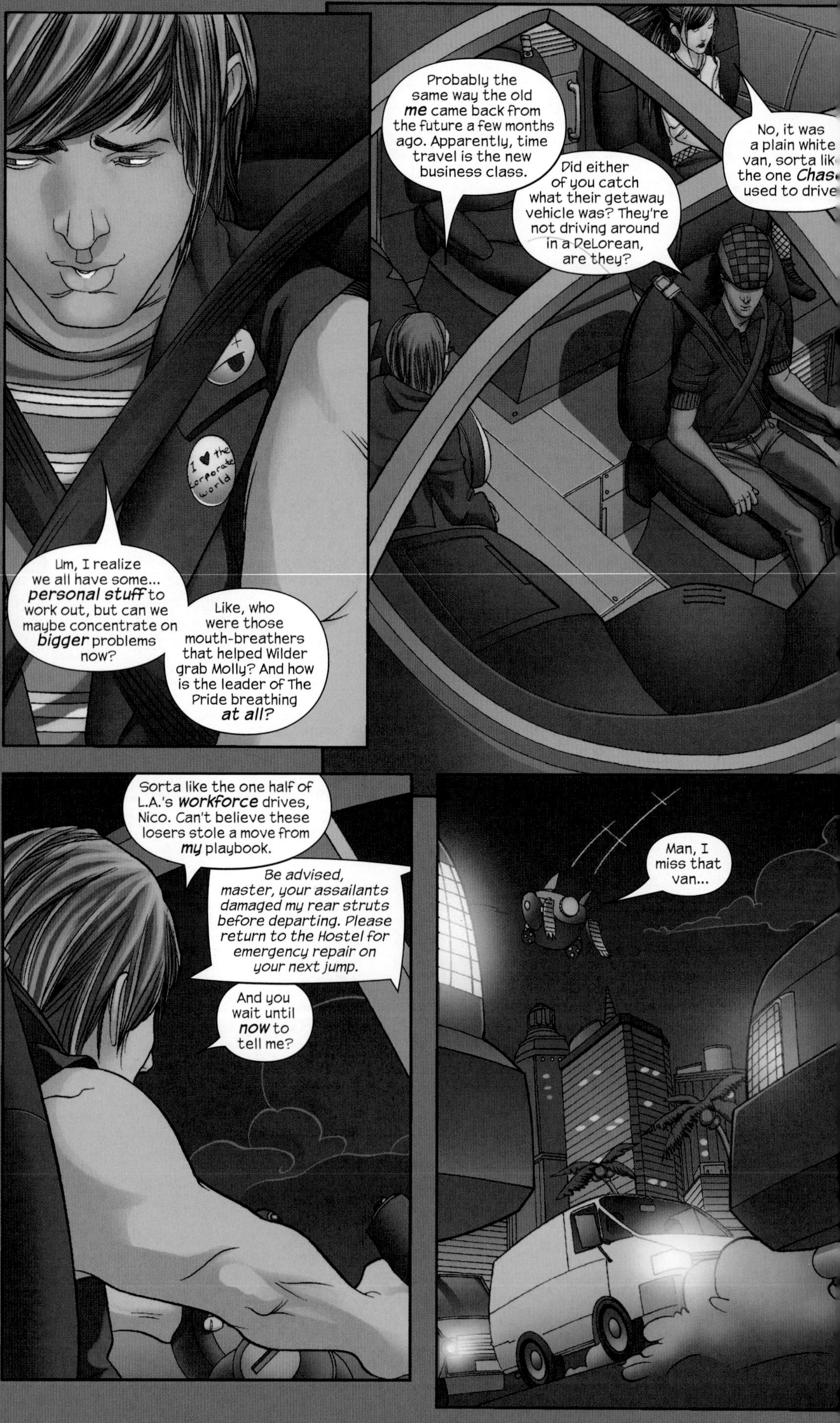
Um, I realize we all have some... *personal stuff* to work out, but can we maybe concentrate on *bigger* problems now?
Like, who were those mouth-breathers that helped Wilder grab Molly? And how is the leader of The Pride breathing *at all?*
I ♥ the corporate world
Probably the same way the old *me* came back from the future a few months ago. Apparently, time travel is the new business class.
Did either of you catch what their getaway vehicle was? They're not driving around in a DeLorean, are they?
No, it was a plain white van, sorta lik the one *Chas* used to drive
Sorta like the one half of L.A.'s *workforce* drives, Nico. Can't believe these losers stole a move from *my* playbook.
Be advised, master, your assailants damaged my rear struts before departing. Please return to the Hostel for emergency repair on your next jump.
And you wait until *now* to tell me?
Man, I miss that van...

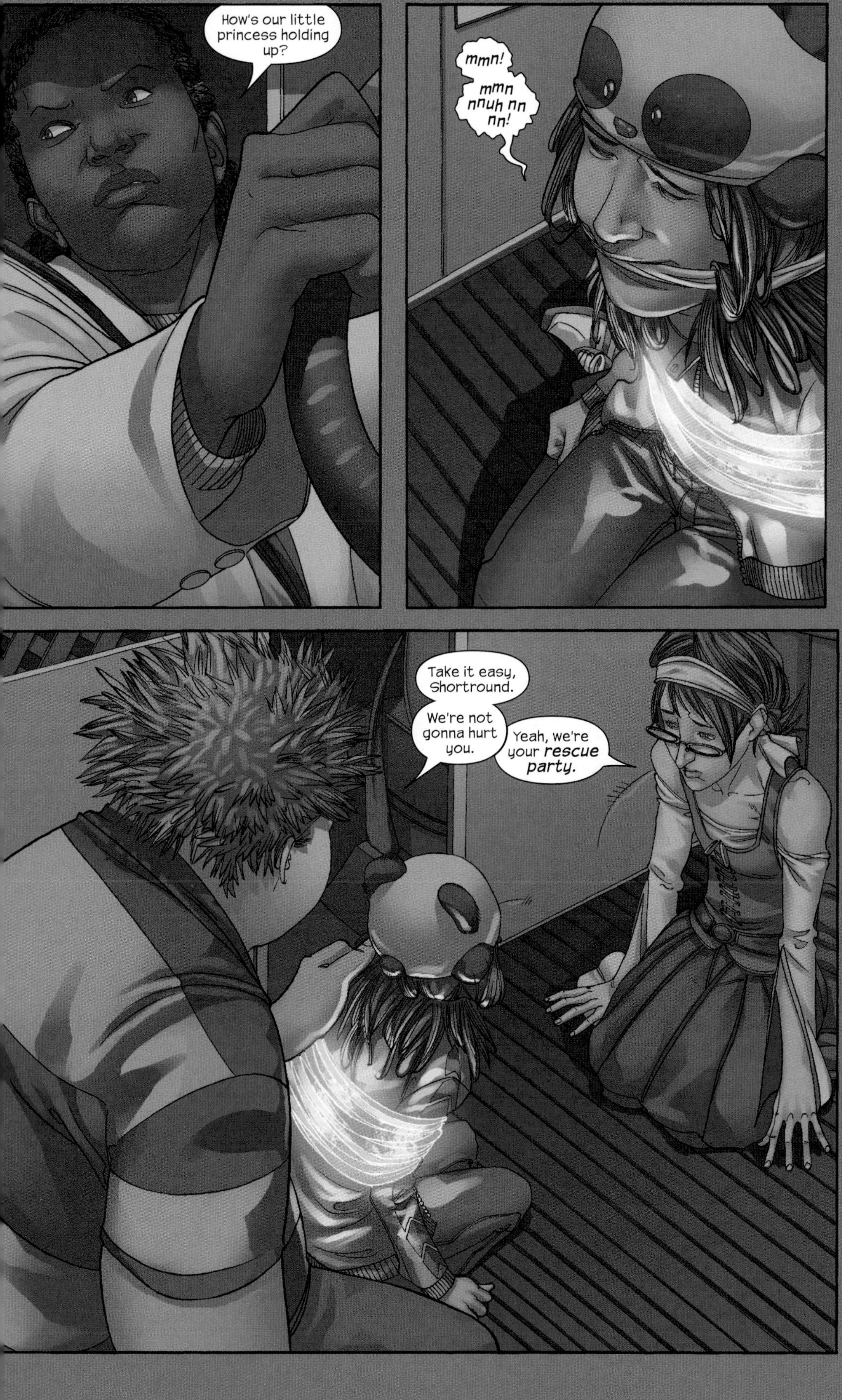
How's our little princess holding up?
mmn!
mmn nnuh nn nn!
Take it easy, Shortround.
We're not gonna hurt you.
Yeah, we're your *rescue party.*

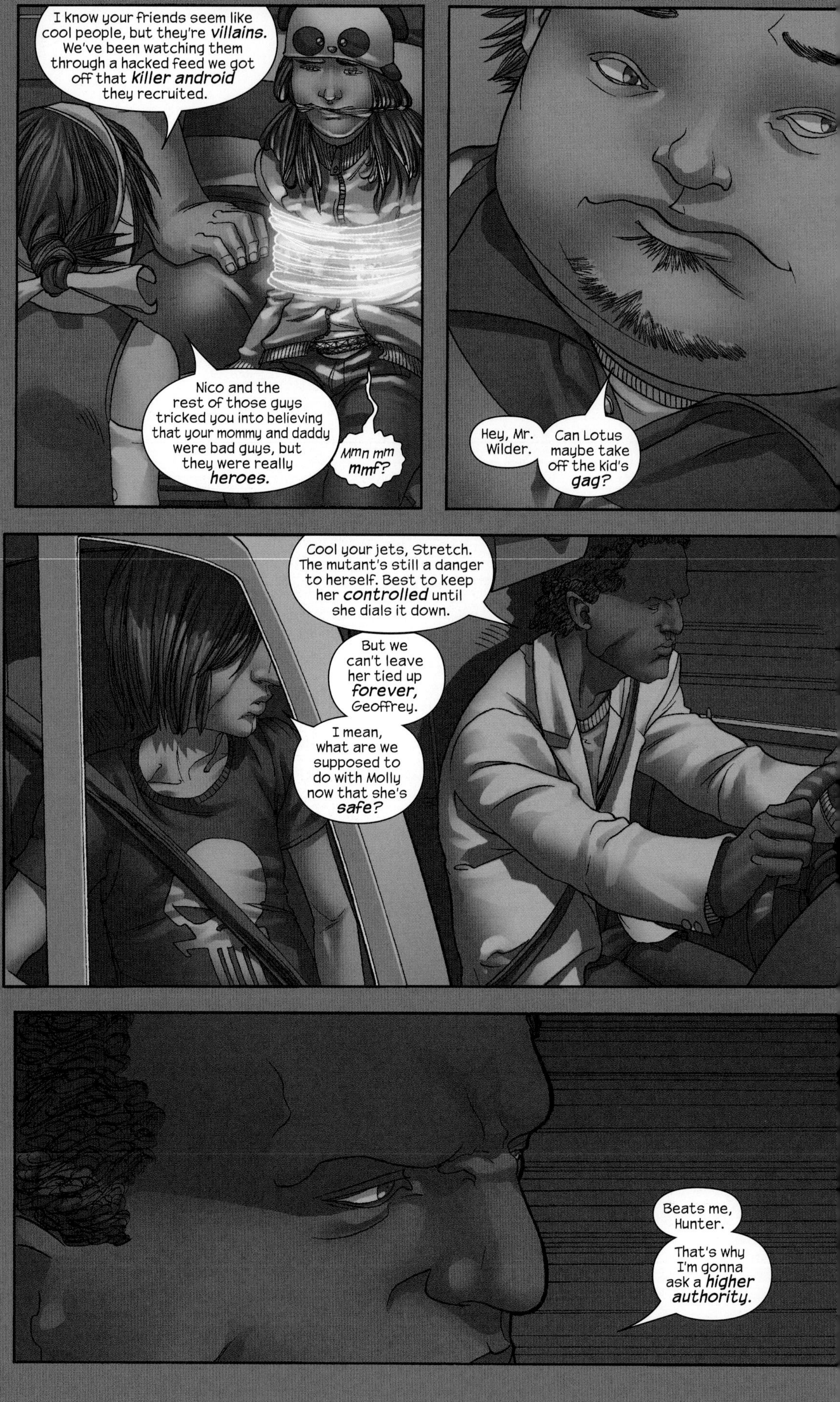

I know your friends seem like cool people, but they're *villains.* We've been watching them through a hacked feed we got off that *killer android* they recruited.
Nico and the rest of those guys tricked you into believing that your mommy and daddy were bad guys, but they were really *heroes.*
Mmn mm mmf?
Hey, Mr. Wilder.
Can Lotus maybe take off the kid's *gag?*
Cool your jets, Stretch. The mutant's still a danger to herself. Best to keep her *controlled* until she dials it down.
But we can't leave her tied up *forever,* Geoffrey.
I mean, what are we supposed to do with Molly now that she's *safe?*
Beats me, Hunter.
That's why I'm gonna ask a *higher authority.*

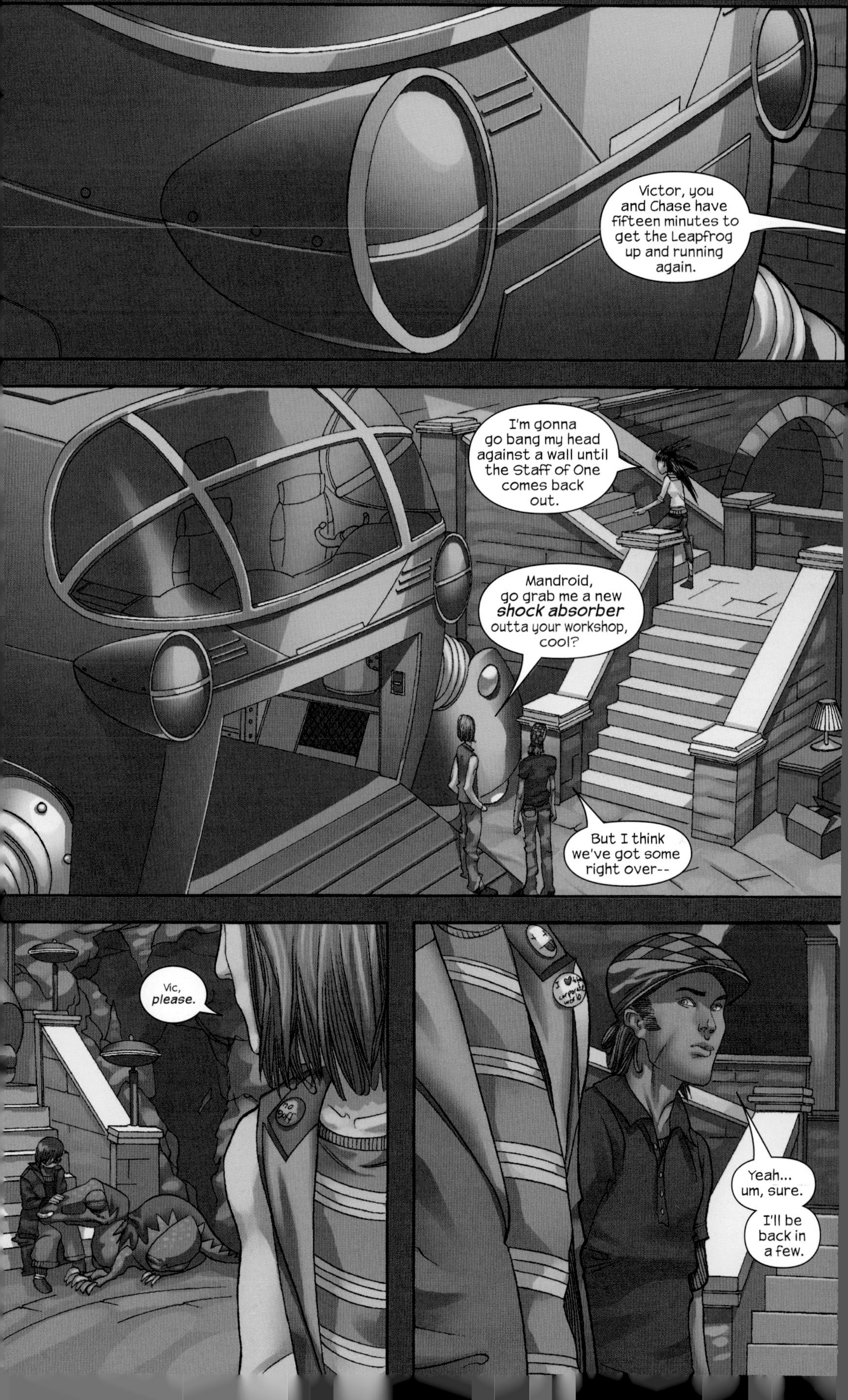
Victor, you and Chase have fifteen minutes to get the Leapfrog up and running again.
I'm gonna go bang my head against a wall until the Staff of One comes back out.
Mandroid, go grab me a new *shock absorber* outta your workshop, cool?
But I think we've got some right over--
Vic, *please.*
Yeah... um, sure.
I'll be back in a few.

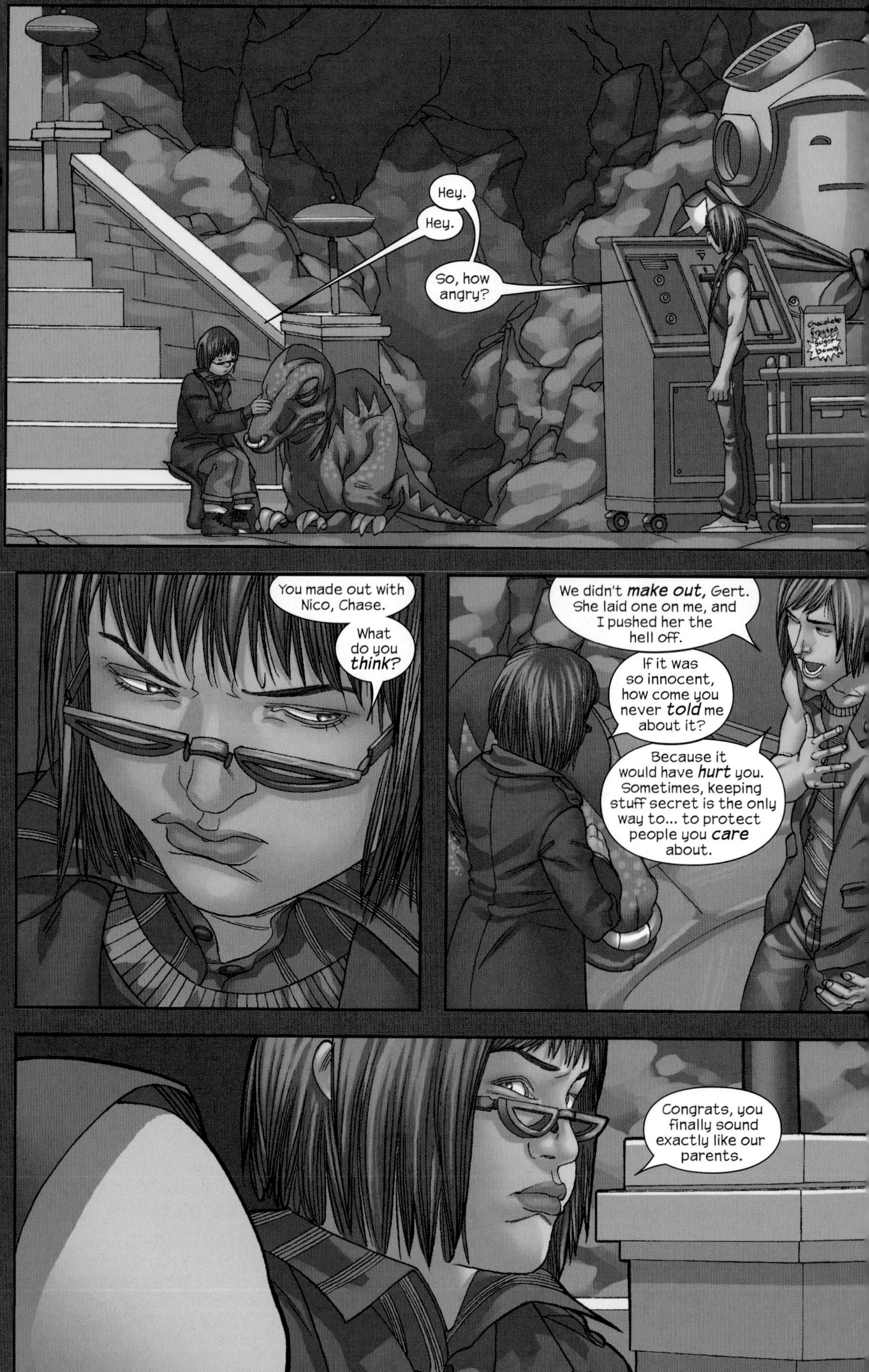
Hey.
Hey.
So, how angry?
You made out with Nico, Chase.
What do you *think?*
We didn't ***make out,*** Gert. She laid one on me, and I pushed her the hell off.
If it was so innocent, how come you never ***told*** me about it?
Because it would have ***hurt*** you. Sometimes, keeping stuff secret is the only way to... to protect people you ***care*** about.
Congrats, you finally sound exactly like our parents.

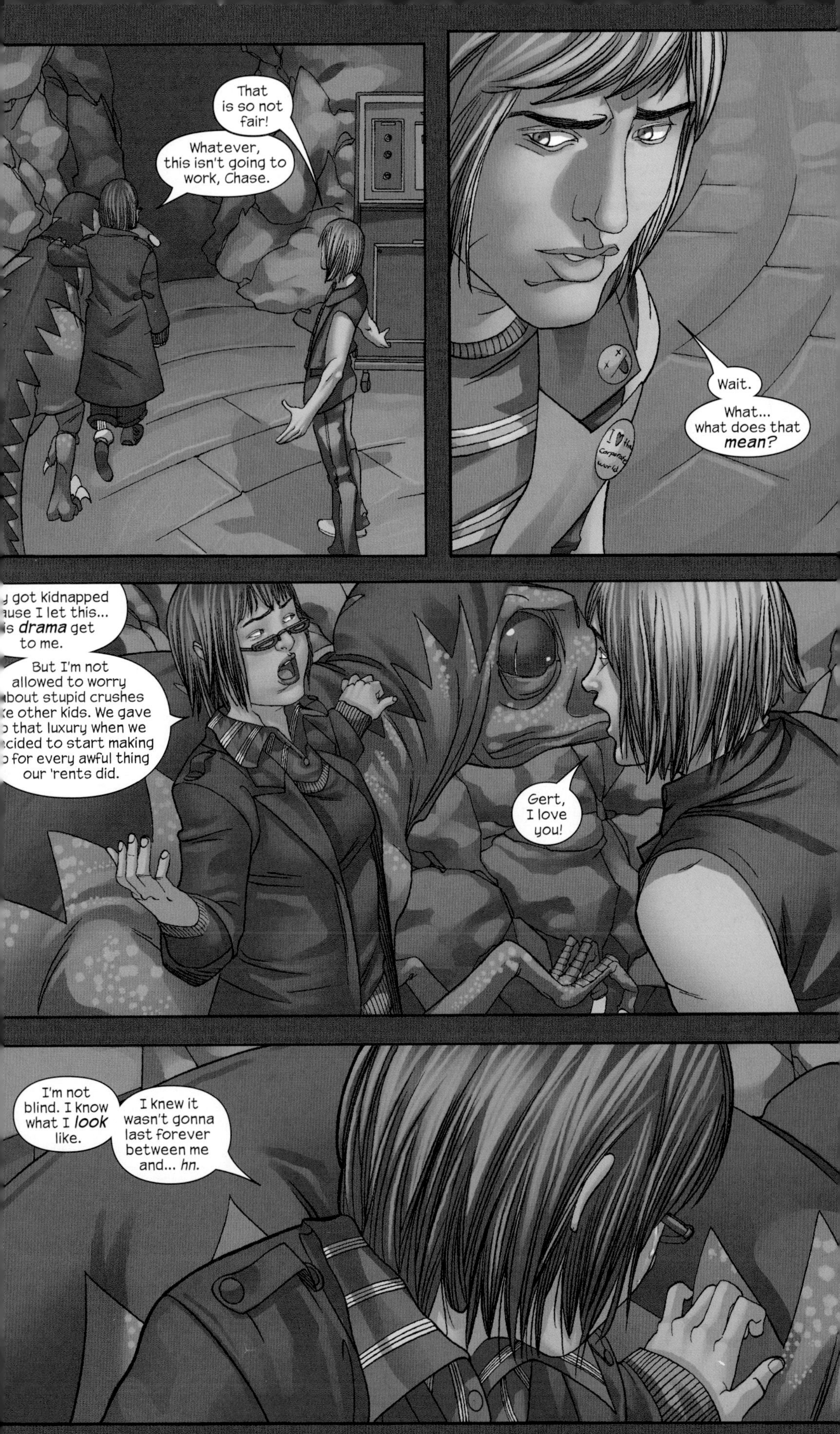

That is so not fair!
Whatever, this isn't going to work, Chase.
Wait.
What... what does that *mean*?
got kidnapped use I let this... is *drama* get to me.
But I'm not allowed to worry bout stupid crushes other kids. We gave that luxury when we cided to start making for every awful thing our 'rents did.
Gert, I love you!
I'm not blind. I know what I *look* like.
I knew it wasn't gonna last forever between me and... *hn.*

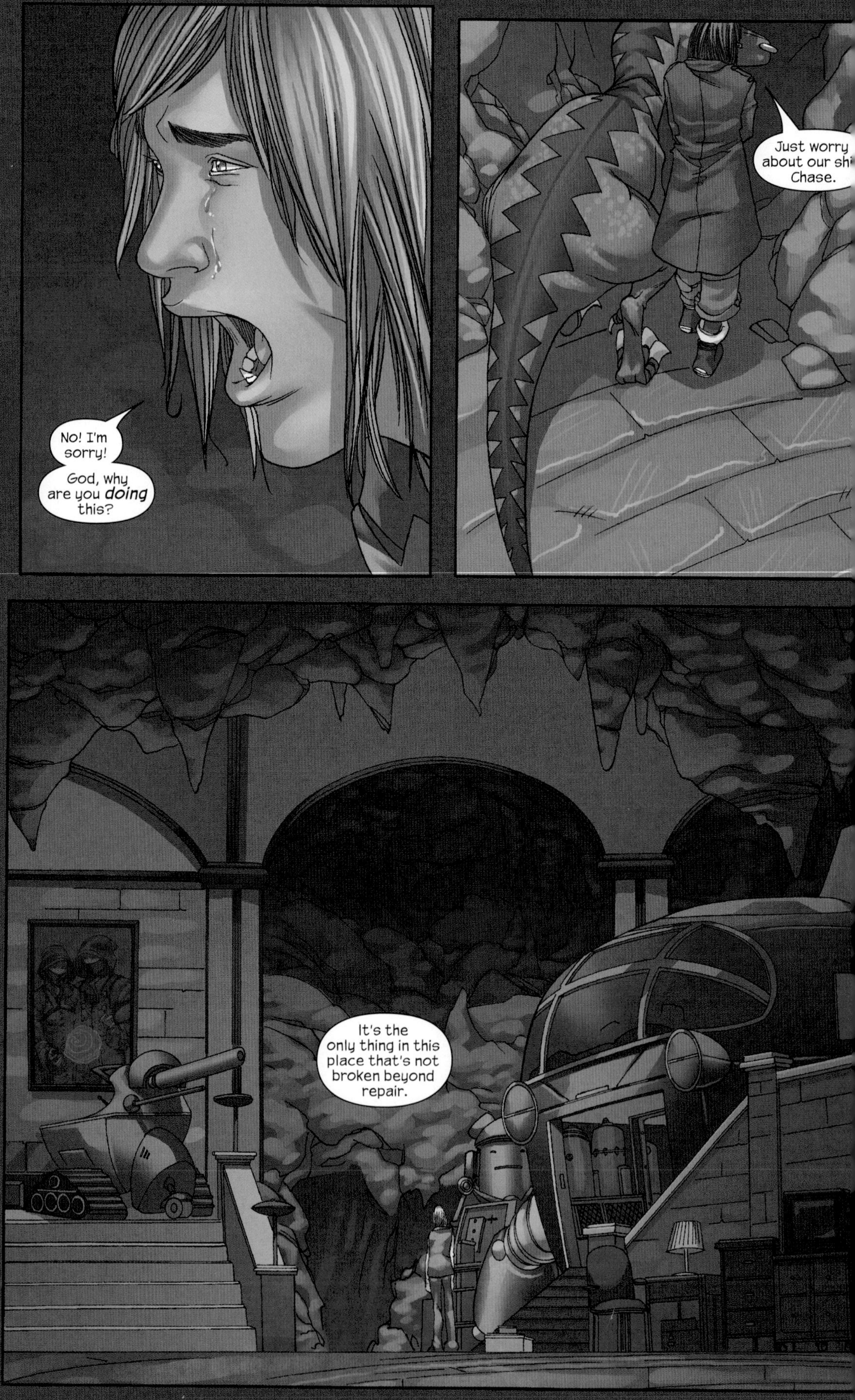
No! I'm sorry!
God, why are you *doing* this?
Just worry about our shi
Chase.
It's the only thing in this place that's not broken beyond repair.

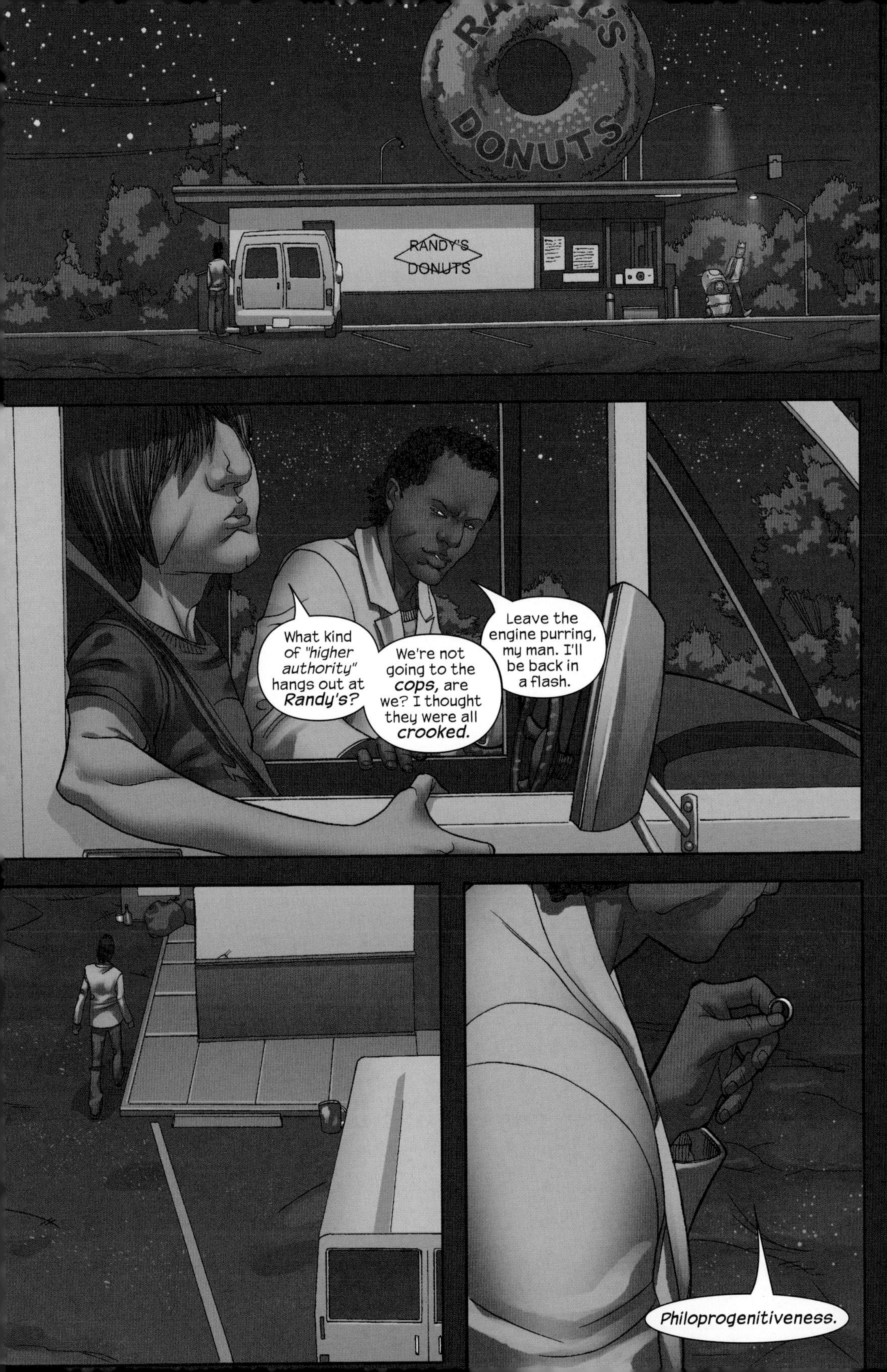
RANDY'S
DONUTS
RANDY'S
DONUTS
What kind of "higher authority" hangs out at Randy's?
We're not going to the cops, are we? I thought they were all crooked.
Leave the engine purring, my man. I'll be back in a flash.
Philoprogenitiveness.

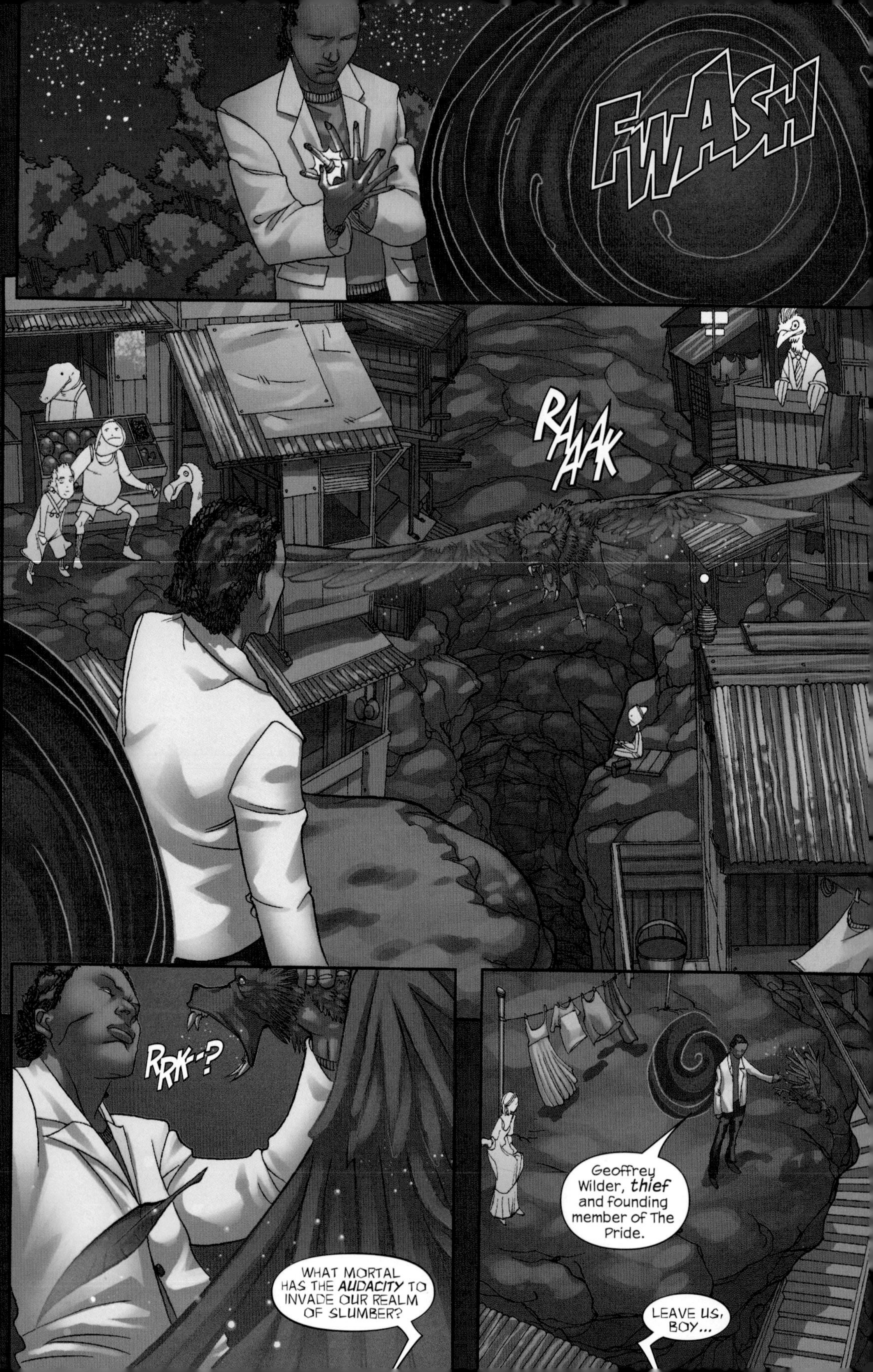
FWASH
RAAAK
RRK--?
WHAT MORTAL HAS THE AUDACITY TO INVADE OUR REALM OF SLUMBER?
Geoffrey Wilder, thief and founding member of The Pride.
LEAVE US, BOY...

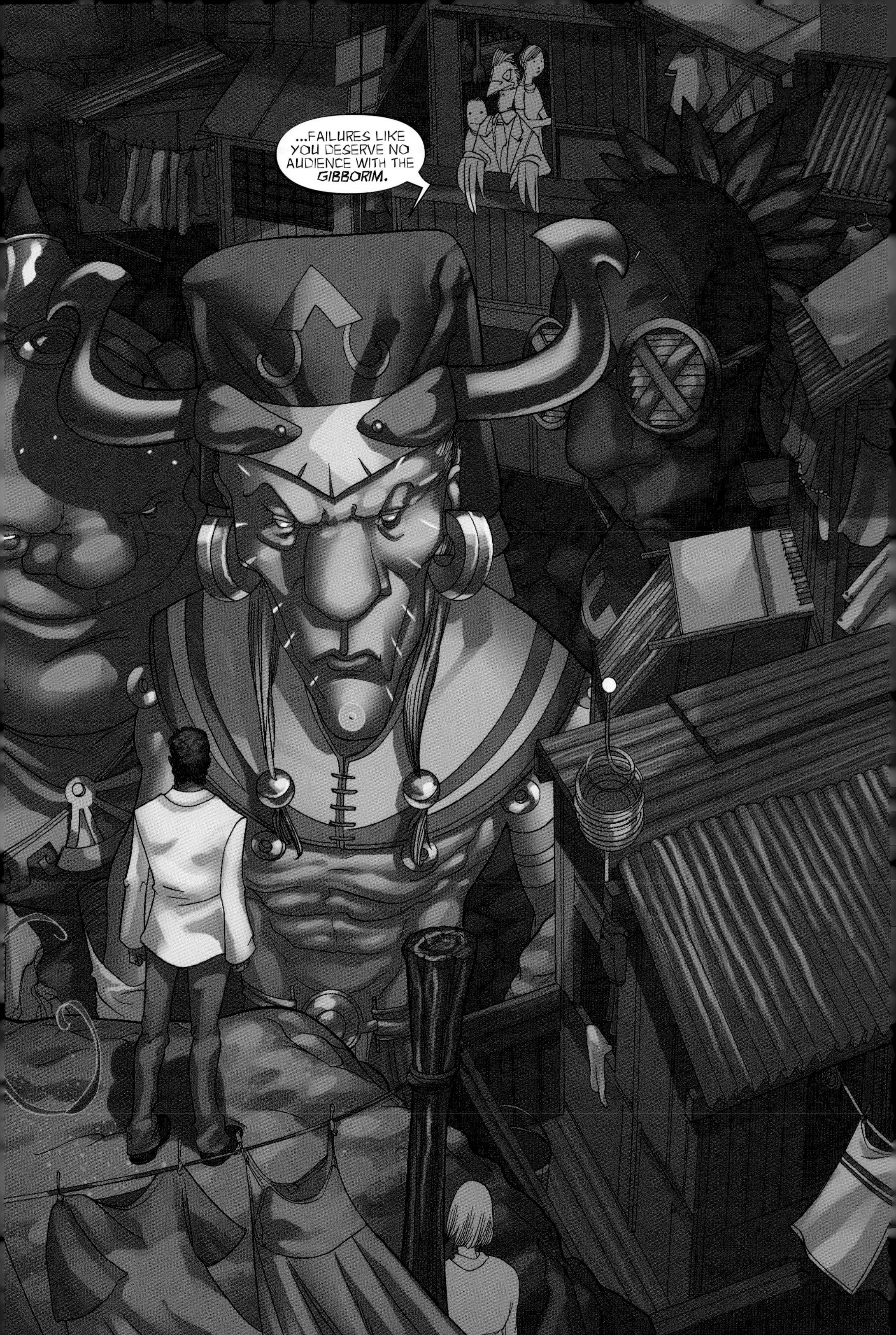
...FAILURES LIKE YOU DESERVE NO AUDIENCE WITH THE GIBBORIM.

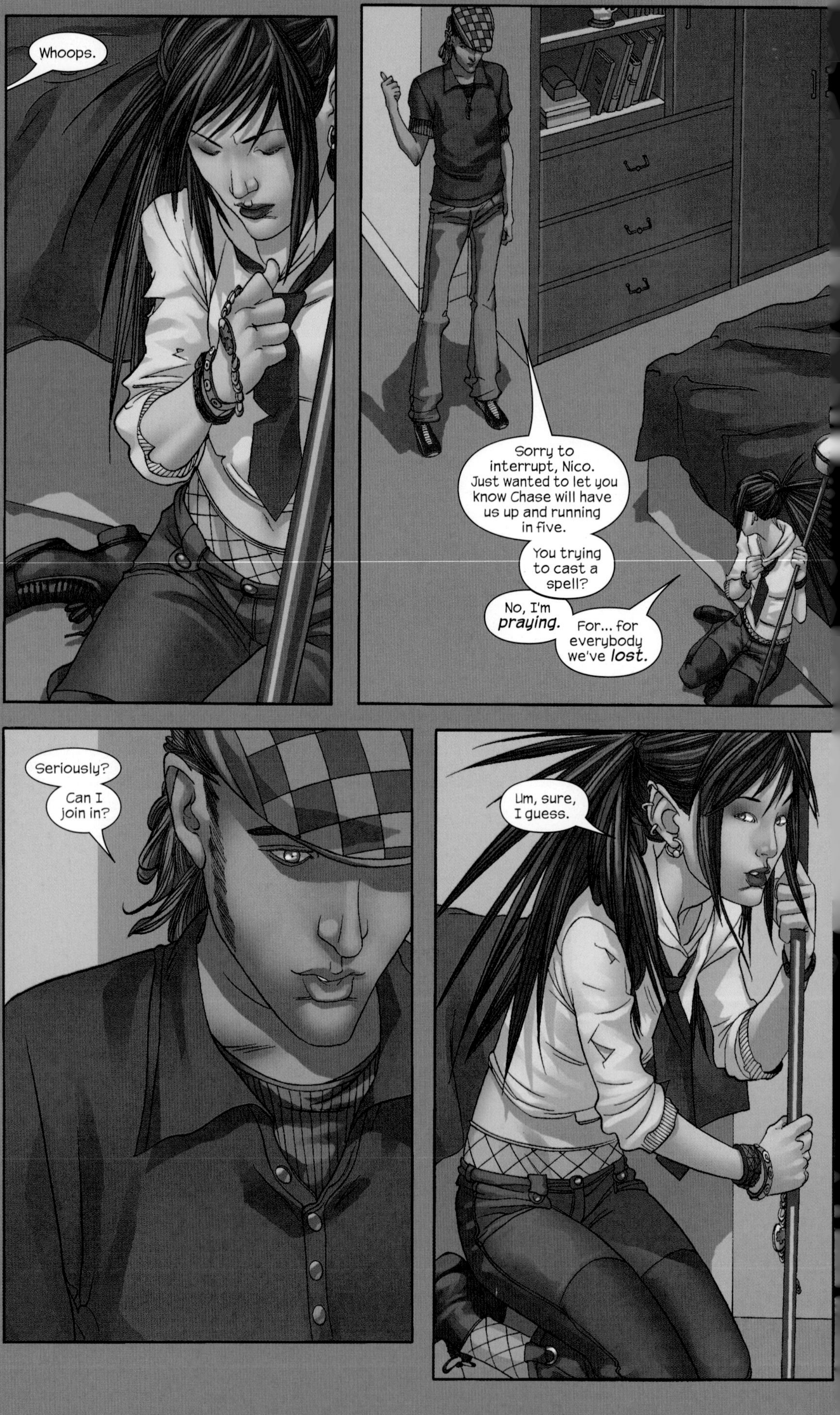
Whoops.
Sorry to interrupt, Nico. Just wanted to let you know Chase will have us up and running in five.
You trying to cast a spell?
No, I'm *praying.*
For... for everybody we've *lost.*
Seriously?
Can I join in?
Um, sure, I guess.

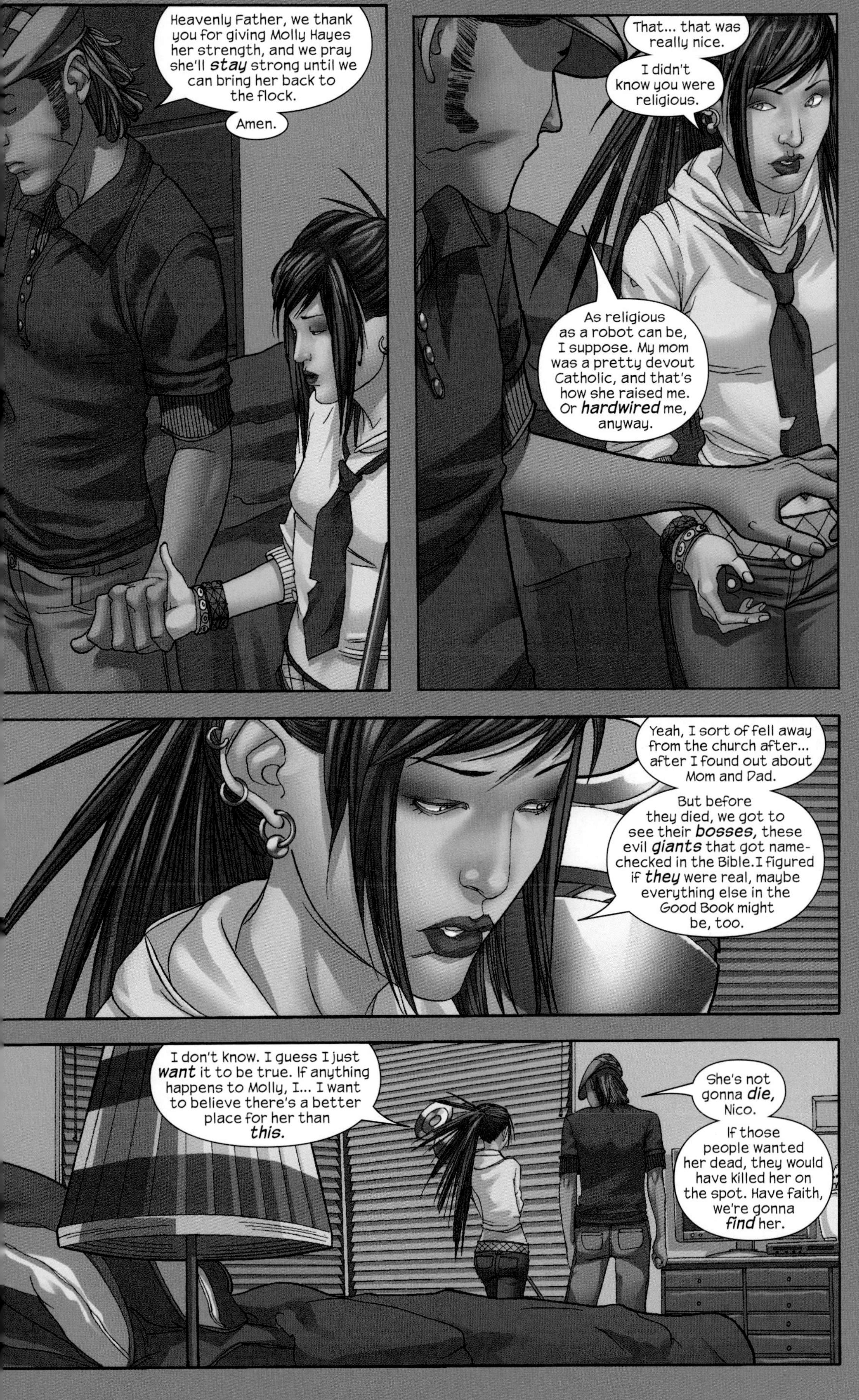

Heavenly Father, we thank you for giving Molly Hayes her strength, and we pray she'll *stay* strong until we can bring her back to the flock.
Amen.
That... that was really nice.
I didn't know you were religious.
As religious as a robot can be, I suppose. My mom was a pretty devout Catholic, and that's how she raised me. Or *hardwired* me, anyway.
Yeah, I sort of fell away from the church after... after I found out about Mom and Dad.
But before they died, we got to see their *bosses,* these evil *giants* that got name-checked in the Bible. I figured if *they* were real, maybe everything else in the Good Book might be, too.
I don't know. I guess I just *want* it to be true. If anything happens to Molly, I... I want to believe there's a better place for her than *this.*
She's not gonna *die,* Nico.
If those people wanted her dead, they would have killed her on the spot. Have faith, we're gonna *find* her.

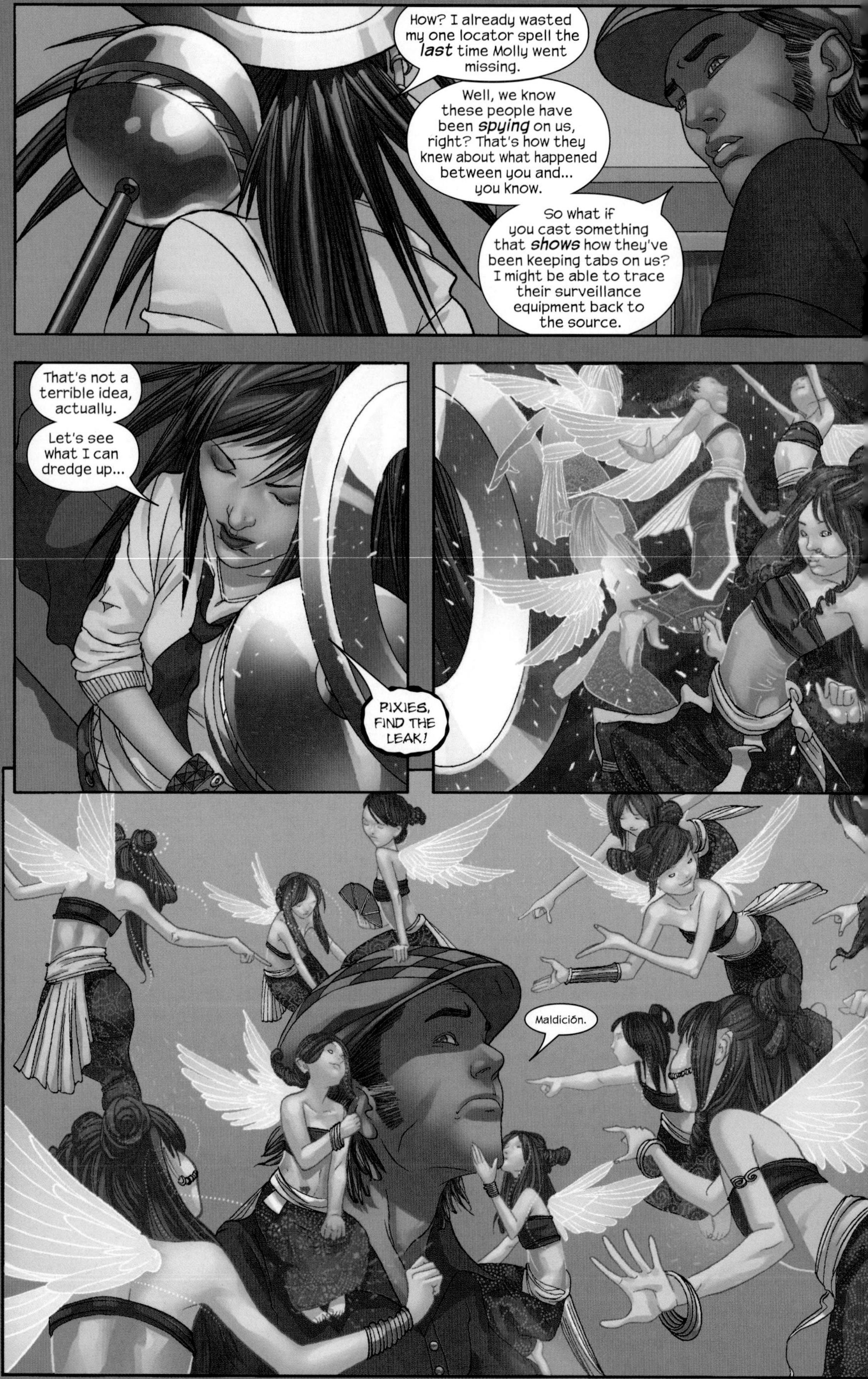
How? I already wasted my one locator spell the last time Molly went missing.
Well, we know these people have been spying on us, right? That's how they knew about what happened between you and... you know.
So what if you cast something that shows how they've been keeping tabs on us? I might be able to trace their surveillance equipment back to the source.
That's not a terrible idea, actually.
Let's see what I can dredge up...
PIXIES, FIND THE LEAK!
Maldición.

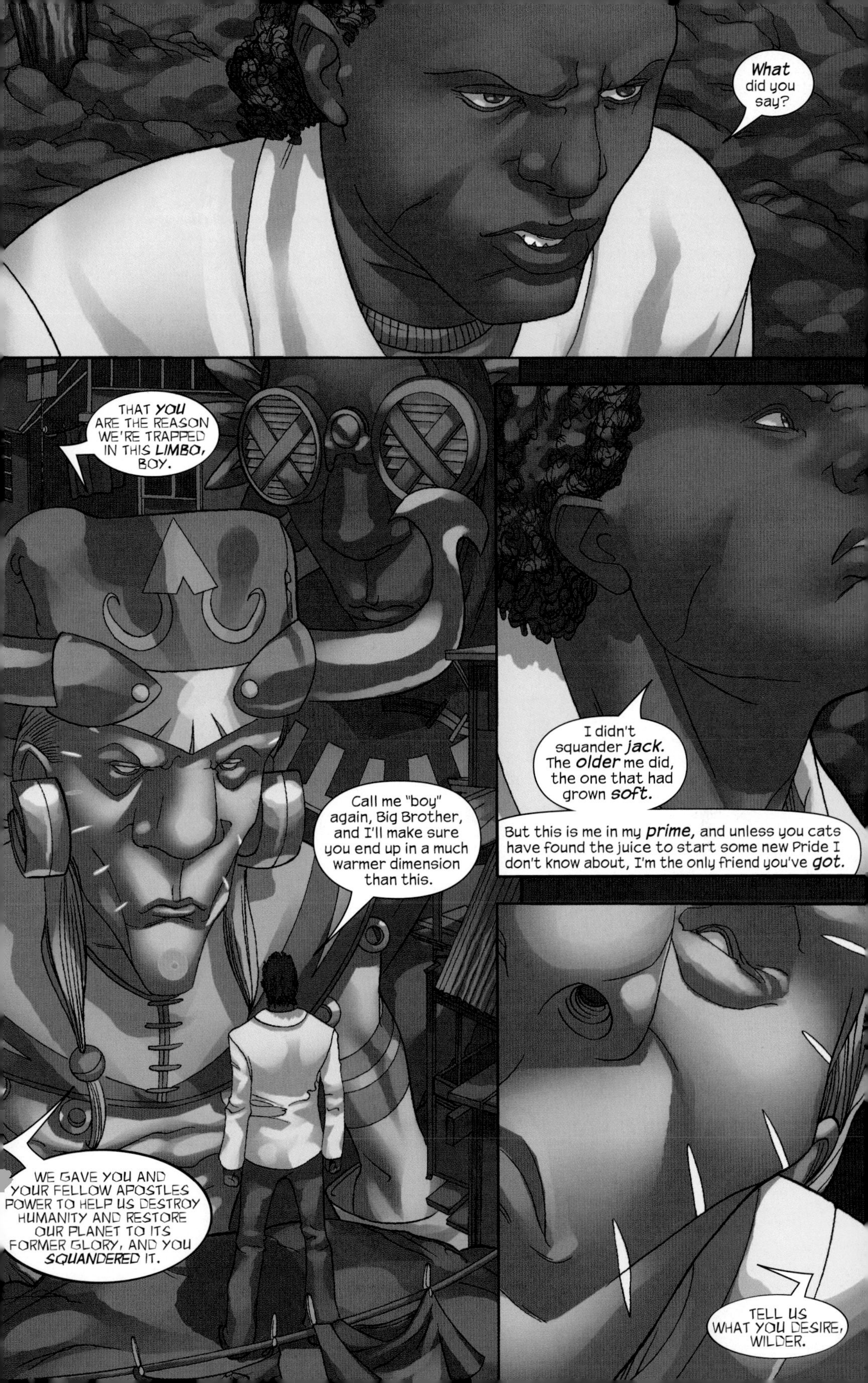
What did you say?
THAT YOU ARE THE REASON WE'RE TRAPPED IN THIS LIMBO, BOY.
WE GAVE YOU AND YOUR FELLOW APOSTLES POWER TO HELP US DESTROY HUMANITY AND RESTORE OUR PLANET TO ITS FORMER GLORY, AND YOU SQUANDERED IT.
Call me "boy" again, Big Brother, and I'll make sure you end up in a much warmer dimension than this.
I didn't squander jack. The older me did, the one that had grown soft.
But this is me in my prime, and unless you cats have found the juice to start some new Pride I don't know about, I'm the only friend you've got.
TELL US WHAT YOU DESIRE, WILDER.

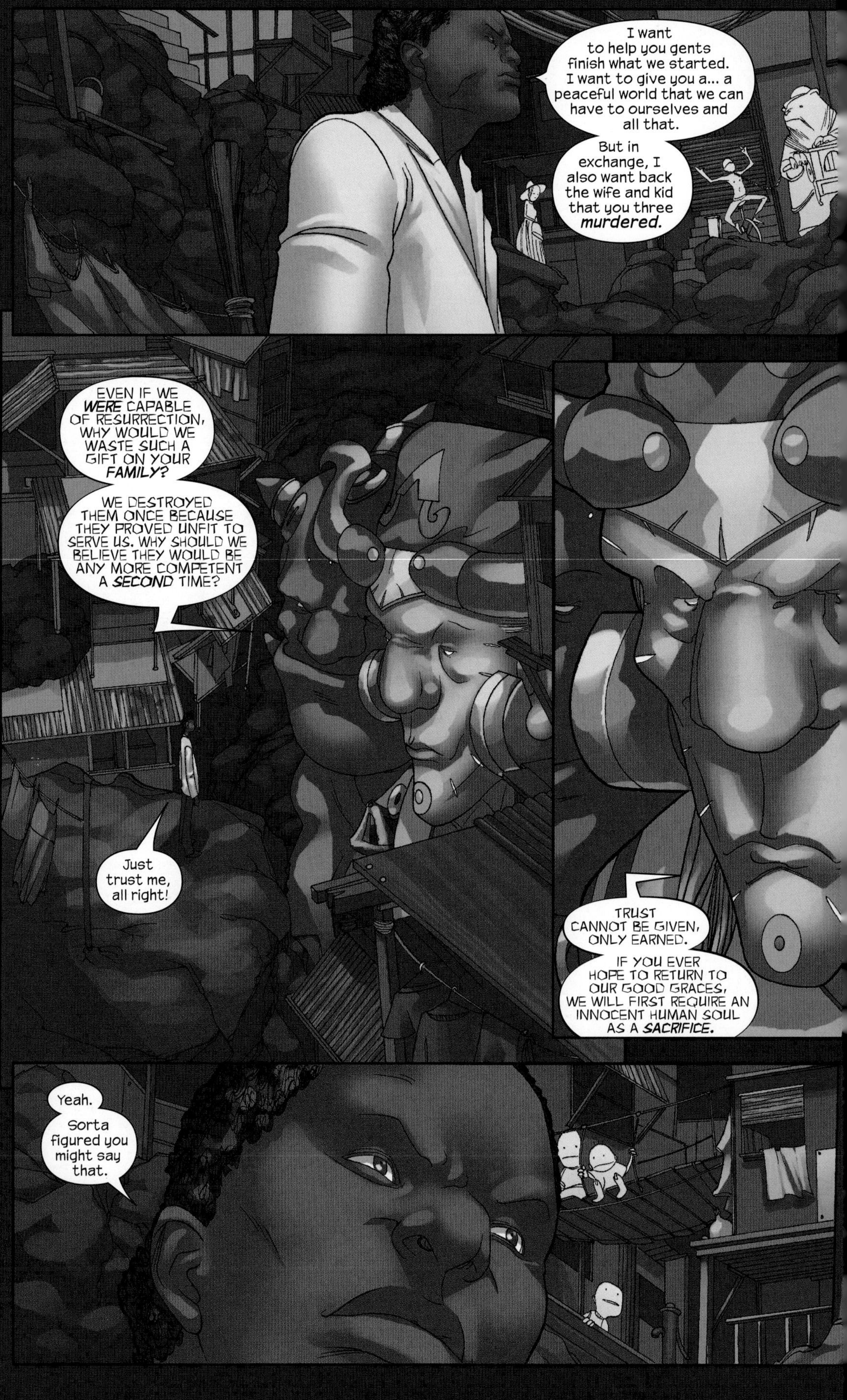

I want to help you gents finish what we started. I want to give you a... a peaceful world that we can have to ourselves and all that.
But in exchange, I also want back the wife and kid that you three murdered.
EVEN IF WE WERE CAPABLE OF RESURRECTION, WHY WOULD WE WASTE SUCH A GIFT ON YOUR FAMILY?
WE DESTROYED THEM ONCE BECAUSE THEY PROVED UNFIT TO SERVE US. WHY SHOULD WE BELIEVE THEY WOULD BE ANY MORE COMPETENT A SECOND TIME?
Just trust me, all right!
TRUST CANNOT BE GIVEN, ONLY EARNED.
IF YOU EVER HOPE TO RETURN TO OUR GOOD GRACES, WE WILL FIRST REQUIRE AN INNOCENT HUMAN SOUL AS A SACRIFICE.
Yeah.
Sorta figured you might say that.

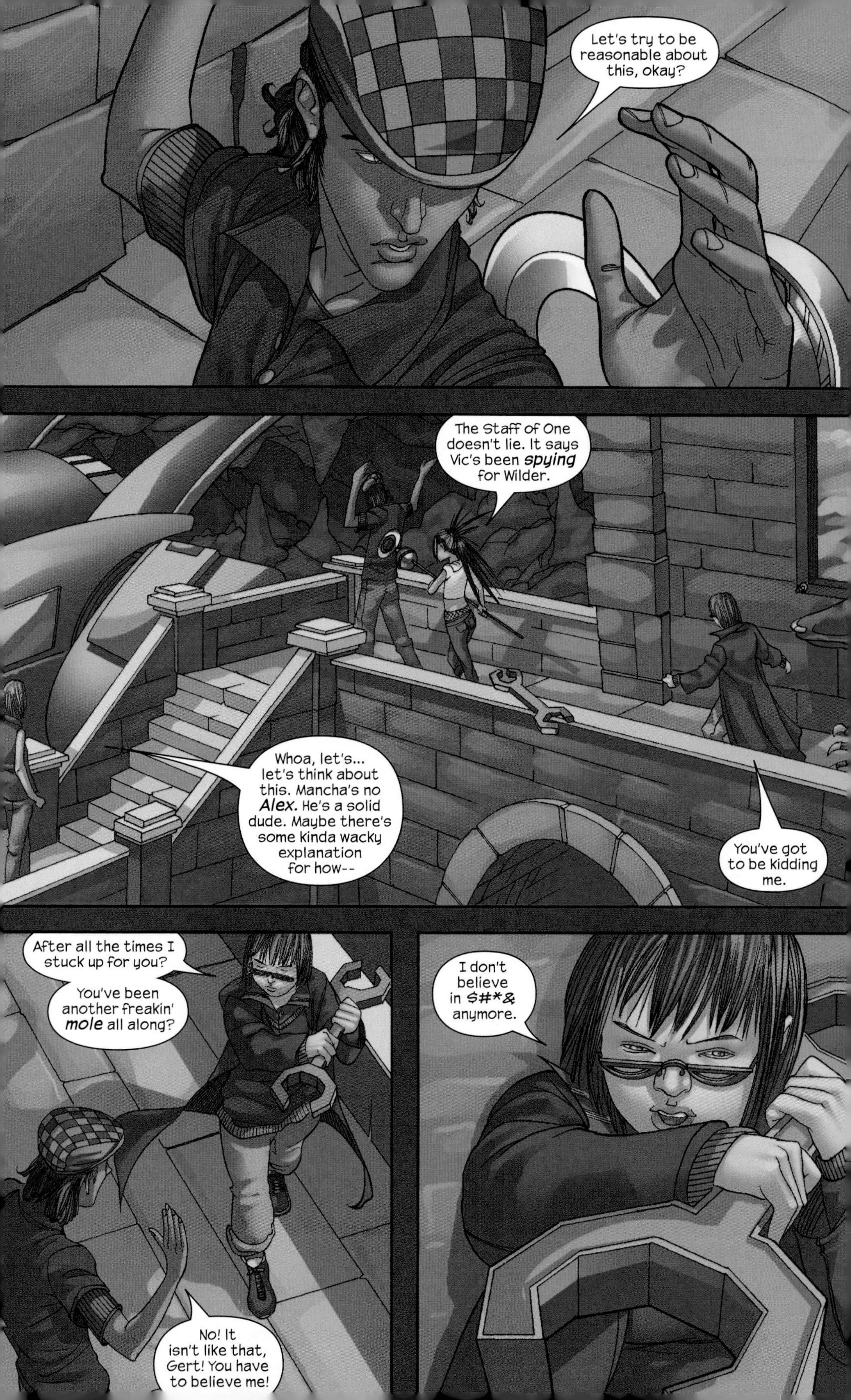
Let's try to be reasonable about this, okay?
The Staff of One doesn't lie. It says Vic's been *spying* for Wilder.
Whoa, let's... let's think about this. Mancha's no *Alex.* He's a solid dude. Maybe there's some kinda wacky explanation for how--
You've got to be kidding me.
After all the times I stuck up for you?
You've been another freakin' *mole* all along?
No! It isn't like that, Gert! You have to believe me!
I don't believe in $#*& anymore.

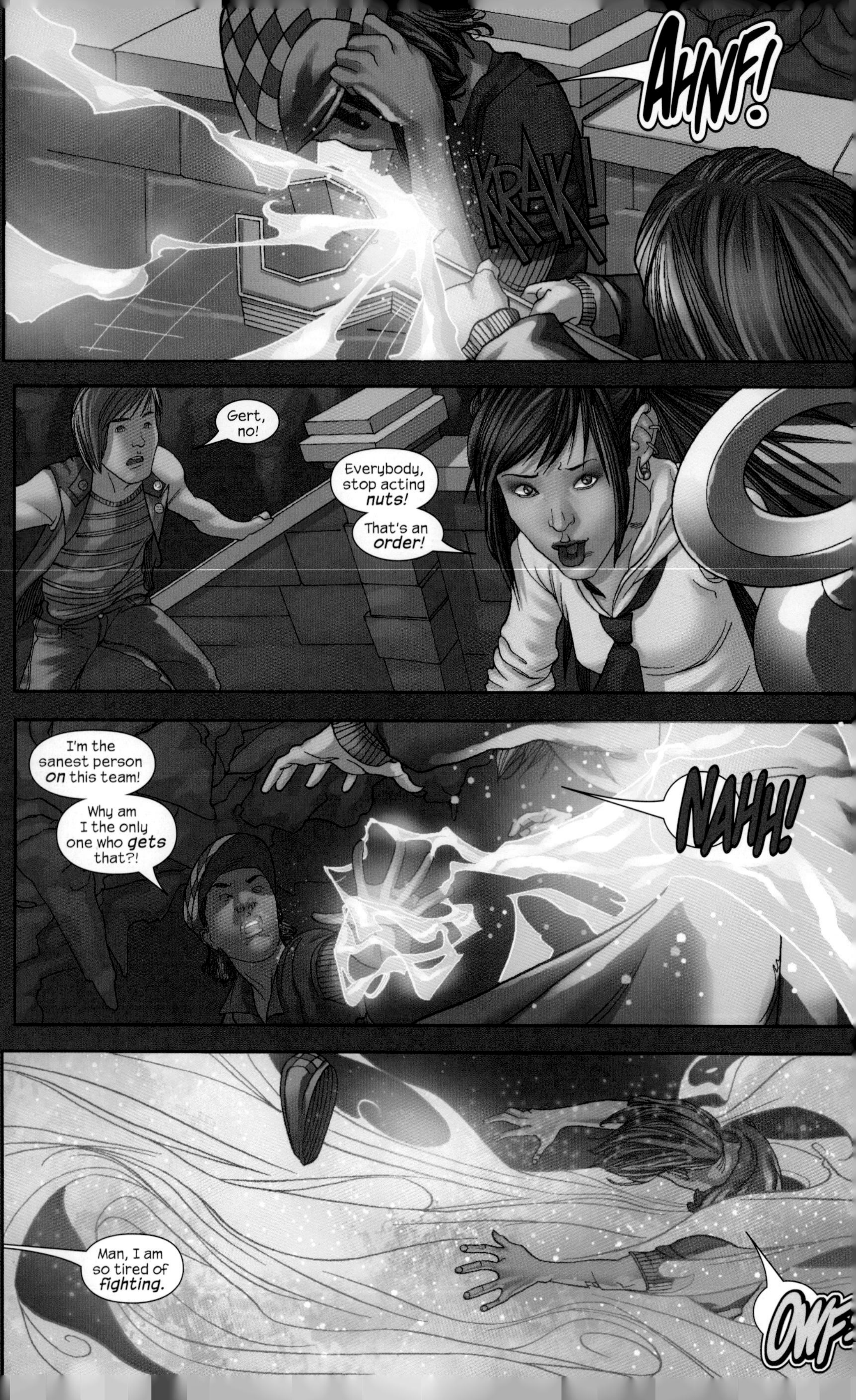
AHNF!
KRAK!
Gert, no!
Everybody, stop acting nuts!
That's an order!
I'm the sanest person on this team!
Why am I the only one who gets that?!
NAHH!
Man, I am so tired of fighting.
OWF

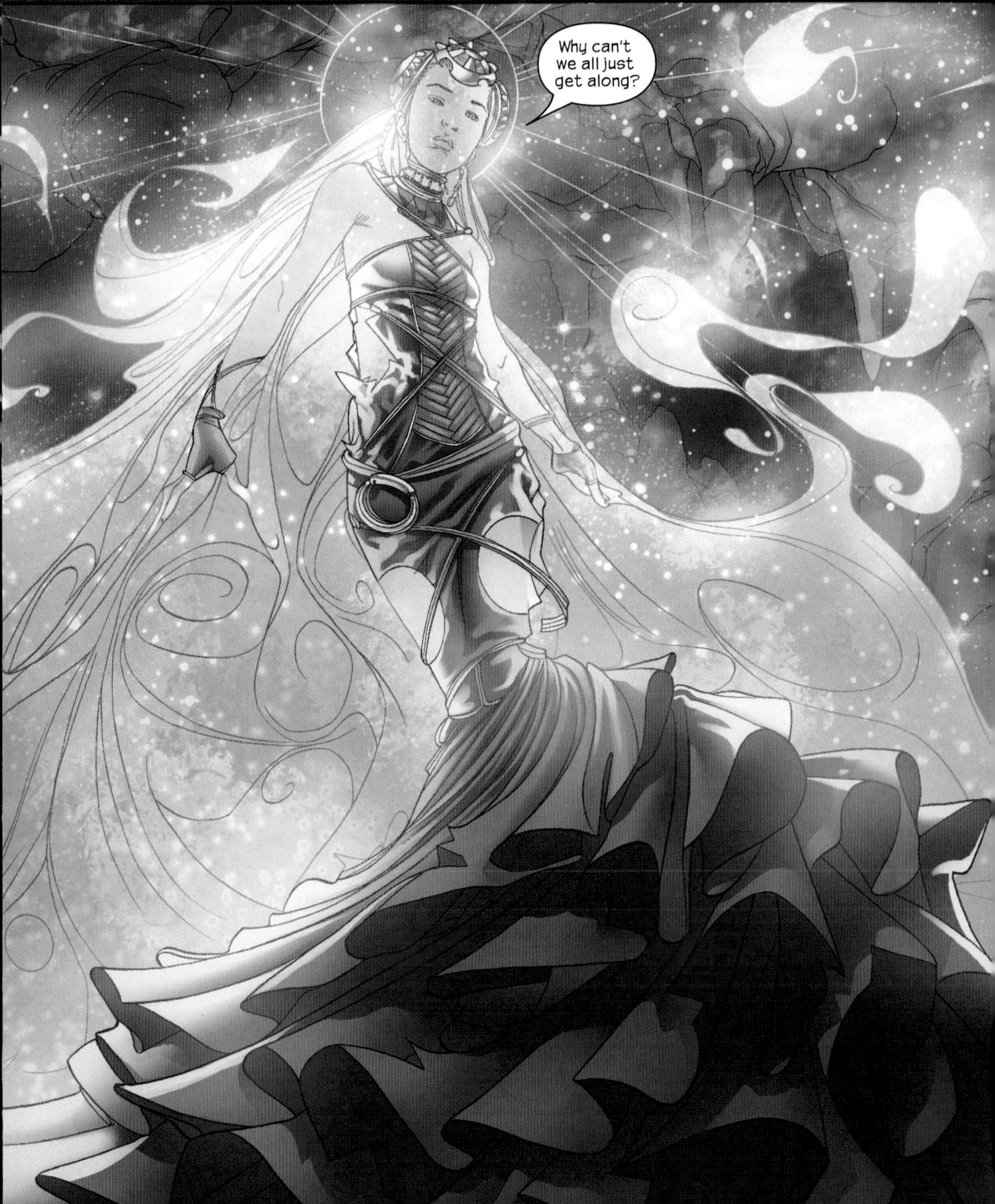
Why can't we all just get along?

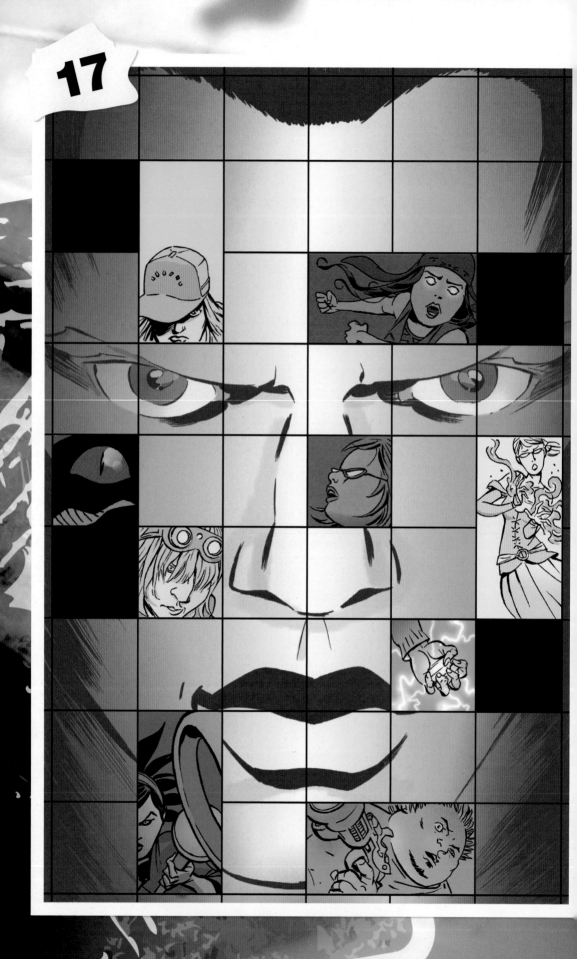

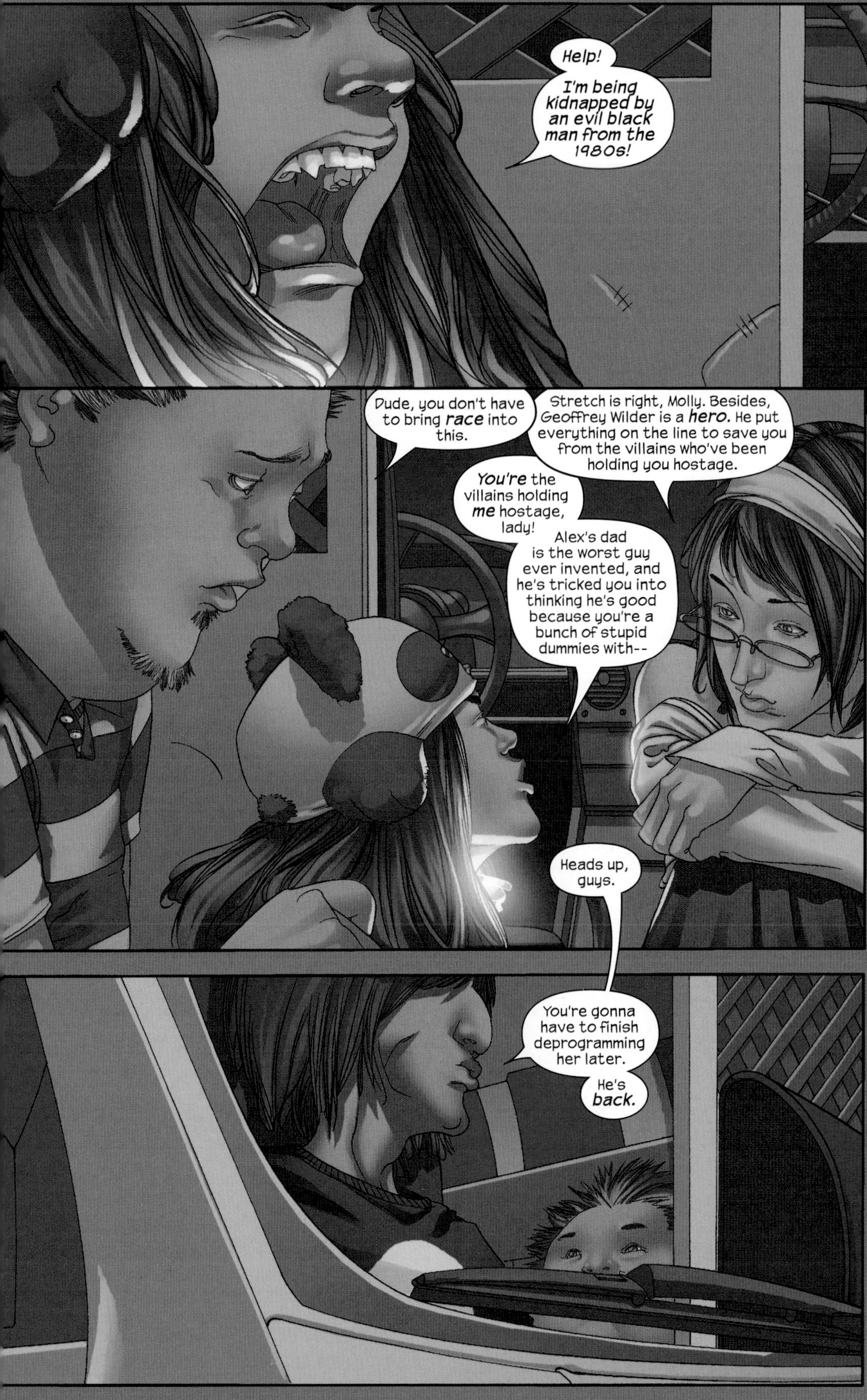

Help!
I'm being kidnapped by an evil black man from the 1980s!
Dude, you don't have to bring *race* into this.
Stretch is right, Molly. Besides, Geoffrey Wilder is a *hero.* He put everything on the line to save you from the villains who've been holding you hostage.
You're the villains holding *me* hostage, lady!
Alex's dad is the worst guy ever invented, and he's tricked you into thinking he's good because you're a bunch of stupid dummies with--
Heads up, guys.
You're gonna have to finish deprogramming her later.
He's *back.*

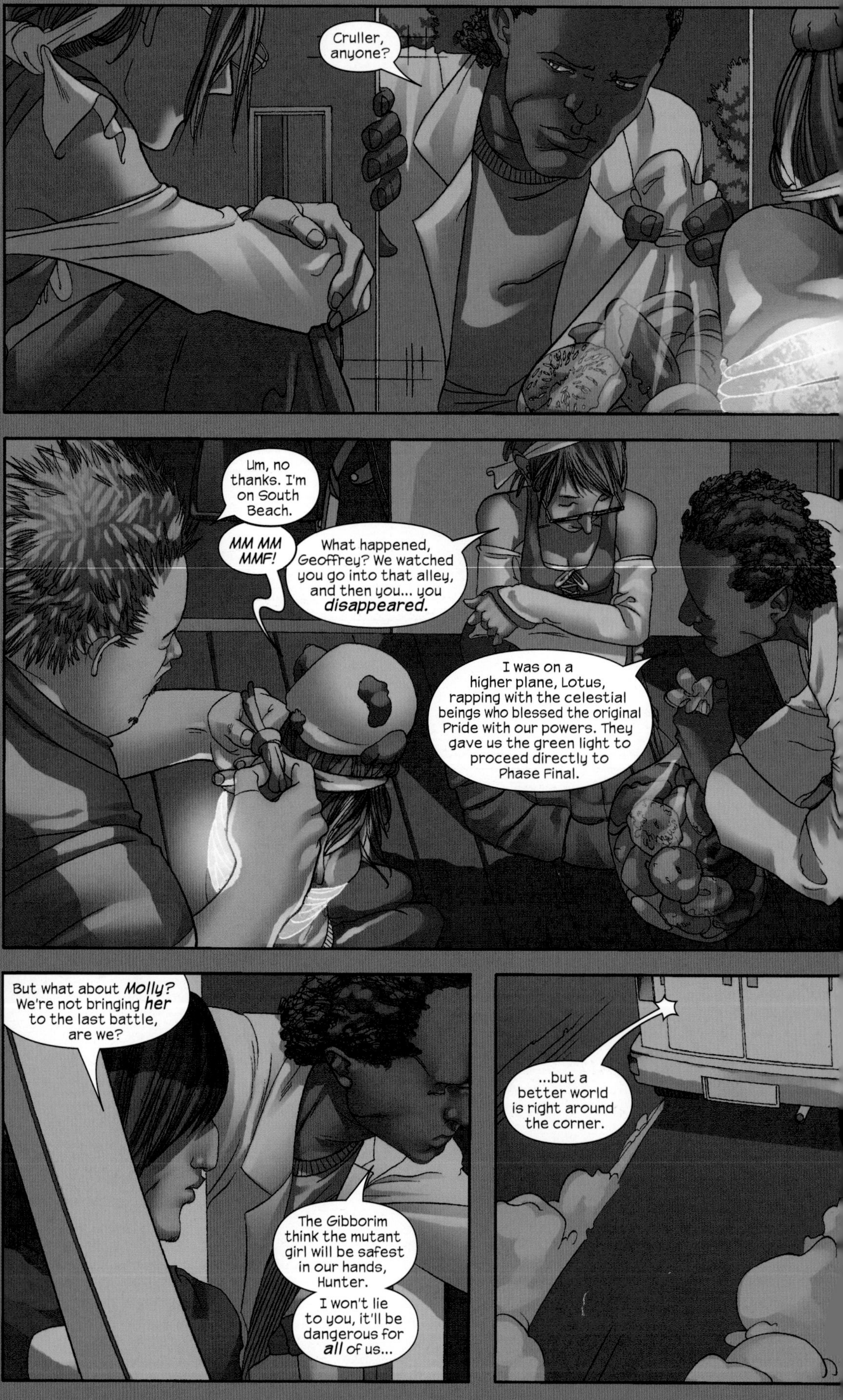
Cruller, anyone?
Um, no thanks. I'm on South Beach.
MM MM MMF!
What happened, Geoffrey? We watched you go into that alley, and then you... you *disappeared.*
I was on a higher plane, Lotus, rapping with the celestial beings who blessed the original Pride with our powers. They gave us the green light to proceed directly to Phase Final.
But what about *Molly*? We're not bringing *her* to the last battle, are we?
The Gibborim think the mutant girl will be safest in our hands, Hunter.
I won't lie to you, it'll be dangerous for *all* of us...
...but a better world is right around the corner.

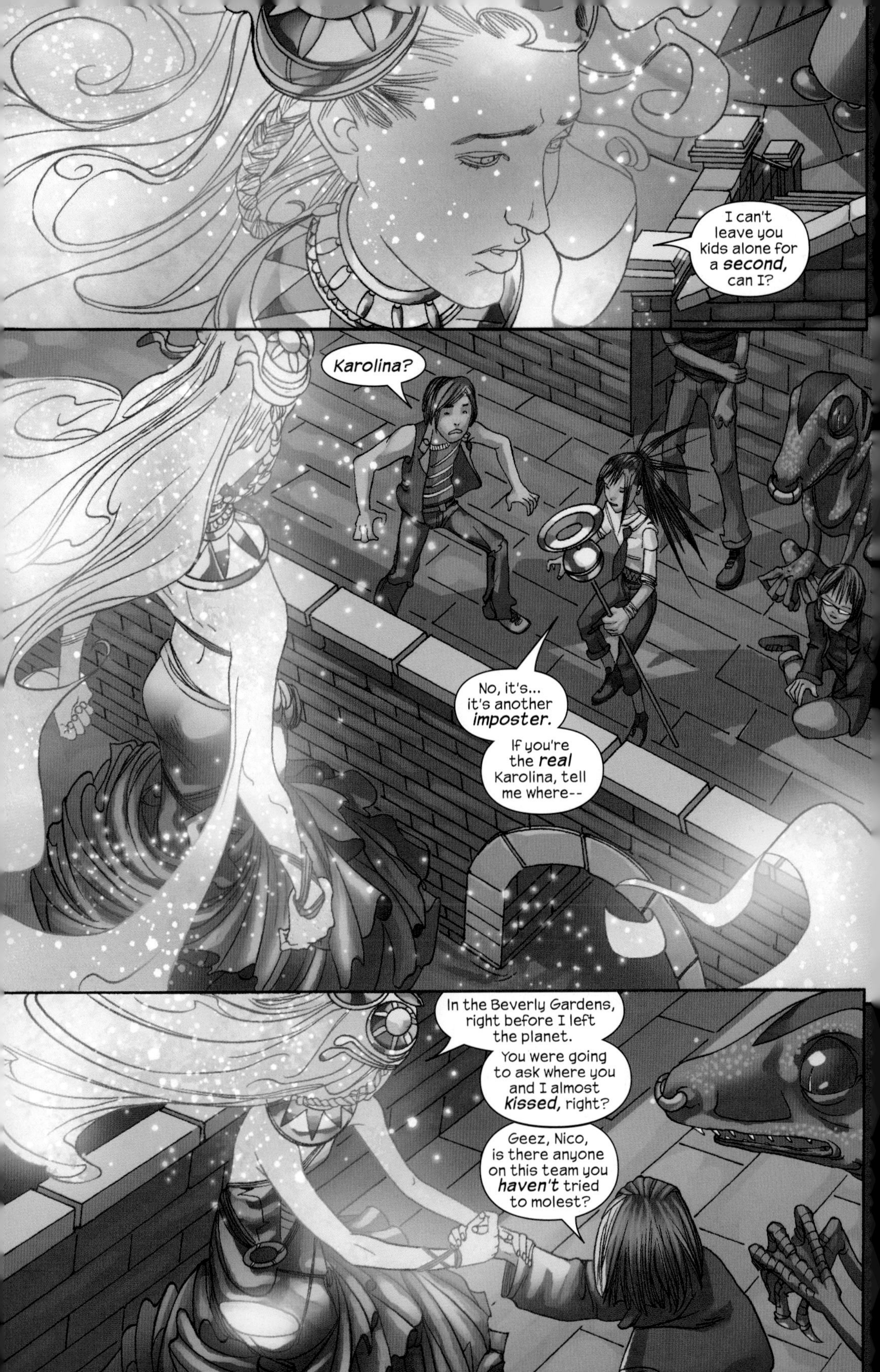
I can't leave you kids alone for a *second,* can I?
Karolina?
No, it's... it's another *imposter.*
If you're the *real* Karolina, tell me where--
In the Beverly Gardens, right before I left the planet.
You were going to ask where you and I almost *kissed,* right?
Geez, Nico, is there anyone on this team you *haven't* tried to molest?

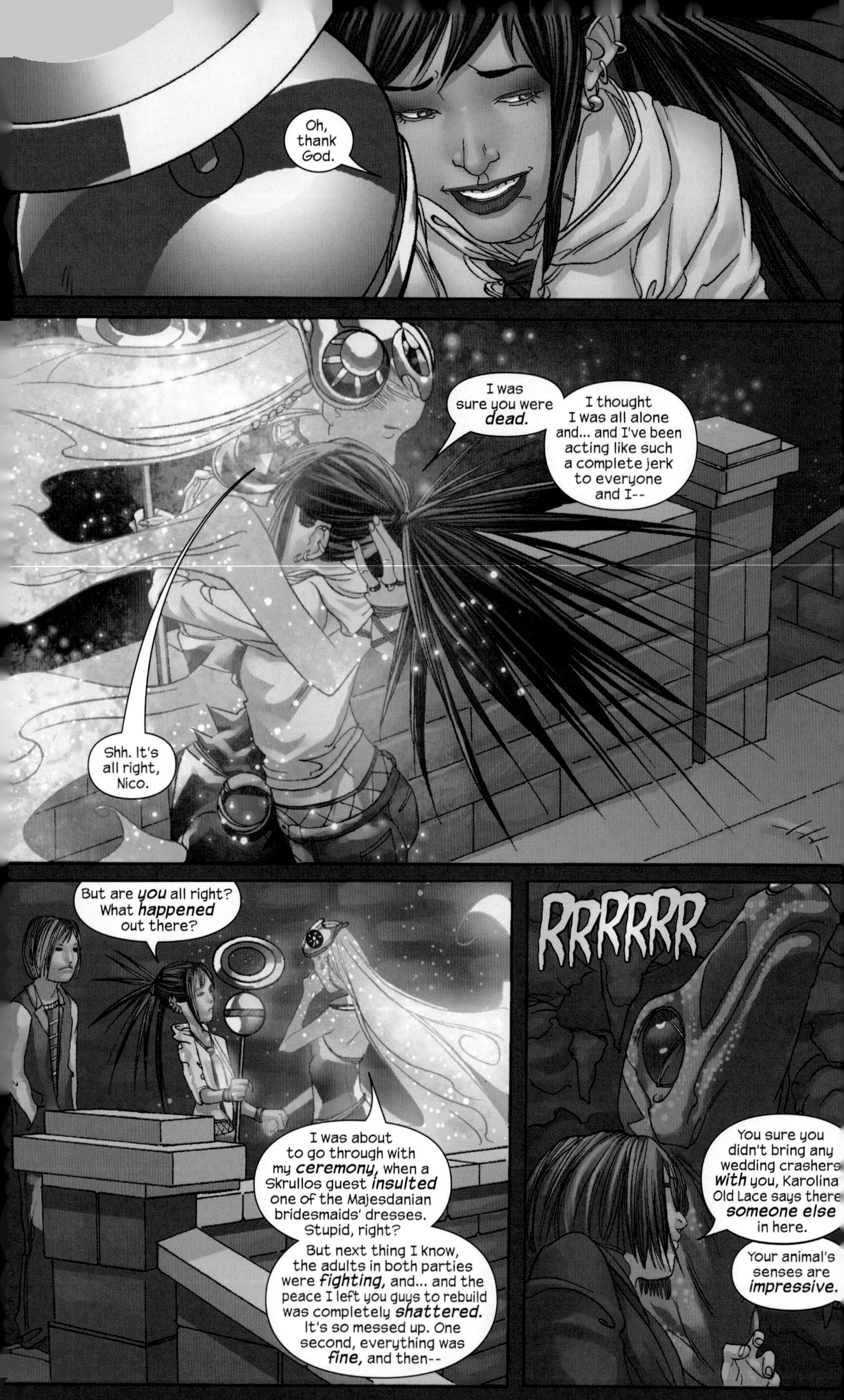
Oh, thank God.
I was sure you were *dead.*
I thought I was all alone and... and I've been acting like such a complete jerk to everyone and I--
Shh. It's all right, Nico.
But are *you* all right? What *happened* out there?
I was about to go through with my *ceremony,* when a Skrullos guest *insulted* one of the Majesdanian bridesmaids' dresses. Stupid, right?
But next thing I know, the adults in both parties were *fighting,* and... and the peace I left you guys to rebuild was completely *shattered.* It's so messed up. One second, everything was *fine,* and then--
RRRRRR
You sure you didn't bring any wedding crashers *with* you, Karolina? Old Lace says there's *someone else* in here.
Your animal's senses are *impressive.*

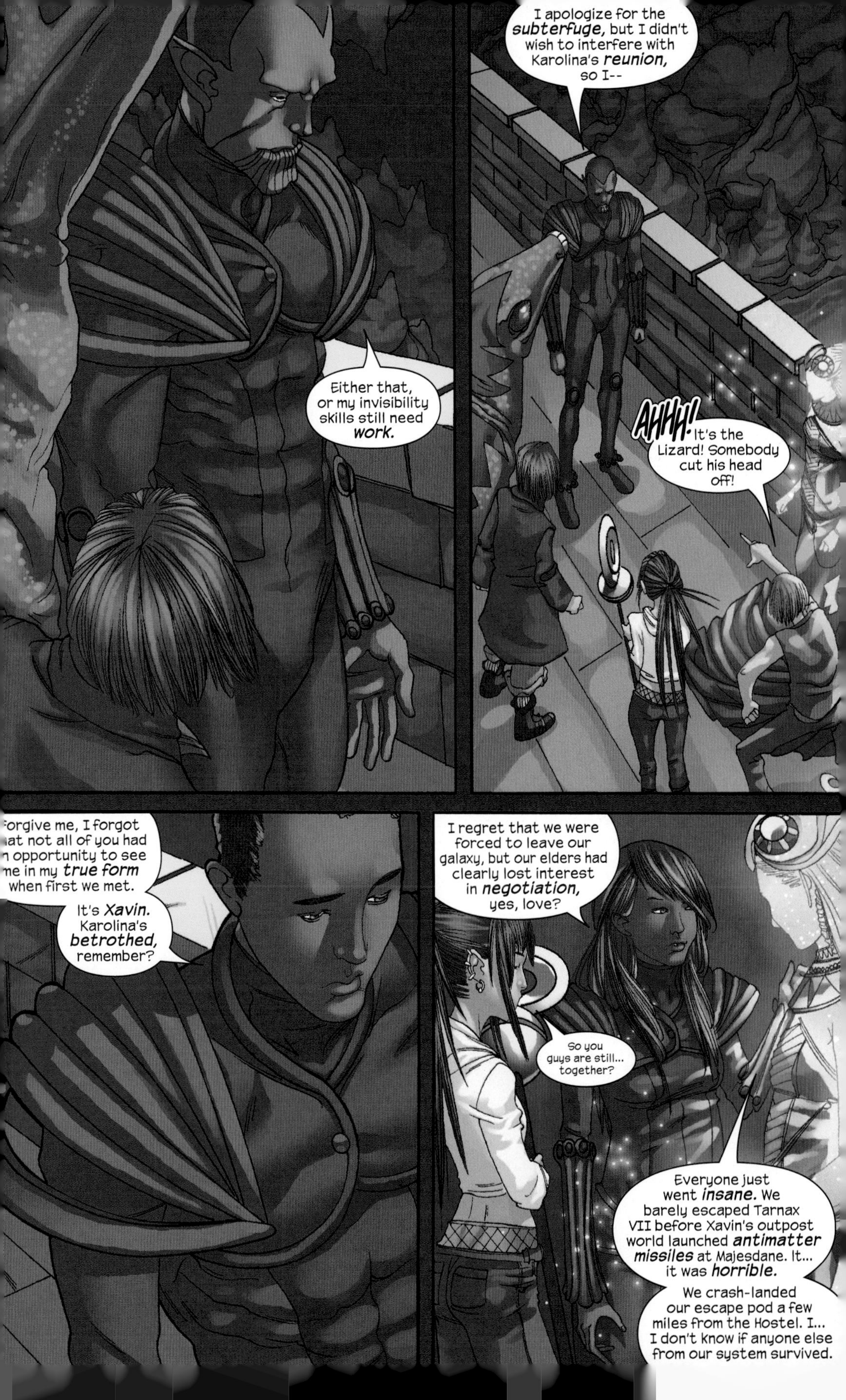
Either that, or my invisibility skills still need *work.*
I apologize for the *subterfuge,* but I didn't wish to interfere with Karolina's *reunion,* so I--
AHHH!
It's the Lizard! Somebody cut his head off!
orgive me, I forgot at not all of you had n opportunity to see me in my *true form* when first we met.
It's *Xavin.* Karolina's *betrothed,* remember?
I regret that we were forced to leave our galaxy, but our elders had clearly lost interest in *negotiation,* yes, love?
So you guys are still... together?
Everyone just went *insane.* We barely escaped Tarnax VII before Xavin's outpost world launched *antimatter missiles* at Majesdane. It... it was *horrible.*
We crash-landed our escape pod a few miles from the Hostel. I... I don't know if anyone else from our system survived.

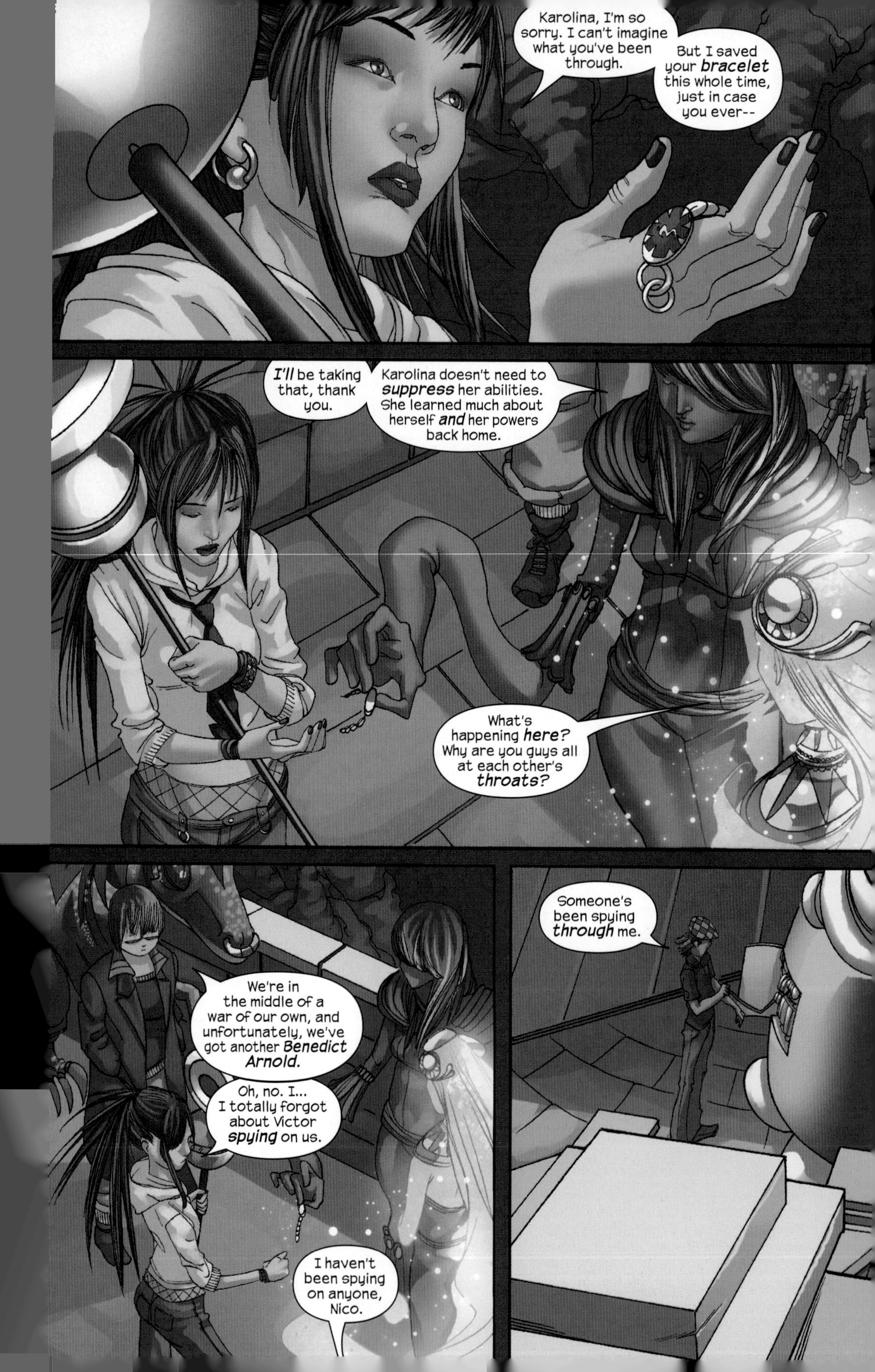
Karolina, I'm so sorry. I can't imagine what you've been through.
But I saved your bracelet this whole time, just in case you ever--
I'll be taking that, thank you.
Karolina doesn't need to suppress her abilities. She learned much about herself and her powers back home.
What's happening here? Why are you guys all at each other's throats?
We're in the middle of a war of our own, and unfortunately, we've got another Benedict Arnold.
Oh, no. I... I totally forgot about Victor spying on us.
I haven't been spying on anyone, Nico.
Someone's been spying through me.

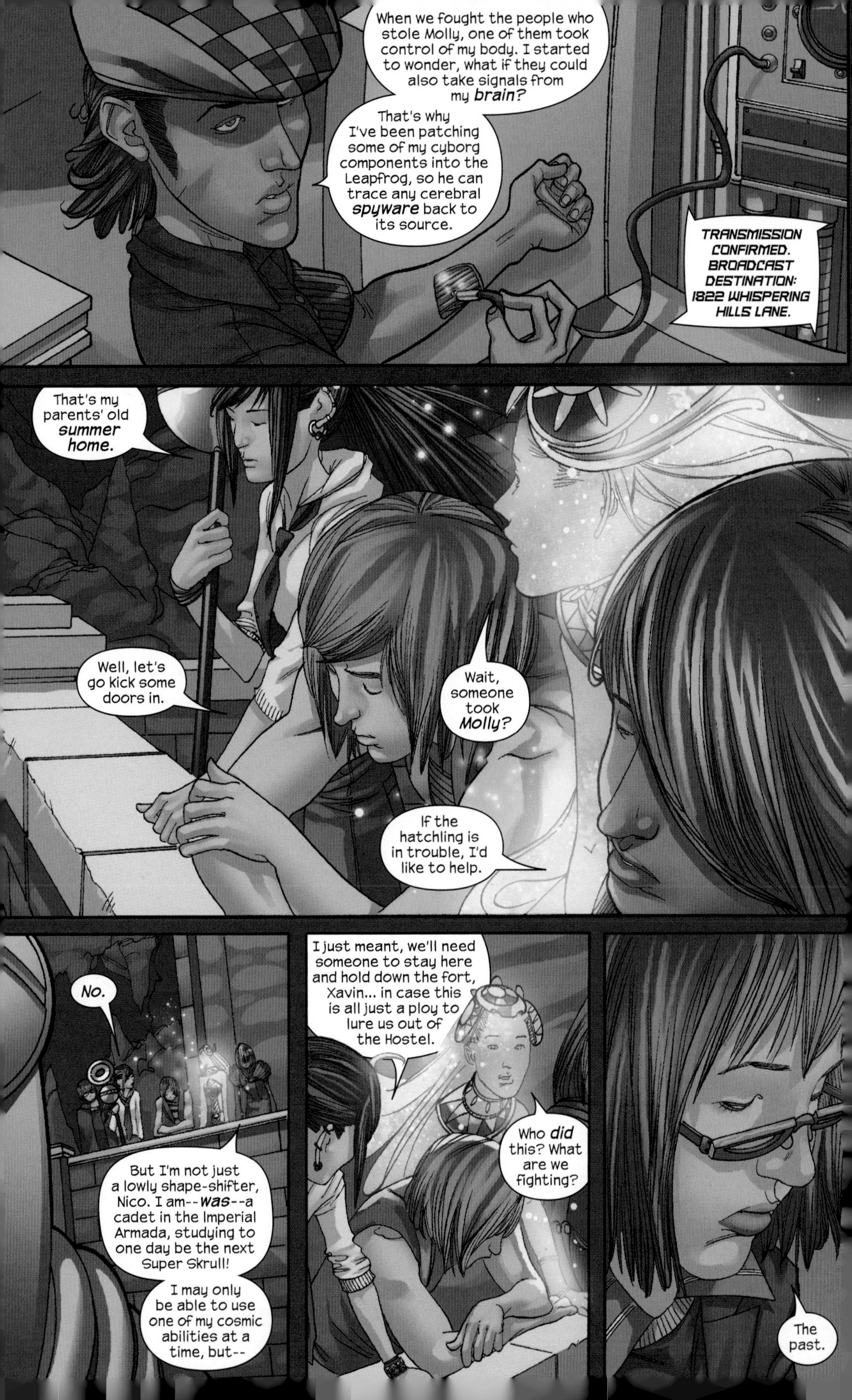
When we fought the people who stole Molly, one of them took control of my body. I started to wonder, what if they could also take signals from my brain?
That's why I've been patching some of my cyborg components into the Leapfrog, so he can trace any cerebral spyware back to its source.
TRANSMISSION CONFIRMED. BROADCAST DESTINATION: 1822 WHISPERING HILLS LANE.
That's my parents' old summer home.
Well, let's go kick some doors in.
Wait, someone took Molly?
If the hatchling is in trouble, I'd like to help.
No.
But I'm not just a lowly shape-shifter, Nico. I am--was--a cadet in the Imperial Armada, studying to one day be the next Super Skrull!
I may only be able to use one of my cosmic abilities at a time, but--
I just meant, we'll need someone to stay here and hold down the fort, Xavin... in case this is all just a ploy to lure us out of the Hostel.
Who did this? What are we fighting?
The past.

So after Not-So-Old Man Wilder's goon squad spilled the beans about my little screwup with Nico, Gert pretty much dumped me forever.

Oh, Chase. I'm sure she's just scared and... and *confused*. Give her time, she'll come around.

Trust me, you two were *made* for each other.

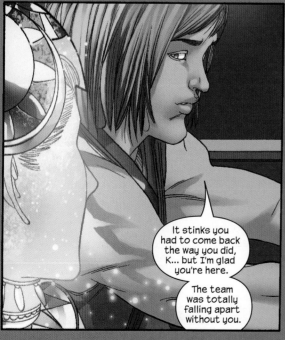

It stinks you had to come back the way you did, K... but I'm glad you're here.

The team was totally falling apart without you.

Each of us has been falling apart since day one, Chase.

We just have to find a way to fall apart *together*.

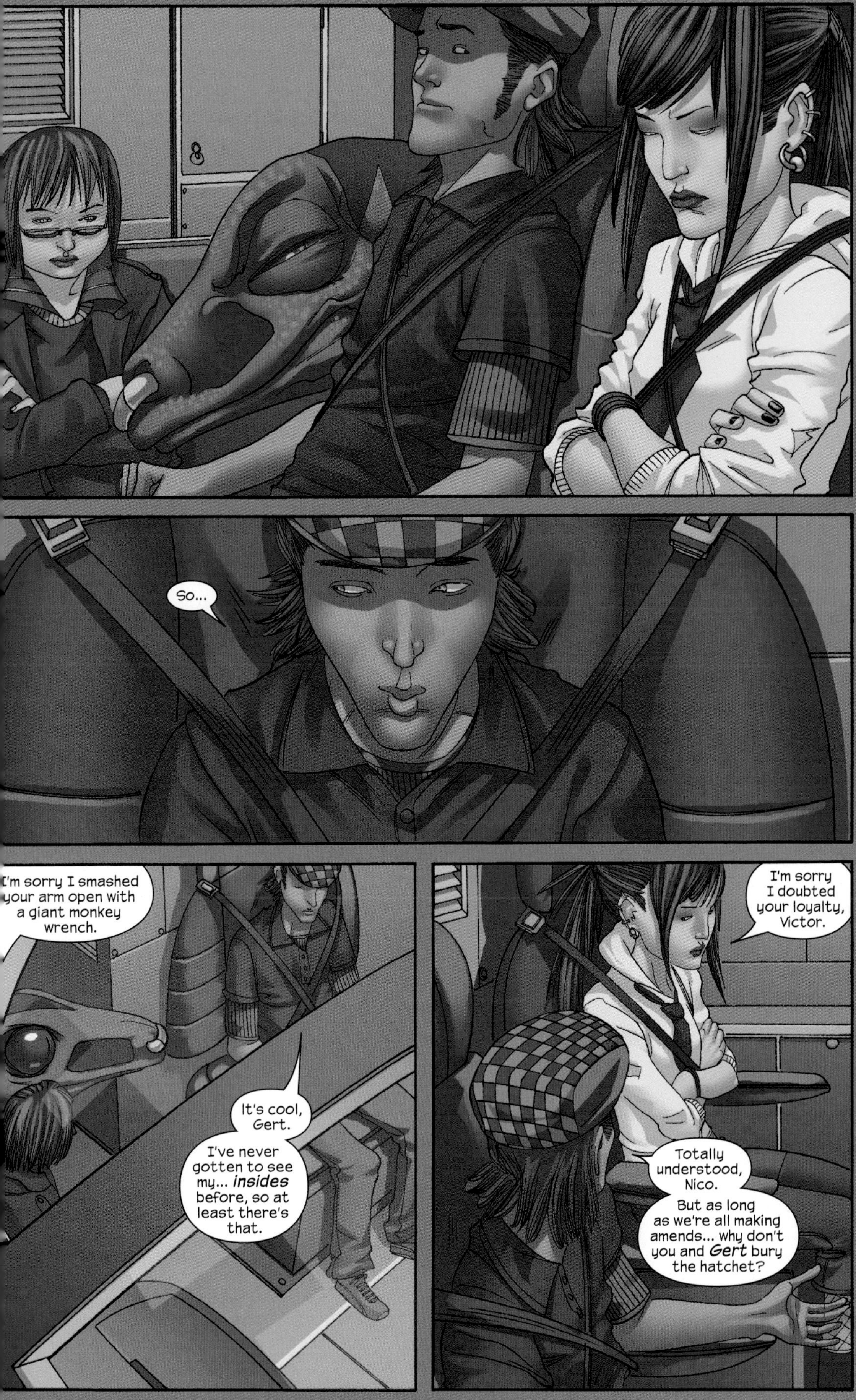
So...
I'm sorry I smashed your arm open with a giant monkey wrench.
It's cool, Gert.
I've never gotten to see my... *insides* before, so at least there's that.
I'm sorry I doubted your loyalty, Victor.
Totally understood, Nico.
But as long as we're all making amends... why don't you and *Gert* bury the hatchet?

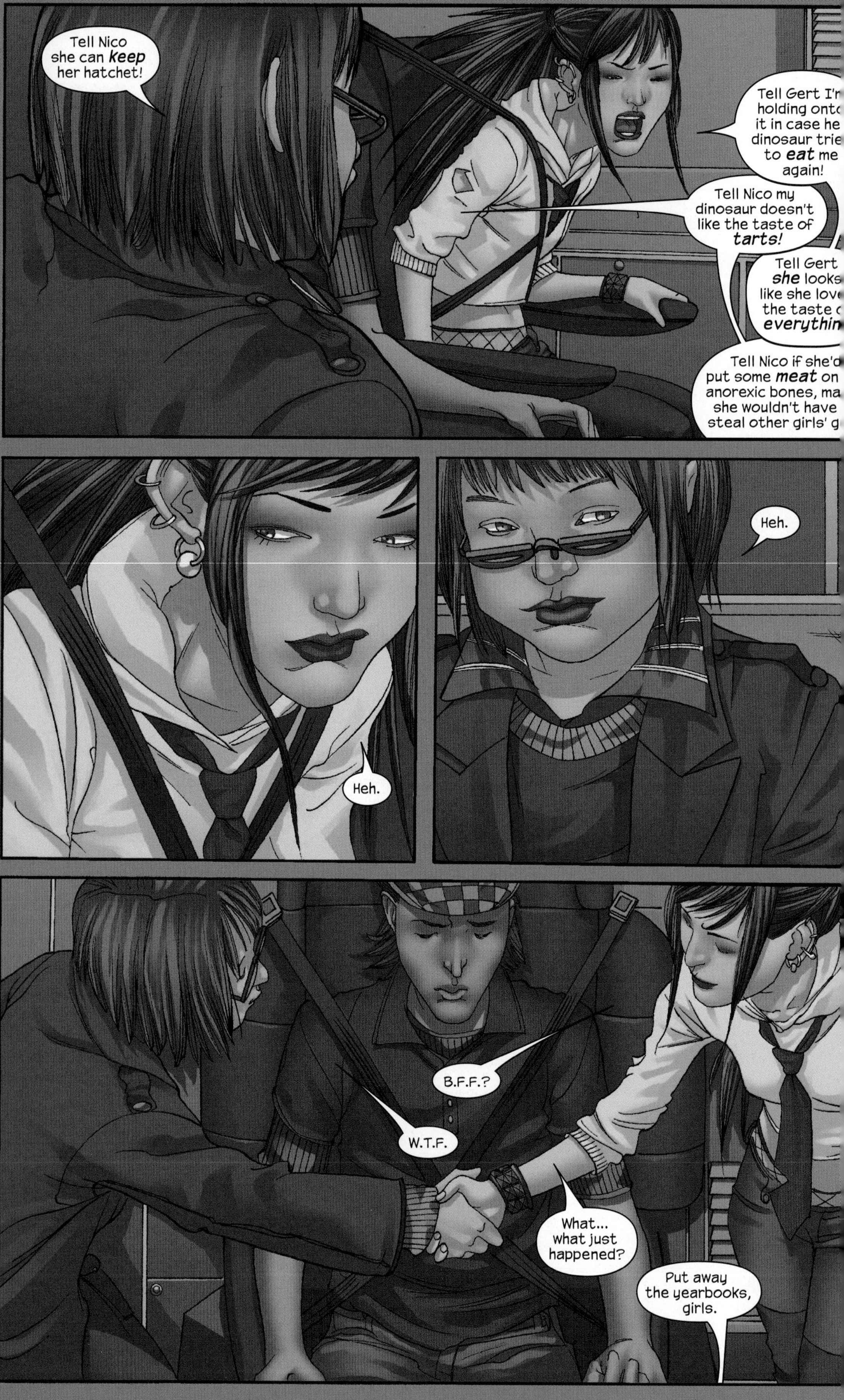

Tell Nico she can *keep* her hatchet!
Tell Gert holding it in case dinosaur to *eat* me again!
Tell Nico my dinosaur doesn't like the taste of *tarts!*
Tell Gert *she* looks like she the taste
Tell Nico if put some *meat* on anorexic bones, she wouldn't have steal other girls'
Heh.
Heh.
B.F.F.?
W.T.F.
What... what just happened?
Put away the yearbooks, girls.

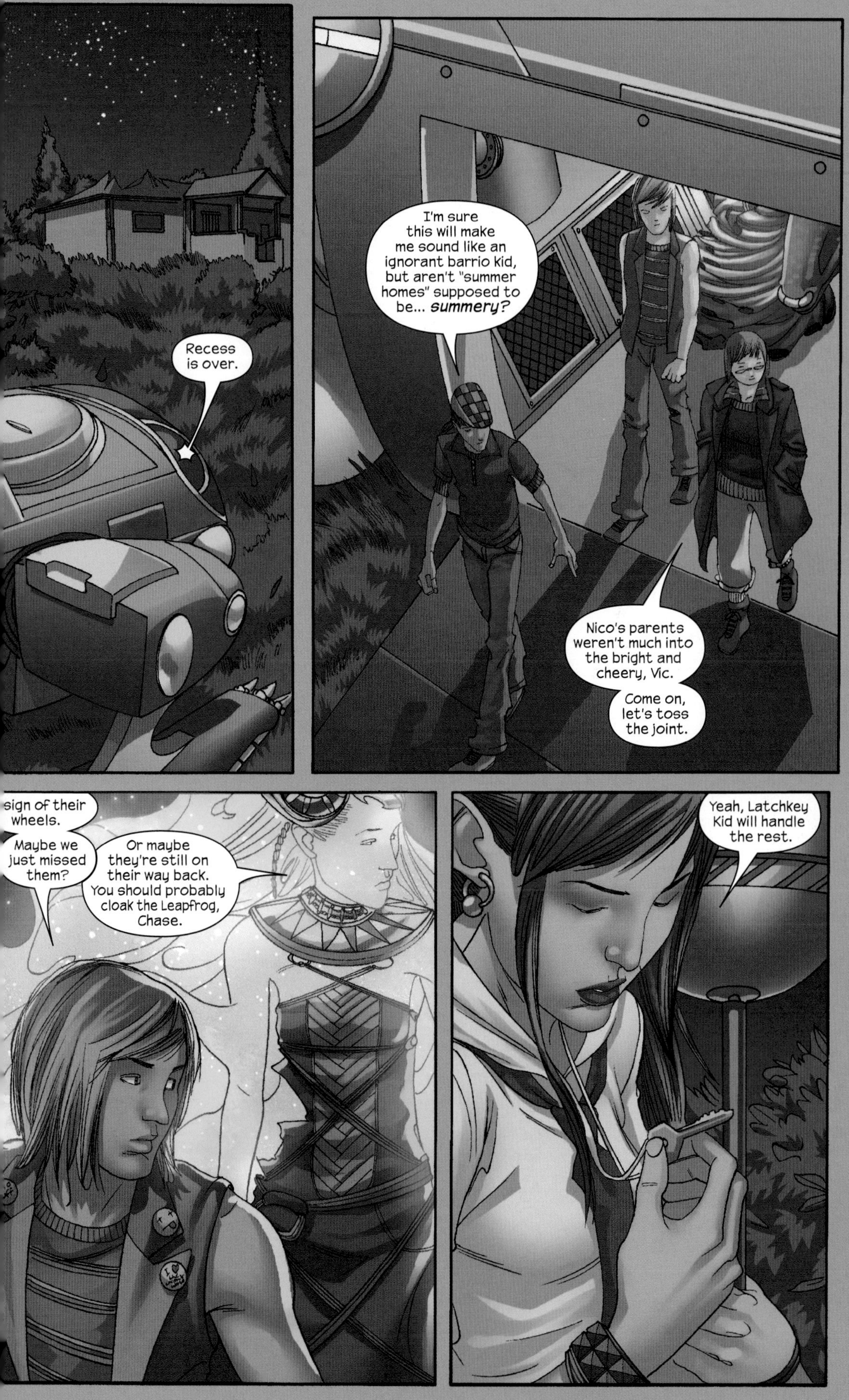
Recess is over.
I'm sure this will make me sound like an ignorant barrio kid, but aren't "summer homes" supposed to be... *summery?*
Nico's parents weren't much into the bright and cheery, Vic.
Come on, let's toss the joint.
sign of their wheels.
Maybe we just missed them?
Or maybe they're still on their way back. You should probably cloak the Leapfrog, Chase.
Yeah, Latchkey Kid will handle the rest.

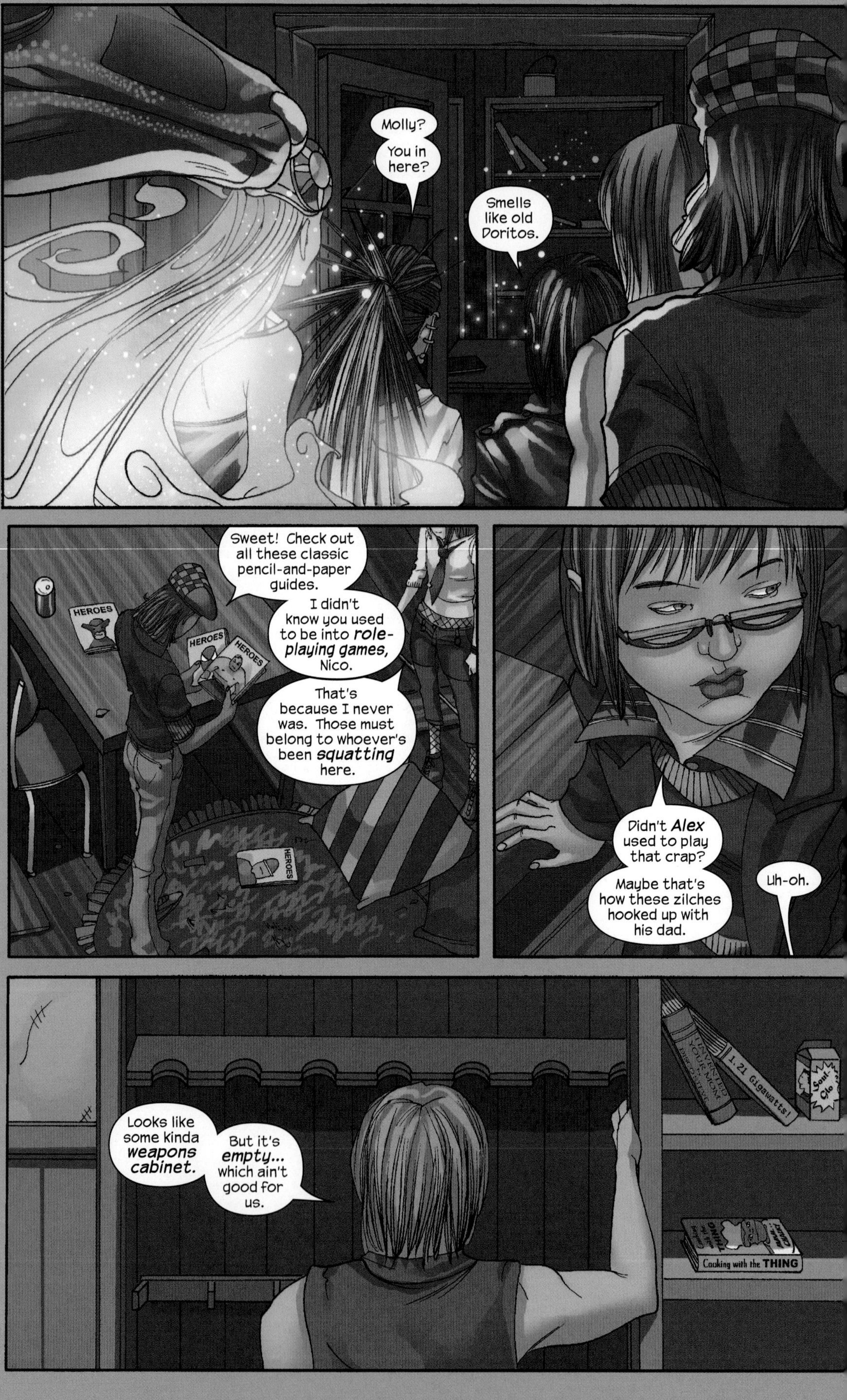
Molly?
You in here?
Smells like old Doritos.
Sweet! Check out all these classic pencil-and-paper guides.
I didn't know you used to be into *role-playing games,* Nico.
That's because I never was. Those must belong to whoever's been *squatting* here.
HEROES
Didn't *Alex* used to play that crap?
Maybe that's how these zilches hooked up with his dad.
Uh-oh.
Looks like some kinda *weapons cabinet.*
But it's *empty...* which ain't good for us.
1.21 Gigawatts!
Cooking with the THING

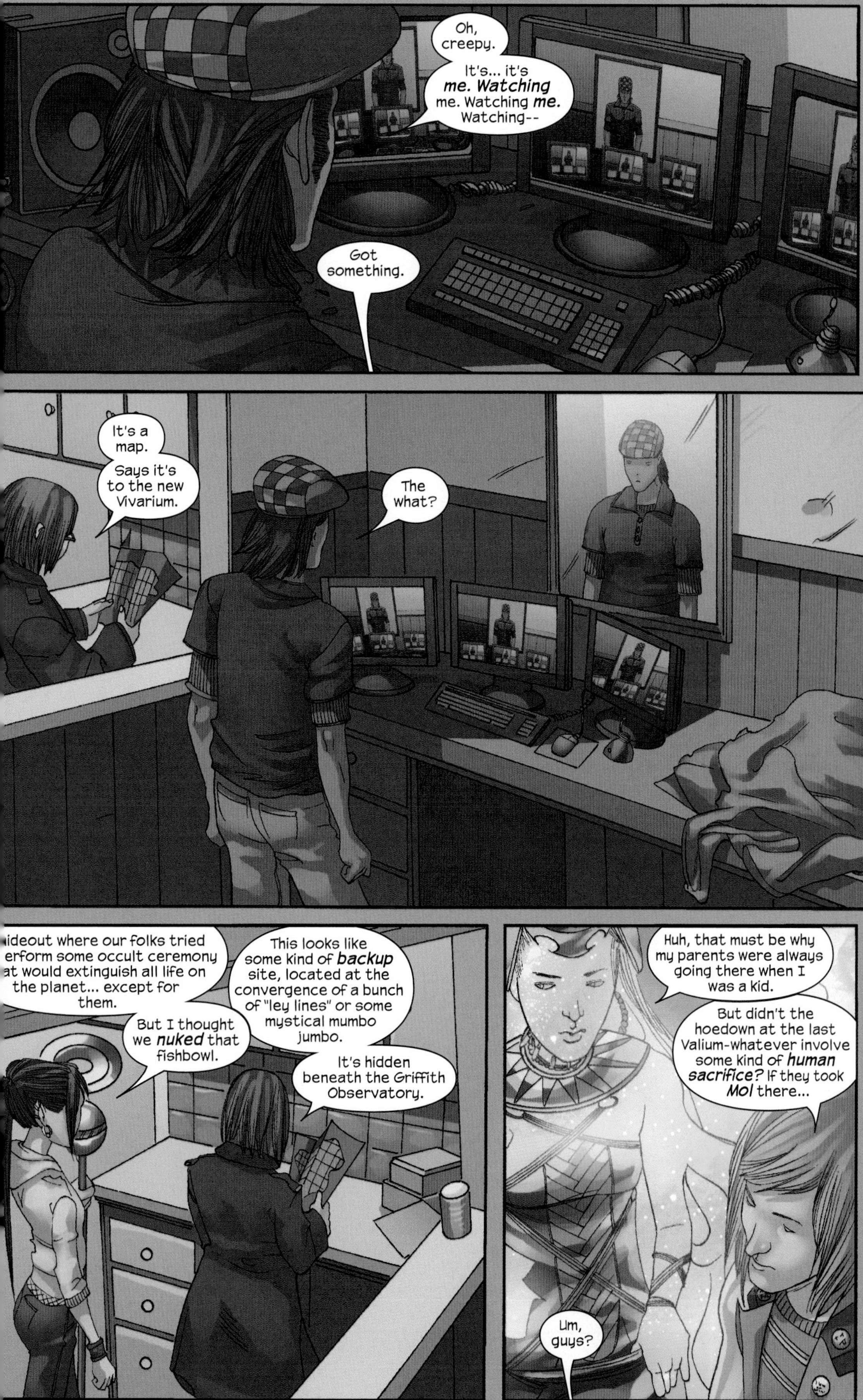

Oh, creepy.
It's... it's *me. Watching* me. Watching *me.* Watching--
Got something.
It's a map.
Says it's to the new Vivarium.
The what?
ideout where our folks tried erform some occult ceremony at would extinguish all life on the planet... except for them.
But I thought we *nuked* that fishbowl.
This looks like some kind of *backup* site, located at the convergence of a bunch of "ley lines" or some mystical mumbo jumbo.
It's hidden beneath the Griffith Observatory.
Huh, that must be why my parents were always going there when I was a kid.
But didn't the hoedown at the last Valium-whatever involve some kind of *human sacrifice?* If they took *Mol* there...
Um, guys?

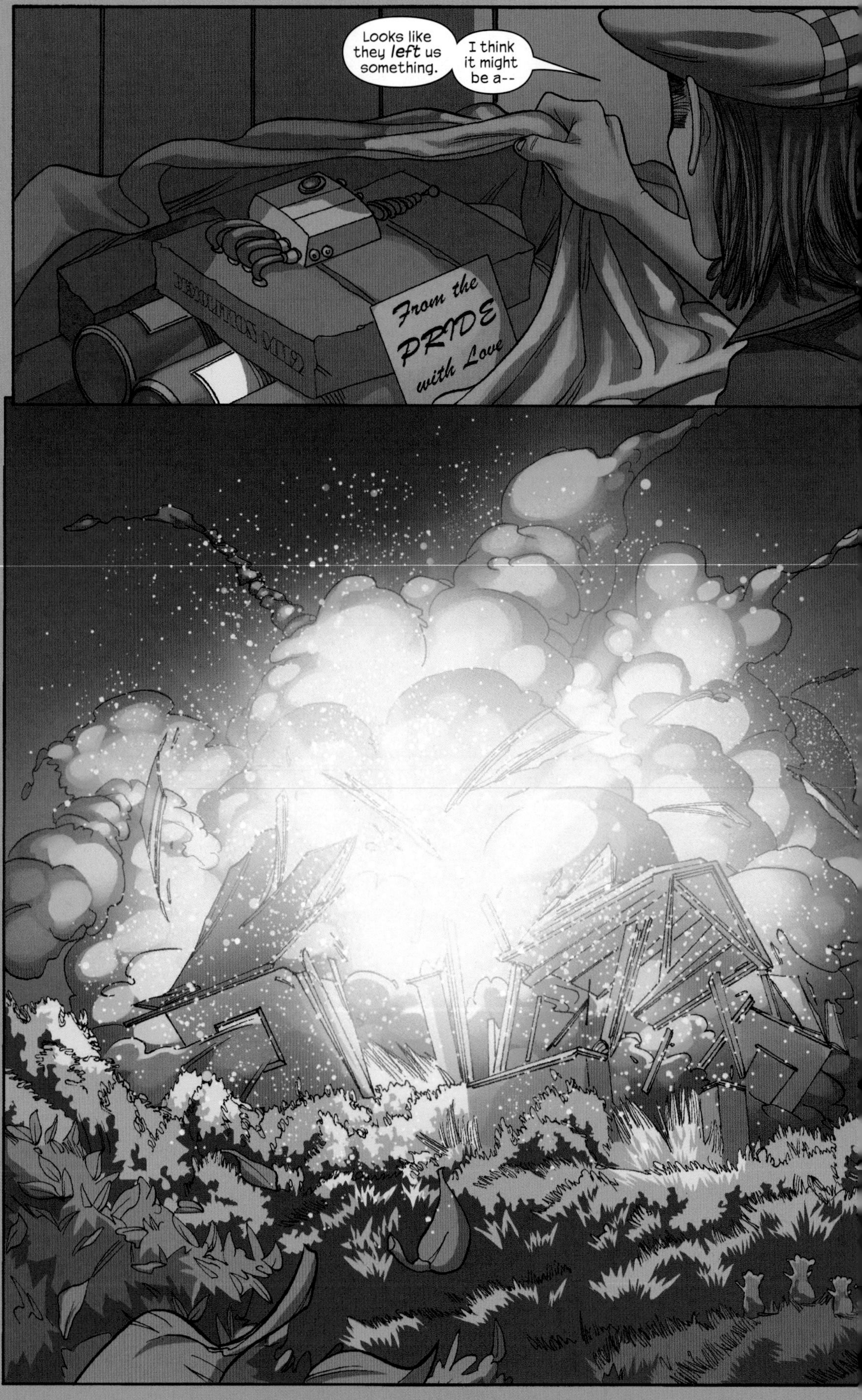
Looks like they *left* us something.
I think it might be a--
From the PRIDE with Love

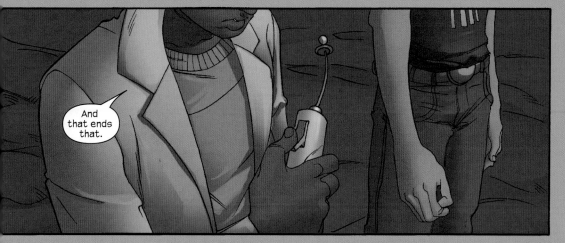

And that ends that.

GRIFFITH OBSE

What are you talking about, Geoffrey?

Just a little something I cooked up to take care of our opponents, so the Pride can get back to doing the Lord's work.

Anyway, make sure Molly's restraints are on tight. I'm gonna take our young charge inside with the Abstract while you three set up a defensive perimeter around the place.

I thought you said the bad guys were taken care of, Mr. Wilder.

Sure, but that's probably what they thought about *me*.

Hope for the best and all that, right?

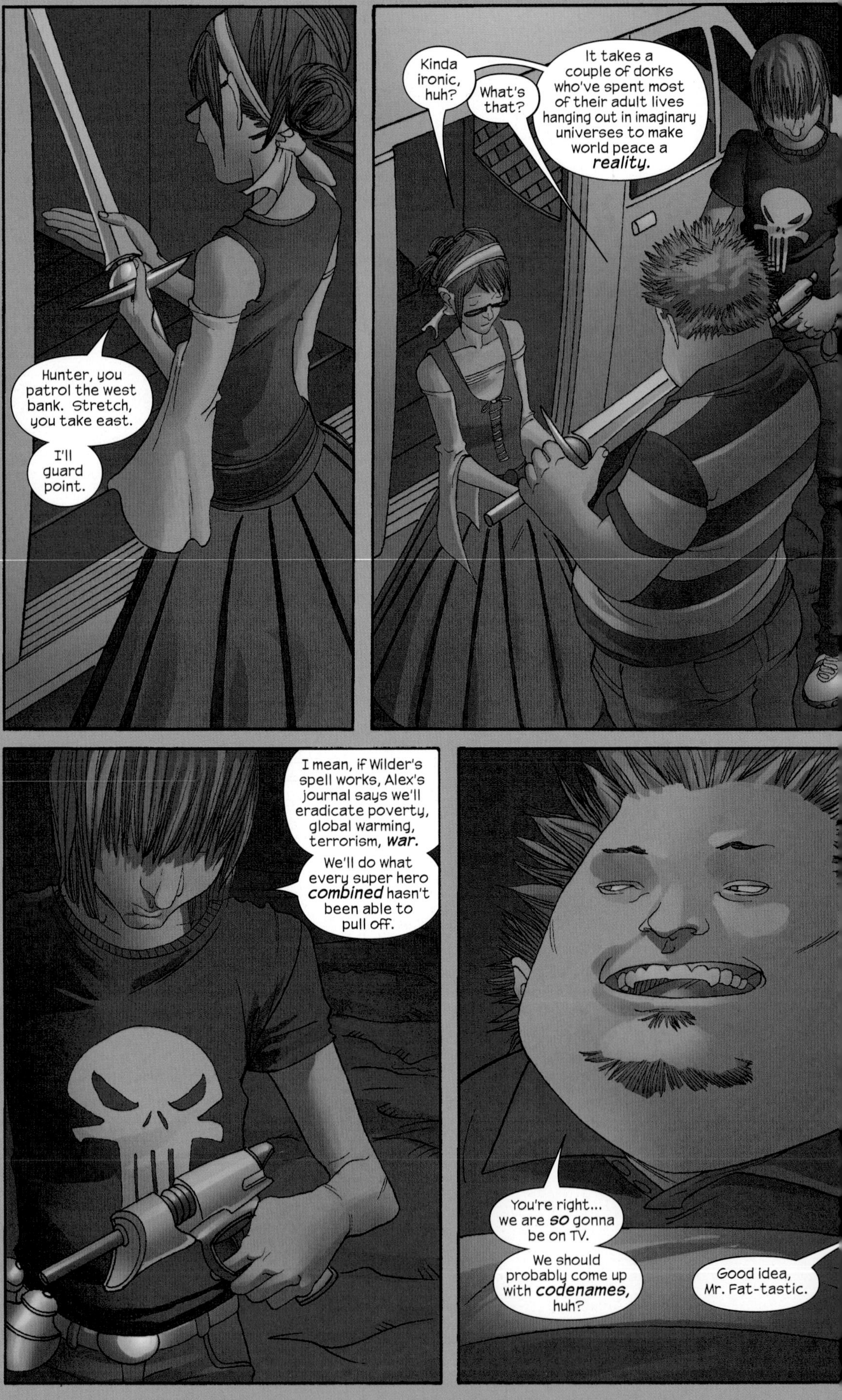
Hunter, you patrol the west bank. Stretch, you take east.
I'll guard point.
Kinda ironic, huh?
What's that?
It takes a couple of dorks who've spent most of their adult lives hanging out in imaginary universes to make world peace a *reality.*
I mean, if Wilder's spell works, Alex's journal says we'll eradicate poverty, global warming, terrorism, *war.*
We'll do what every super hero *combined* hasn't been able to pull off.
You're right... we are *so* gonna be on TV.
We should probably come up with *codenames,* huh?
Good idea, Mr. Fat-tastic.

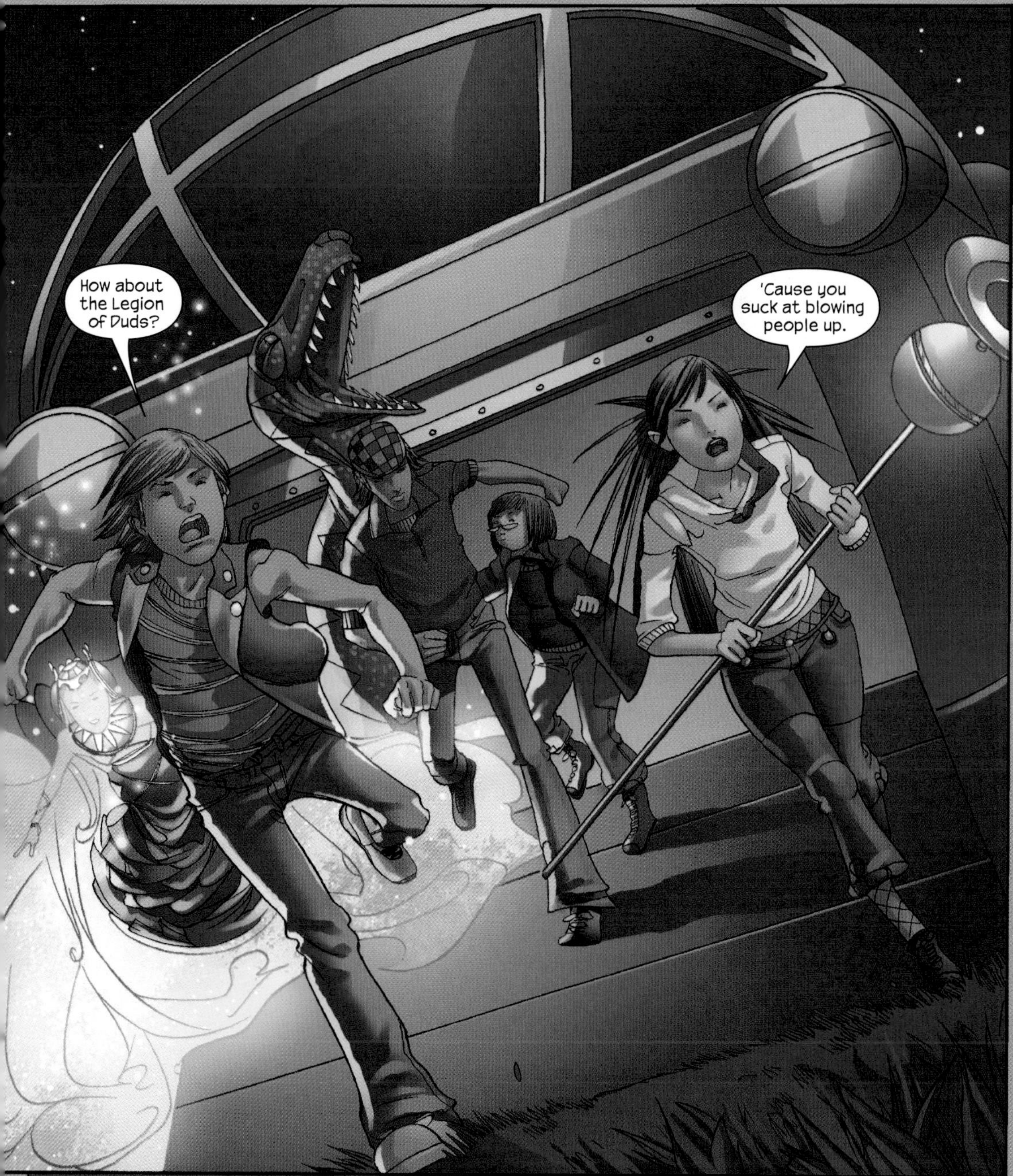
How about the Legion of Duds?
'Cause you suck at blowing people up.

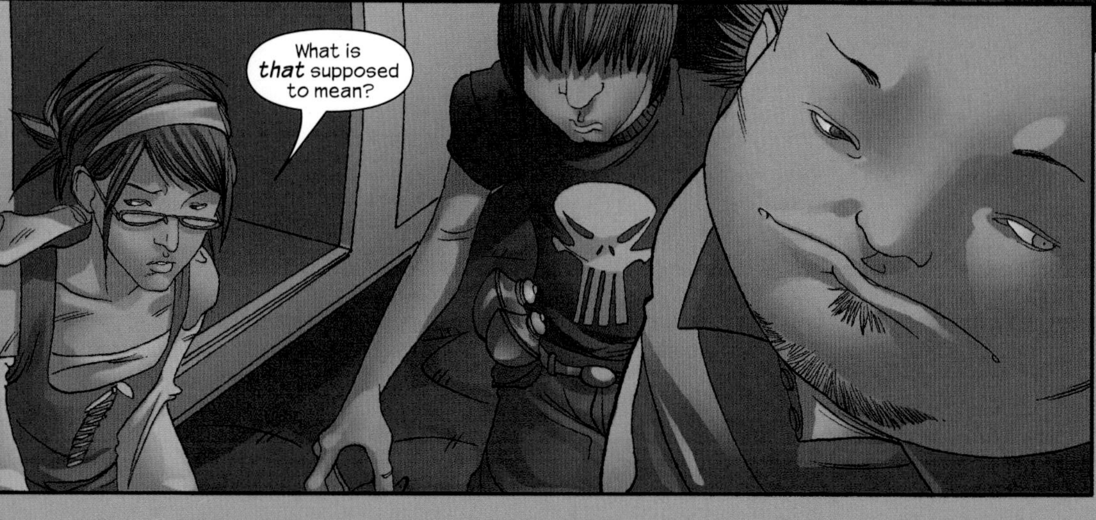
What is *that* supposed to mean?

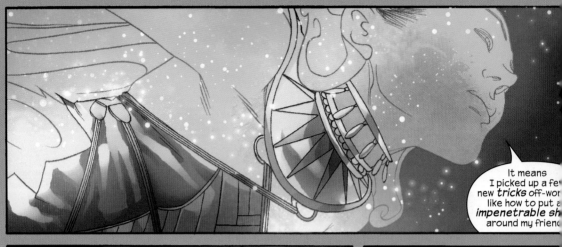

It means I picked up a few new *tricks* off-worl[d] like how to put a[n] *impenetrable sh*[ield] around my frien[ds.]

Thankfully, it works on *enemies*, too.

KA SH NK

So the *alien* invades again, huh? Mr. Wilder said the Abstract *warned* you might show your face.

Which is why we forged a *sword* out of the material that dampens your energy points.

See, this is what happens when you mess with *masters.*

BEEP BOO[P]

Sorry, I set up an internal *firewall* so you can't hack into my mainframe again.

Not trying to hack into *you*, Borg Queen.

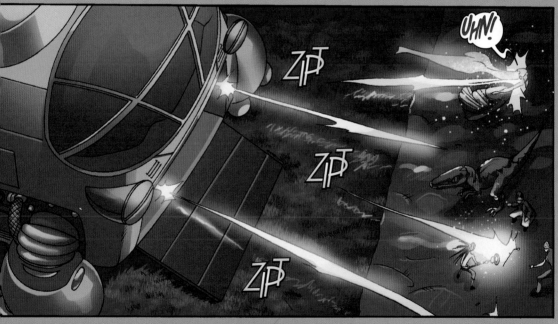

ZIP

ZIP

ZIP

UHN!

Gert, can you--

Go, Chase and I will try to buy you some time!

Just find *Molly!*

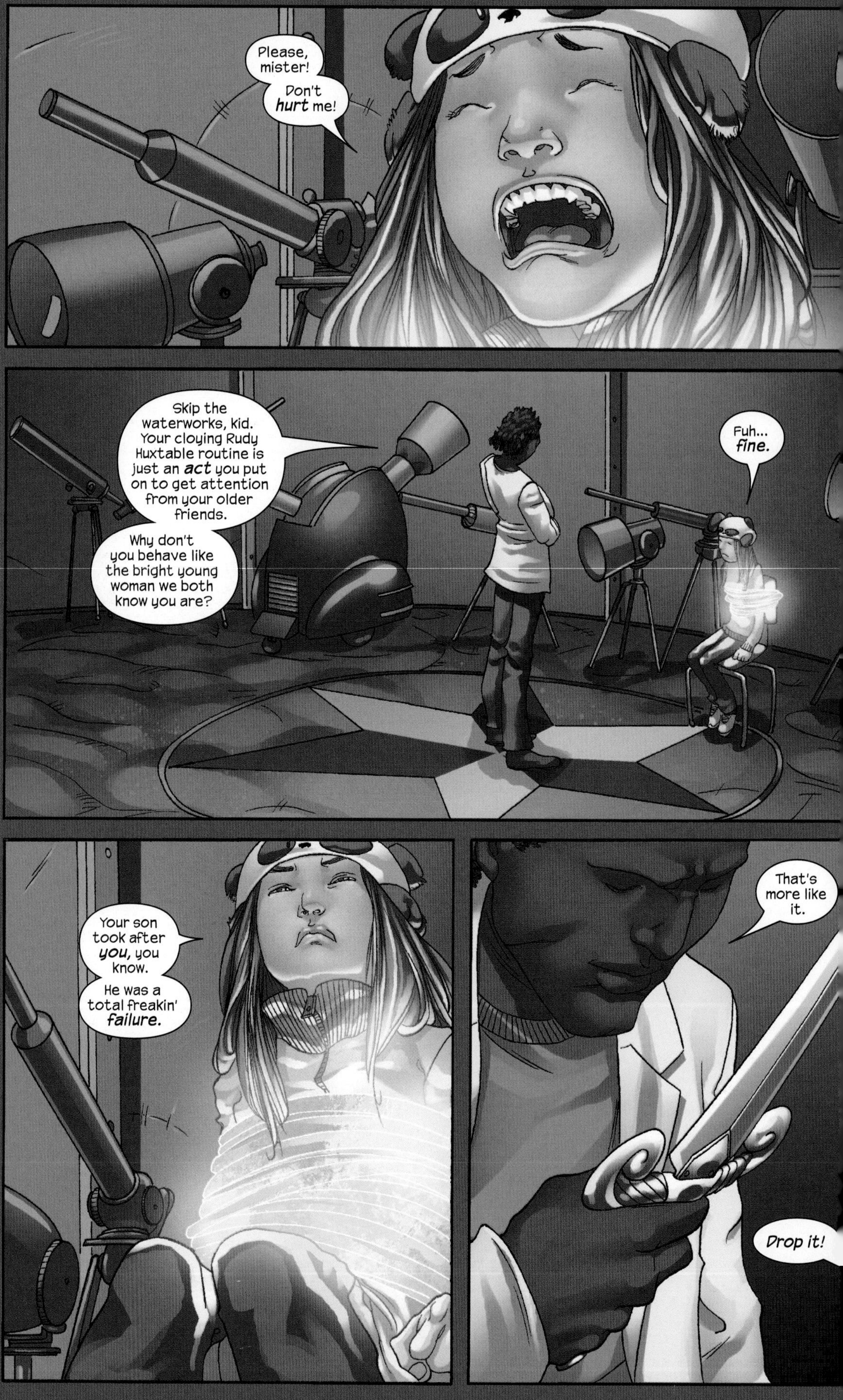

Please, mister!
Don't *hurt* me!
Skip the waterworks, kid. Your cloying Rudy Huxtable routine is just an *act* you put on to get attention from your older friends.
Why don't you behave like the bright young woman we both know you are?
Fuh... *fine.*
Your son took after *you*, you know.
He was a total freakin' *failure.*
That's more like it.
Drop it!

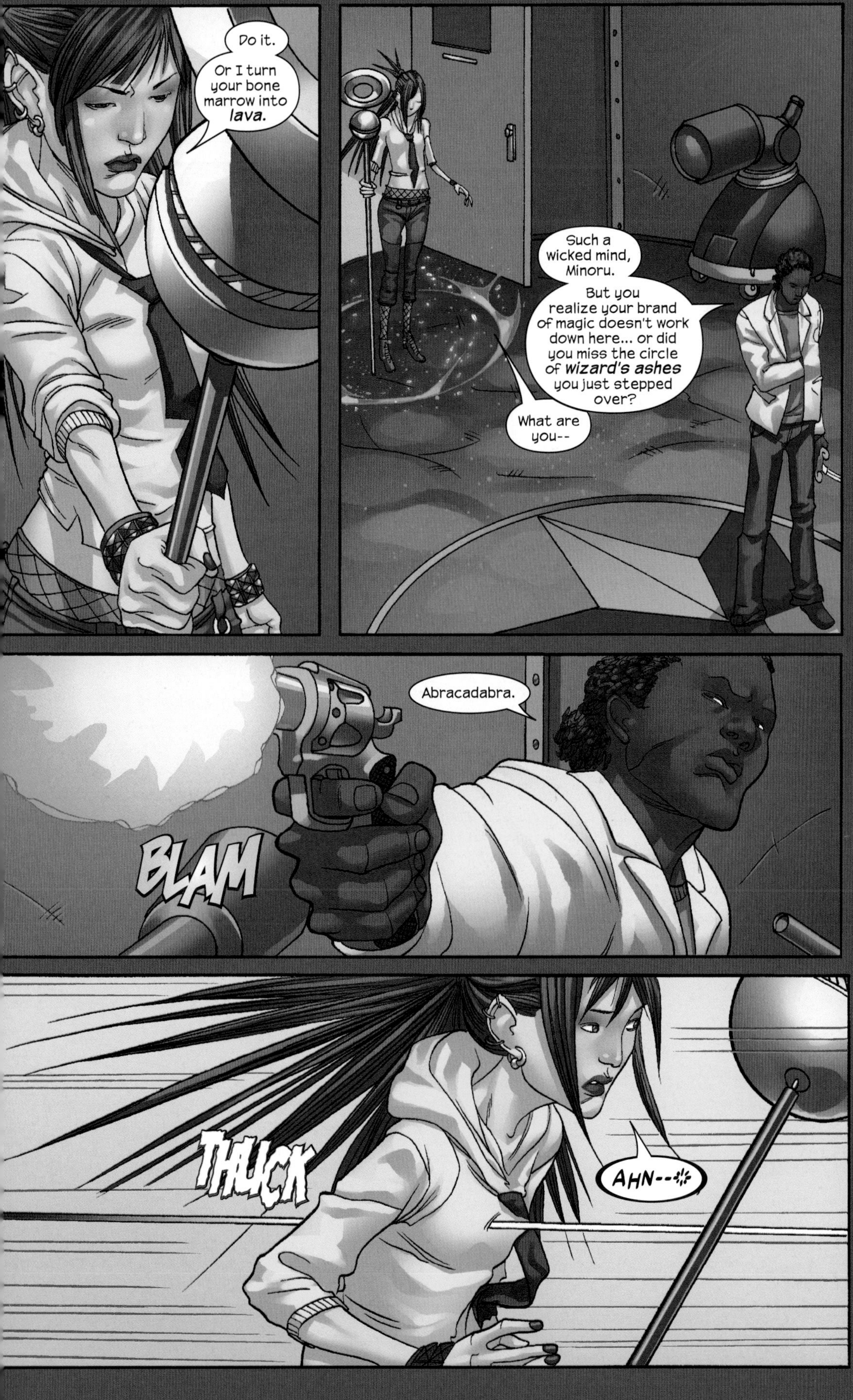
Do it.
Or I turn your bone marrow into *lava.*
Such a wicked mind, Minoru.
But you realize your brand of magic doesn't work down here... or did you miss the circle of ***wizard's ashes*** you just stepped over?
What are you--
Abracadabra.
BLAM
THUCK
AHN--

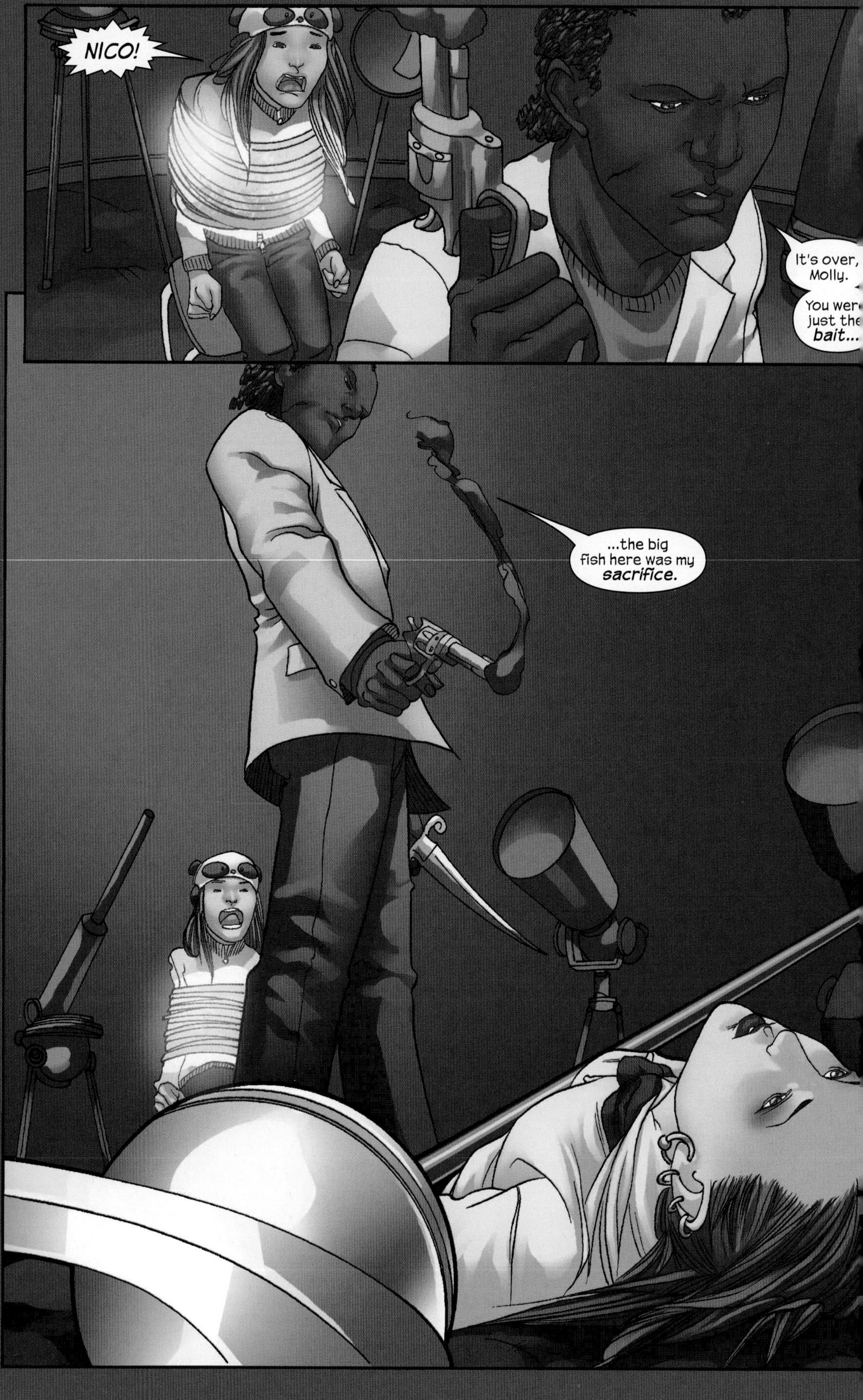
NICO!
It's over, Molly.
You wer just the bait...
...the big fish here was my sacrifice.

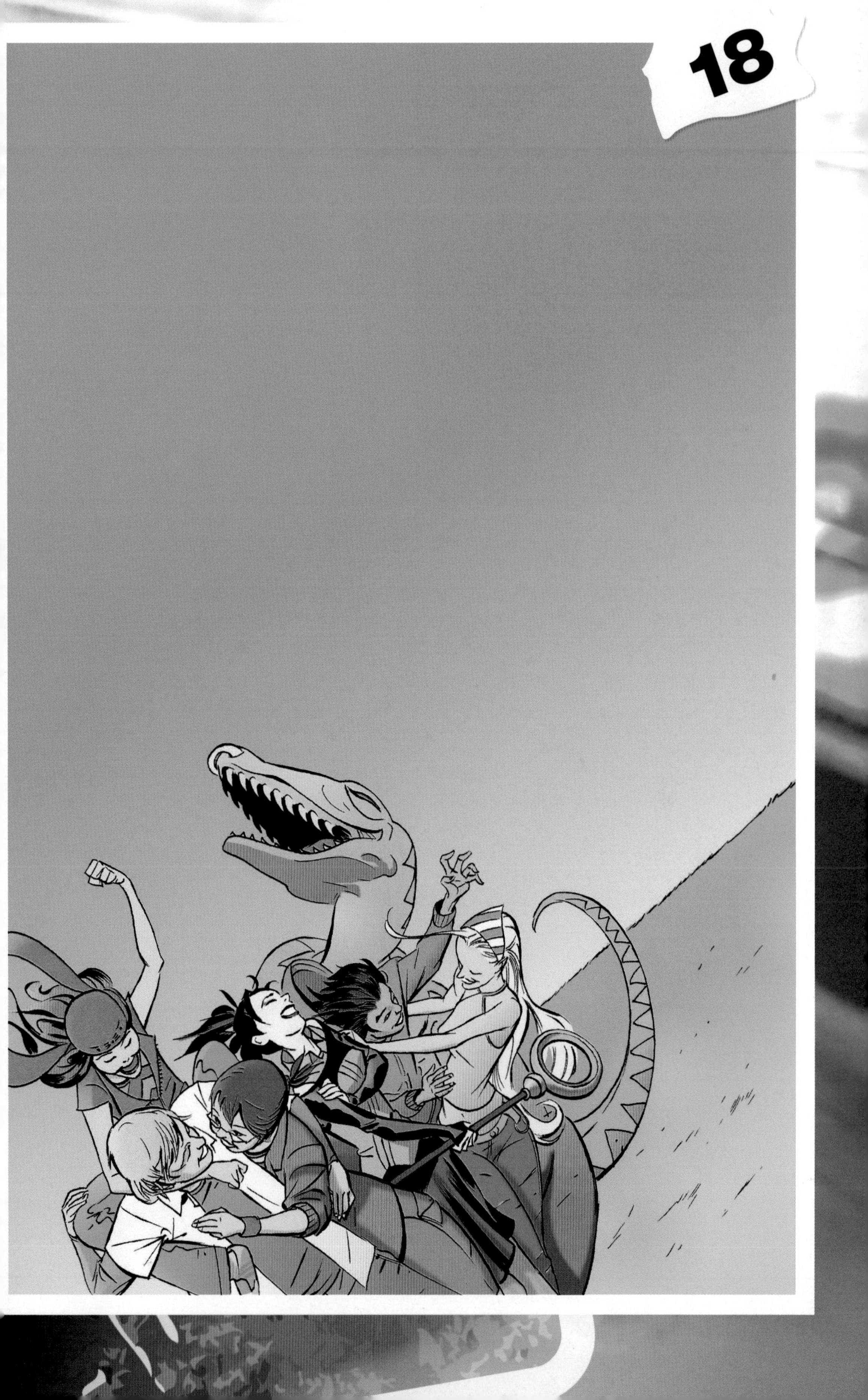
18

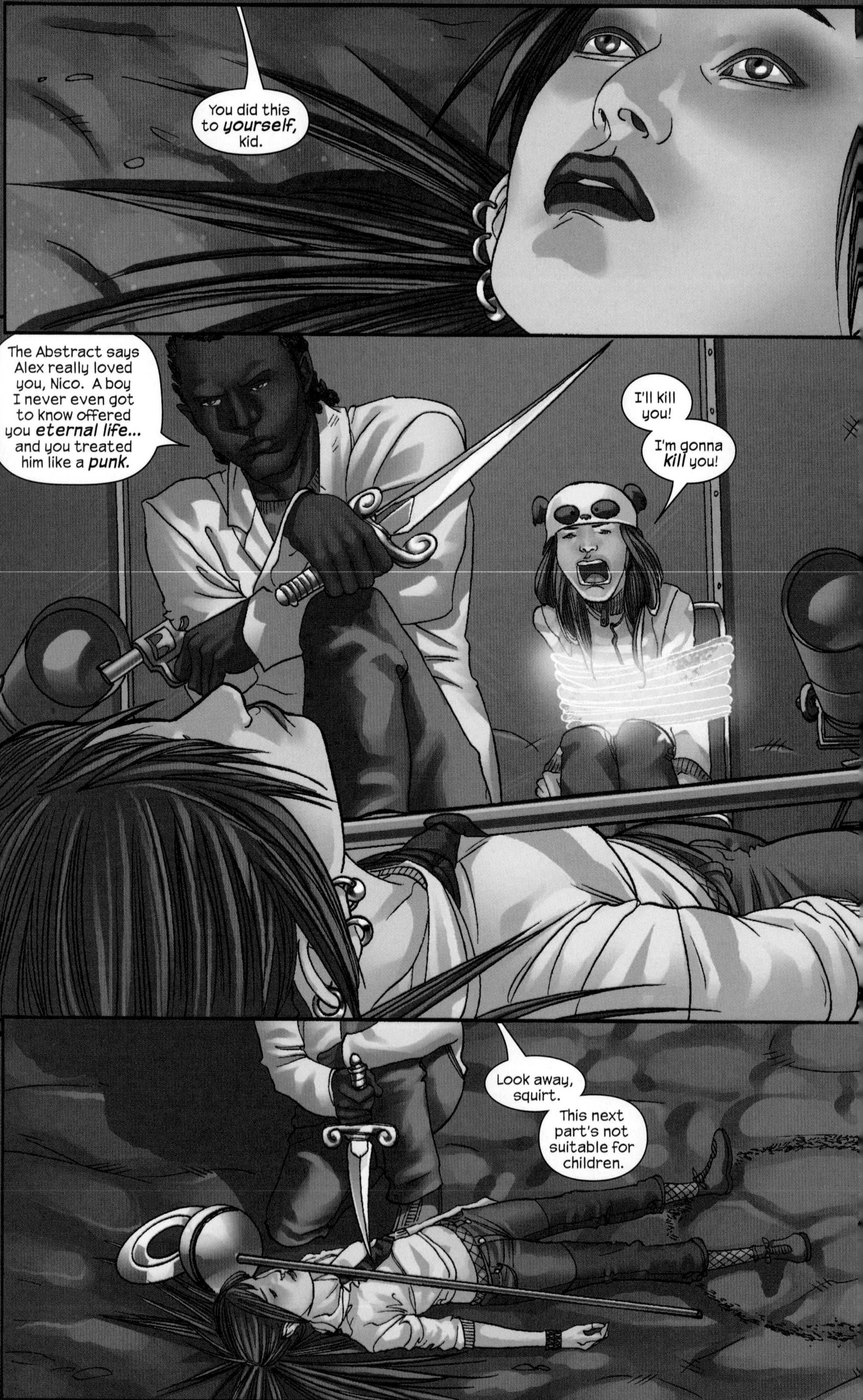
You did this to *yourself,* kid.
The Abstract says Alex really loved you, Nico. A boy I never even got to know offered you *eternal life...* and you treated him like a *punk.*
I'll kill you!
I'm gonna *kill* you!
Look away, squirt.
This next part's not suitable for children.

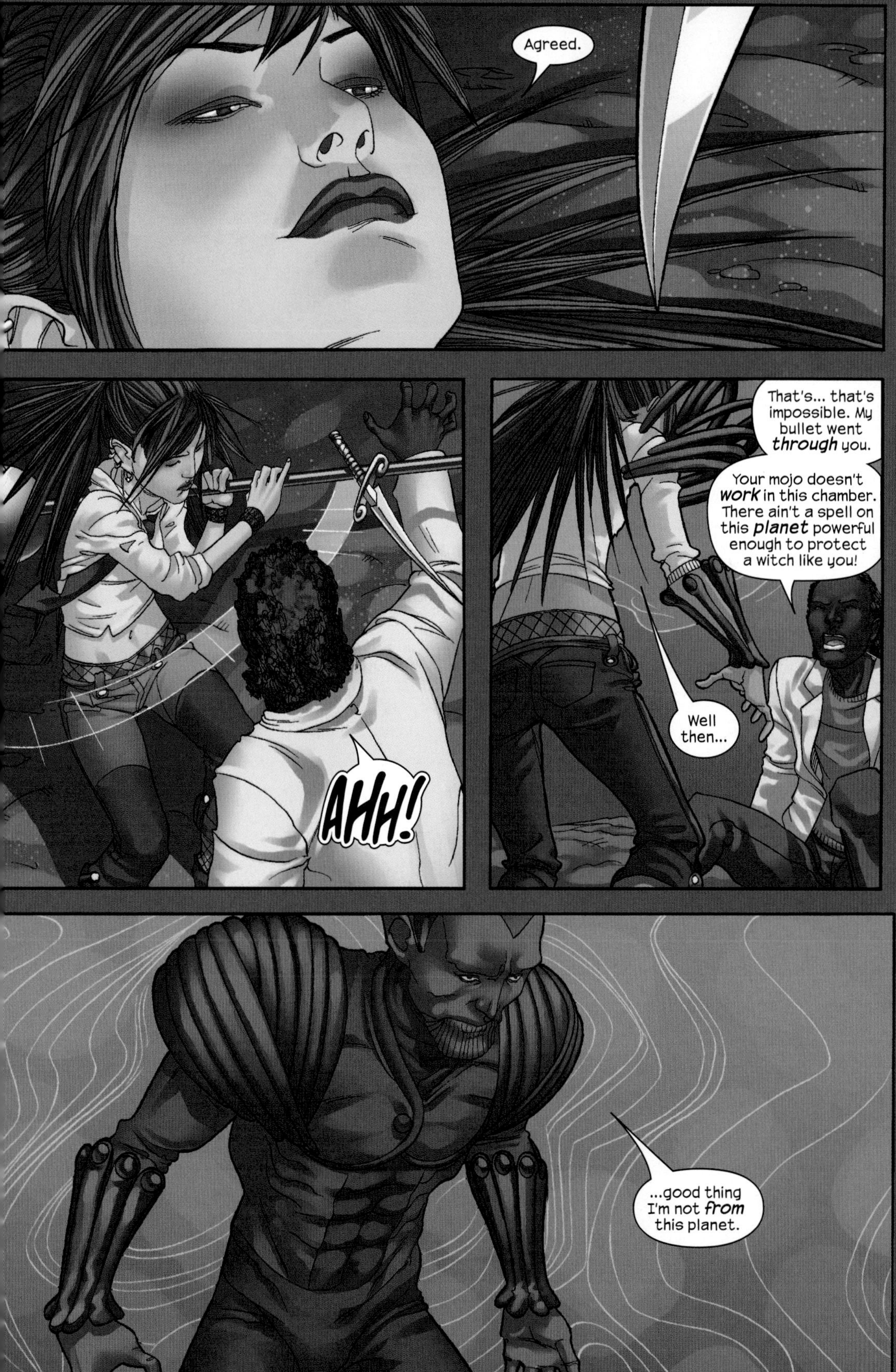
Agreed.
AHH!
That's... that's impossible. My bullet went *through* you.
Your mojo doesn't *work* in this chamber. There ain't a spell on this *planet* powerful enough to protect a witch like you!
Well then...
...good thing I'm not *from* this planet.

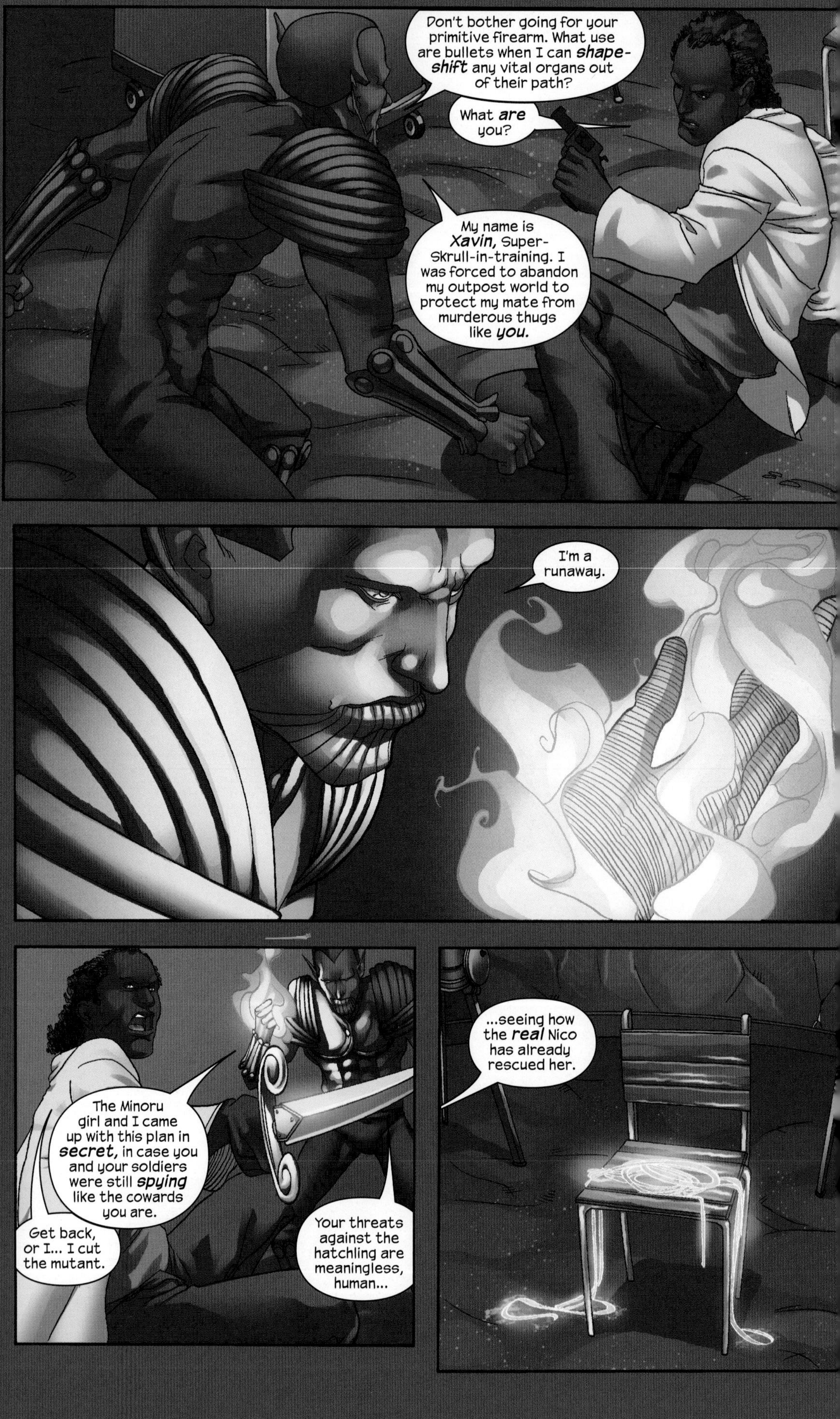
Don't bother going for your primitive firearm. What use are bullets when I can *shape-shift* any vital organs out of their path?
What *are* you?
My name is *Xavin,* Super-Skrull-in-training. I was forced to abandon my outpost world to protect my mate from murderous thugs like *you.*
I'm a runaway.
The Minoru girl and I came up with this plan in *secret,* in case you and your soldiers were still *spying* like the cowards you are.
Get back, or I... I cut the mutant.
Your threats against the hatchling are meaningless, human...
...seeing how the *real* Nico has already rescued her.

This can't be *happening!*

The Abstract never said anything about freaks like you. My ring decoded every word!

Yes, well, the best-laid plans of Kree and men...

I used an invisible shield to cloak Nico while I performed the... what do you people call the Dance of Deception?

You got a big mouth, E.T.

Big *ears*, too.

Wonder how they'll handle a few thousand *decibels.*

EEEEEEEEEEEEEEEEEEEEEEEEEEEEEEEEEEEE

NAHHH!

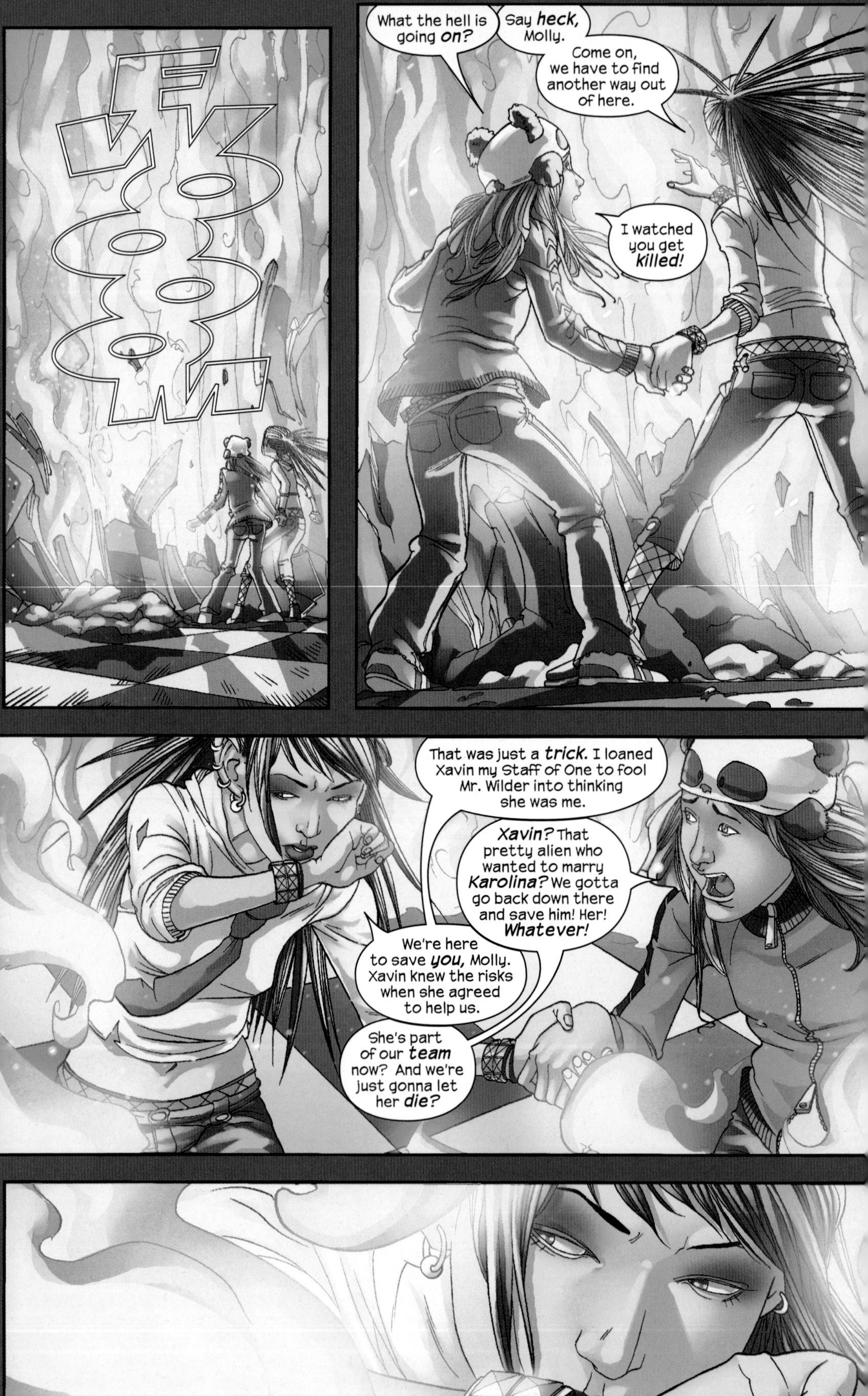
FWOOOM
What the hell is going on?
Say heck, Molly.
Come on, we have to find another way out of here.
I watched you get killed!
That was just a trick. I loaned Xavin my Staff of One to fool Mr. Wilder into thinking she was me.
Xavin? That pretty alien who wanted to marry Karolina? We gotta go back down there and save him! Her! Whatever!
We're here to save you, Molly. Xavin knew the risks when she agreed to help us.
She's part of our team now? And we're just gonna let her die?

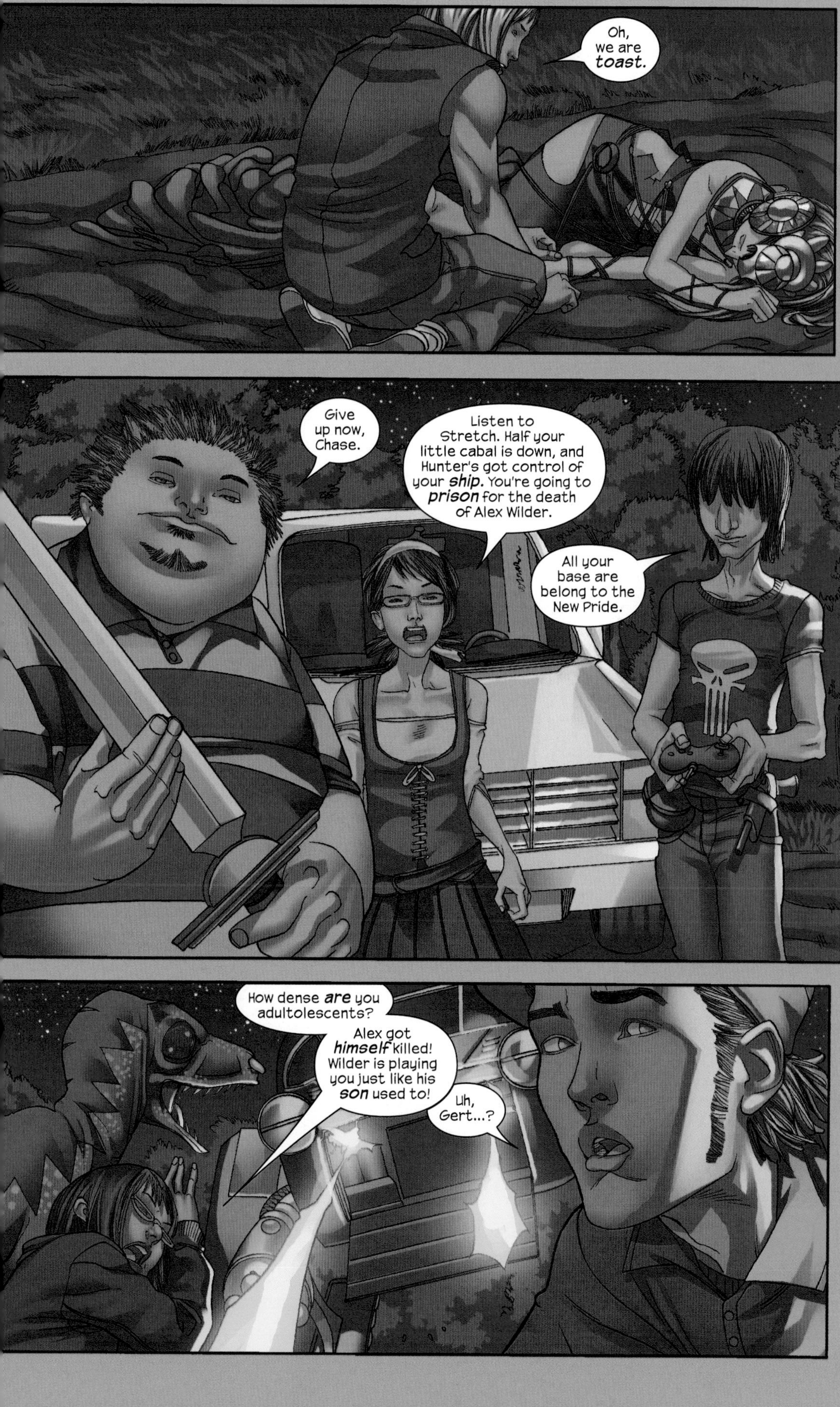
Oh, we are *toast.*
Give up now, Chase.
Listen to Stretch. Half your little cabal is down, and Hunter's got control of your *ship.* You're going to *prison* for the death of Alex Wilder.
All your base are belong to the New Pride.
How dense *are* you adultolescents?
Alex got *himself* killed! Wilder is playing you just like his *son* used to!
Uh, Gert...?

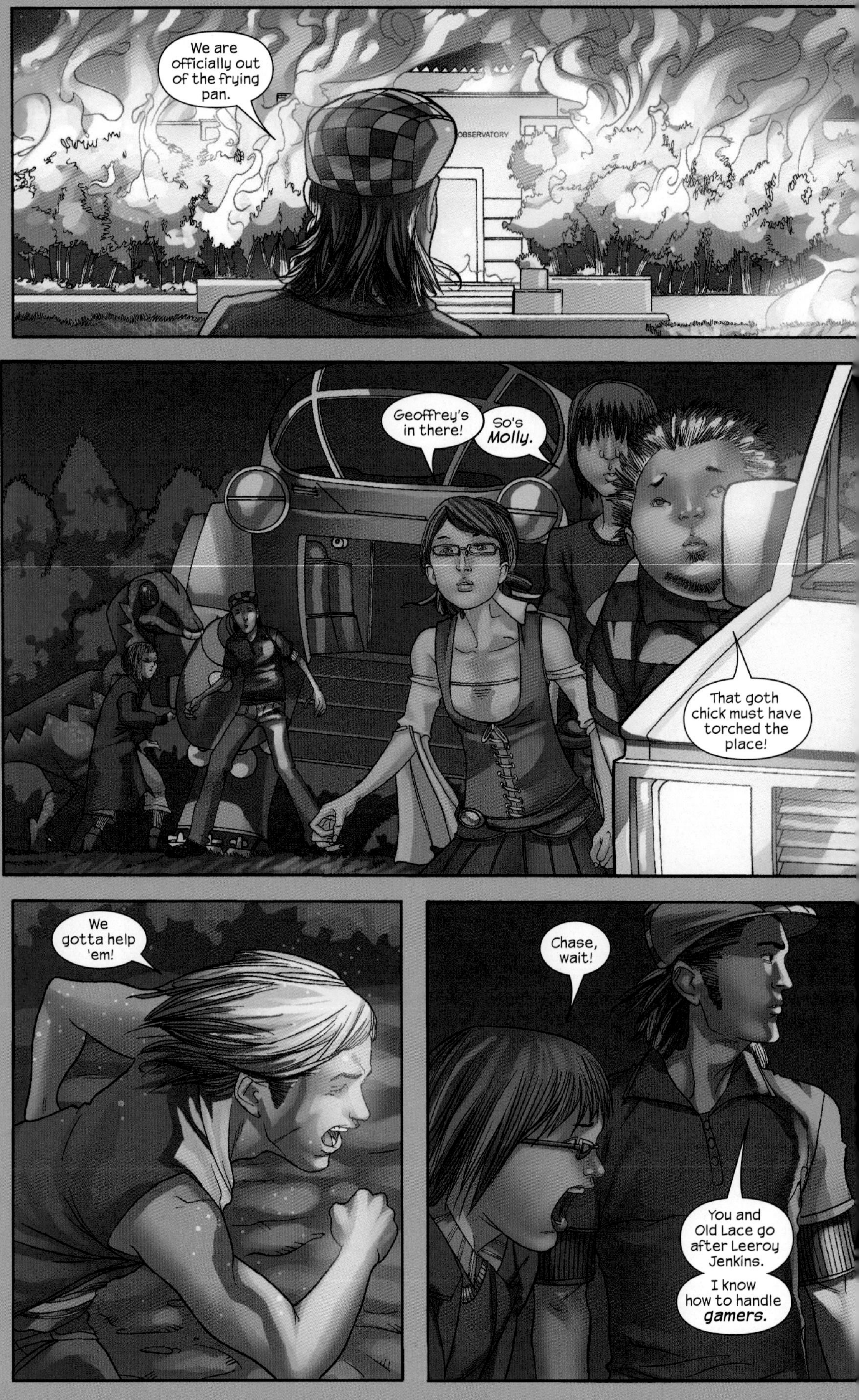

We are officially out of the frying pan.
Geoffrey's in there!
So's *Molly.*
That goth chick must have torched the place!
We gotta help 'em!
Chase, wait!
You and Old Lace go after Leeroy Jenkins.
I know how to handle *gamers.*

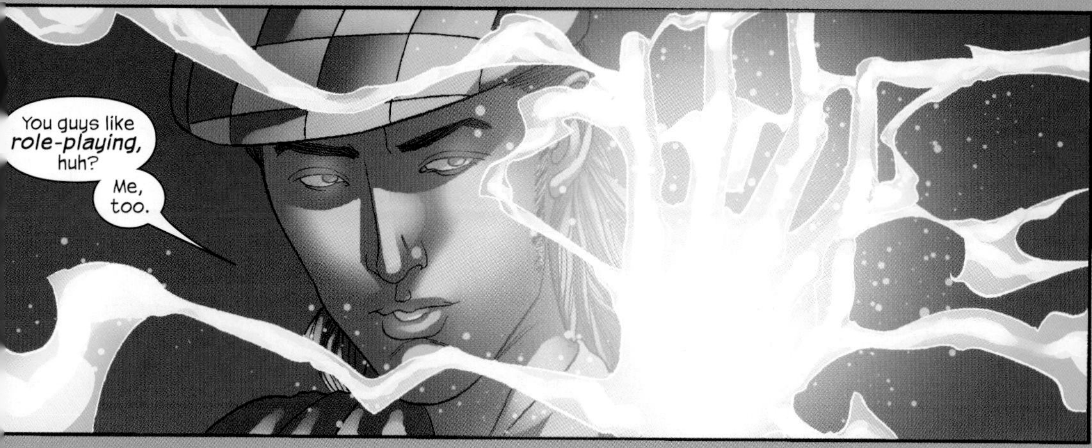
You guys like *role-playing,* huh?
Me, too.

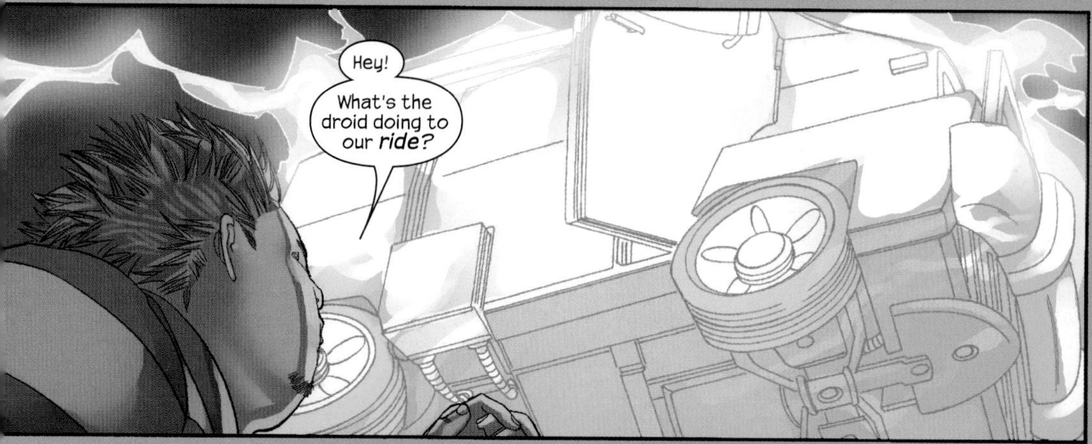
Hey!
What's the droid doing to our *ride?*

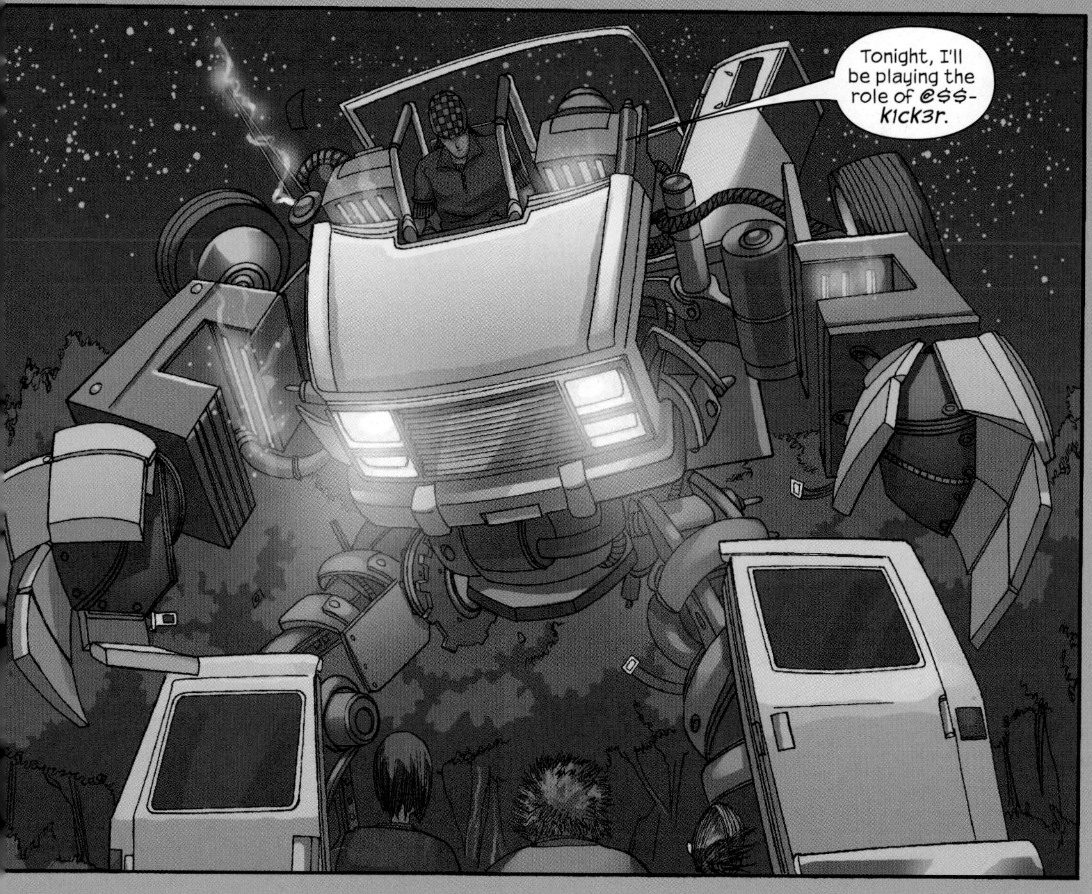
Tonight, I'll be playing the role of @$$-k1ck3r.

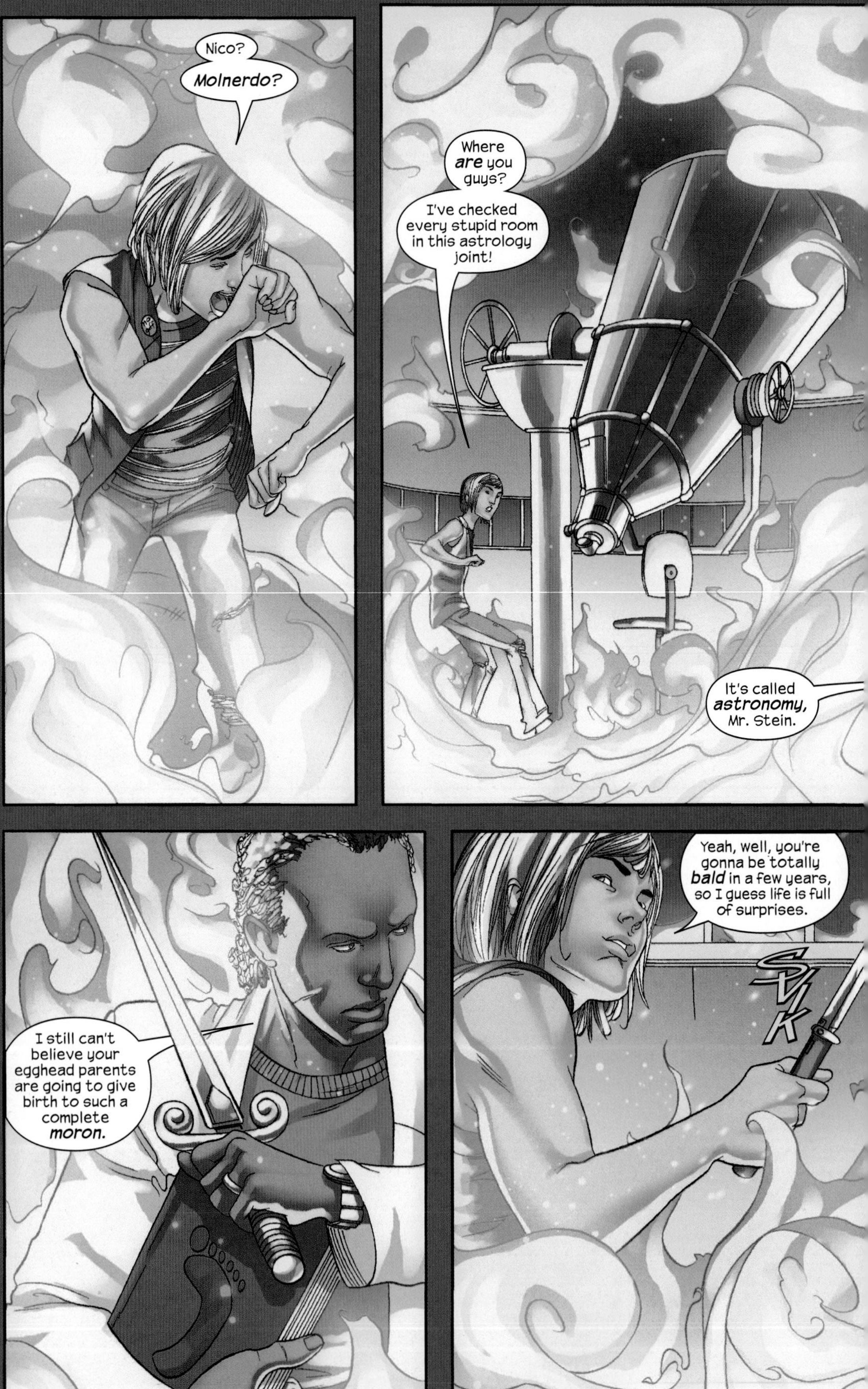

Nico?
Molnerdo?
Where are you guys?
I've checked every stupid room in this astrology joint!
It's called astronomy, Mr. Stein.
I still can't believe your egghead parents are going to give birth to such a complete moron.
Yeah, well, you're gonna be totally bald in a few years, so I guess life is full of surprises.
SNIK

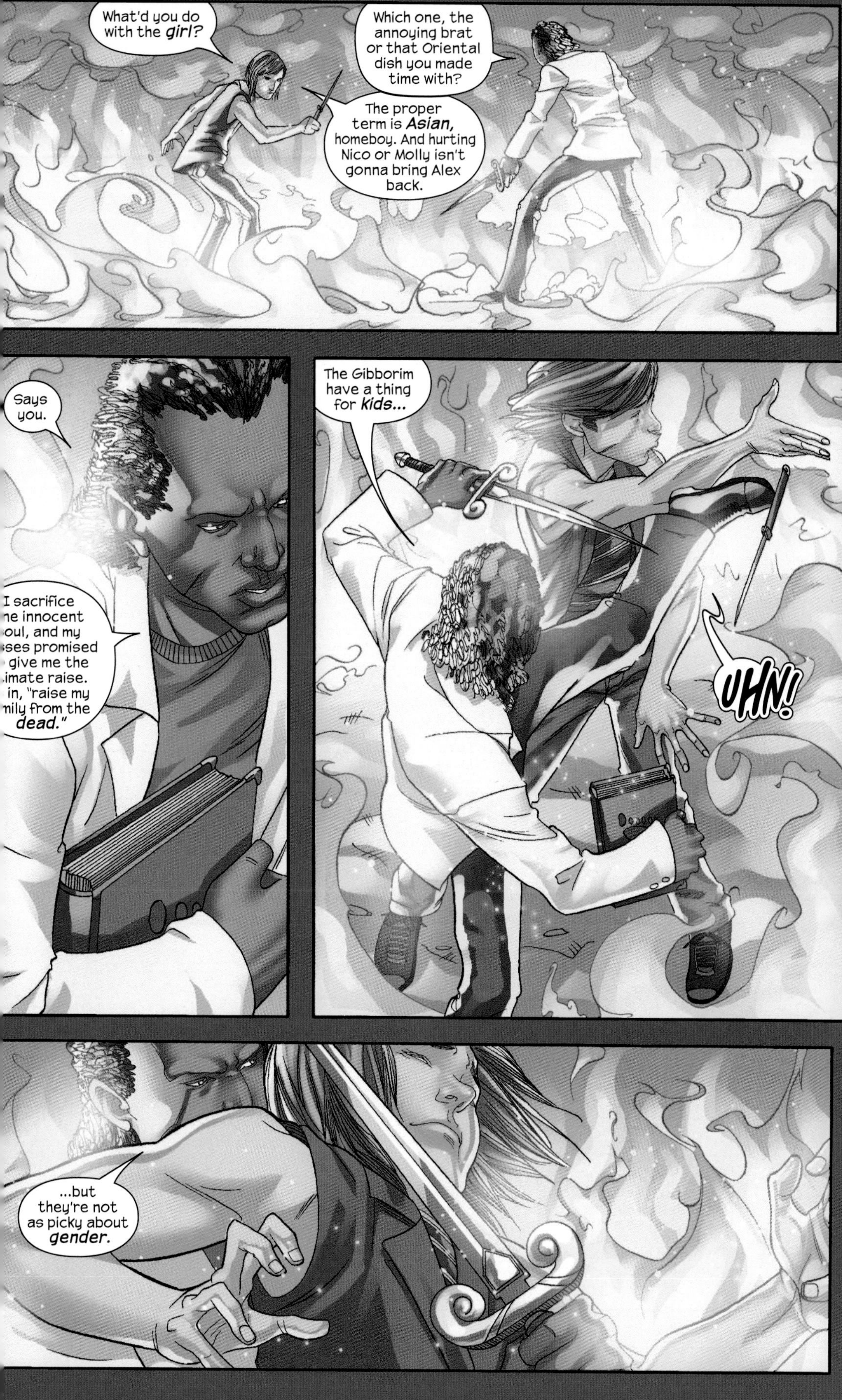

What'd you do with the *girl?*
Which one, the annoying brat or that Oriental dish you made time with?
The proper term is ***Asian,*** homeboy. And hurting Nico or Molly isn't gonna bring Alex back.
Says you.
I sacrifice ne innocent oul, and my sses promised give me the imate raise. in, "raise my mily from the ***dead."***
The Gibborim have a thing for ***kids...***
UHN!
...but they're not as picky about ***gender.***

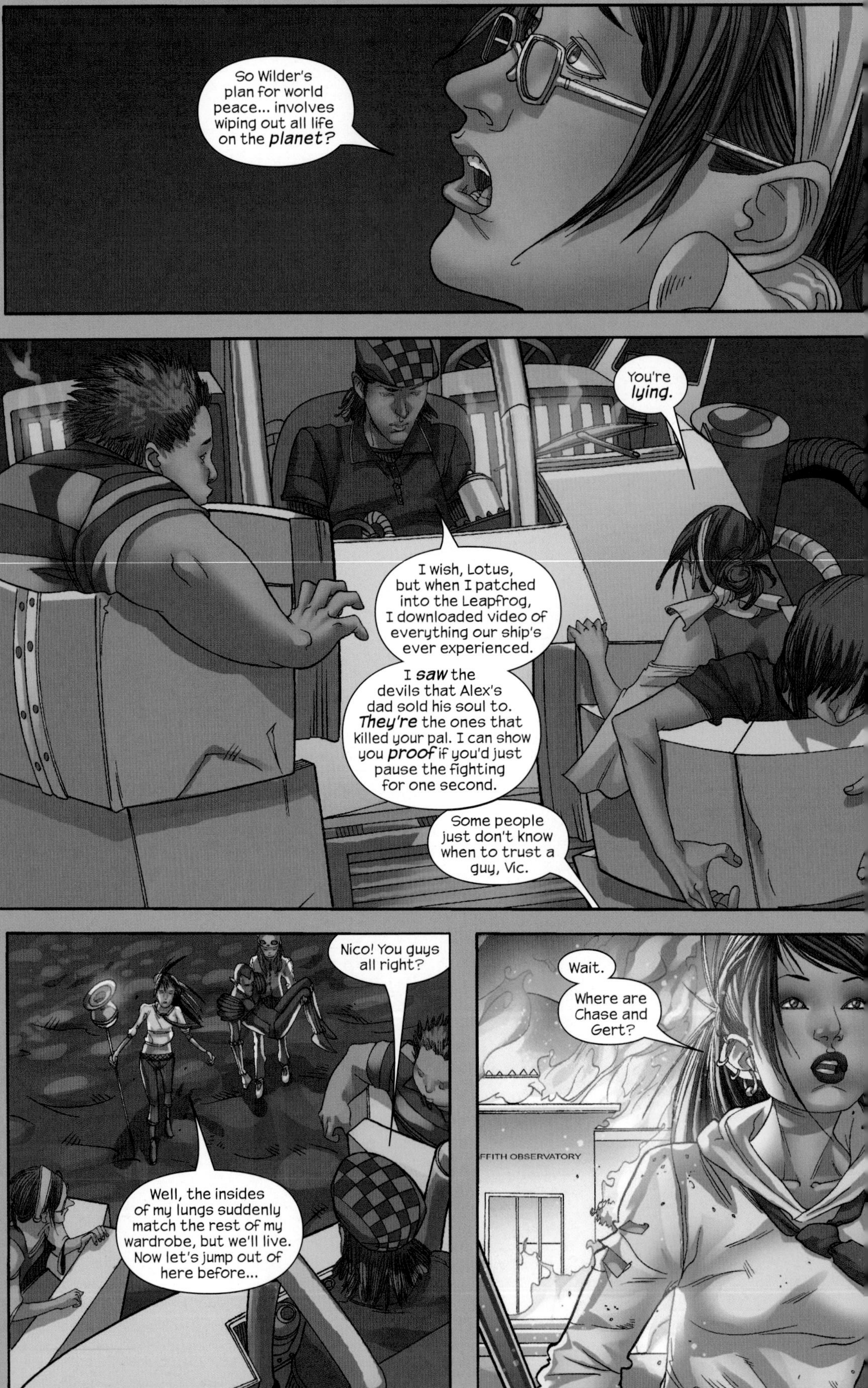

So Wilder's plan for world peace... involves wiping out all life on the *planet?*
You're *lying.*
I wish, Lotus, but when I patched into the Leapfrog, I downloaded video of everything our ship's ever experienced.
I *saw* the devils that Alex's dad sold his soul to. *They're* the ones that killed your pal. I can show you *proof* if you'd just pause the fighting for one second.
Some people just don't know when to trust a guy, Vic.
Nico! You guys all right?
Well, the insides of my lungs suddenly match the rest of my wardrobe, but we'll live. Now let's jump out of here before...
Wait.
Where are Chase and Gert?

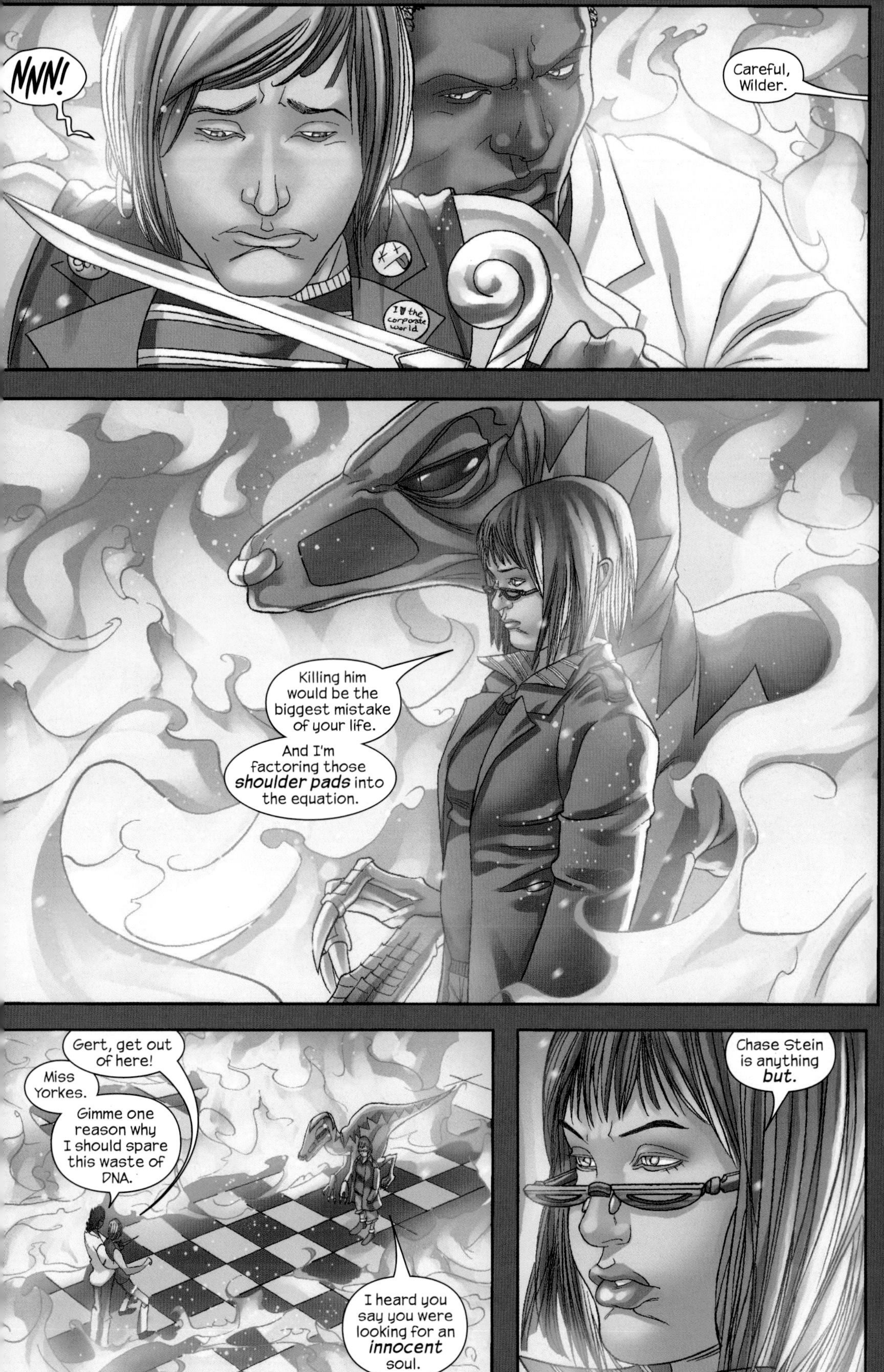
NNN!
Careful, Wilder.
I ♥ the corporate world
Killing him would be the biggest mistake of your life.
And I'm factoring those **shoulder pads** into the equation.
Gert, get out of here!
Miss Yorkes.
Gimme one reason why I should spare this waste of DNA.
I heard you say you were looking for an *innocent* soul.
Chase Stein is anything **but.**

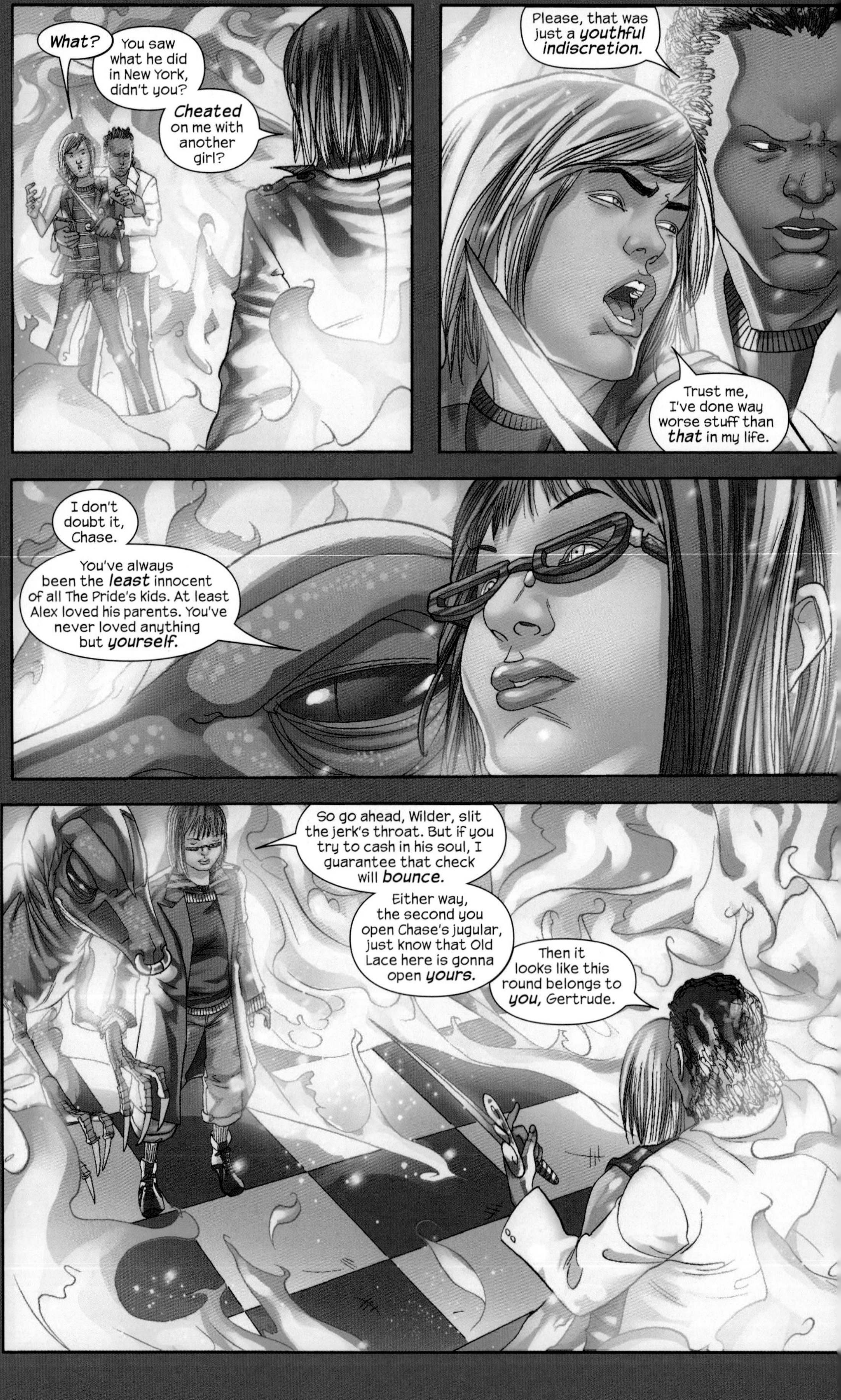
What?
You saw what he did in New York, didn't you?
Cheated on me with another girl?
Please, that was just a youthful indiscretion.
Trust me, I've done way worse stuff than that in my life.
I don't doubt it, Chase.
You've always been the least innocent of all The Pride's kids. At least Alex loved his parents. You've never loved anything but yourself.
So go ahead, Wilder, slit the jerk's throat. But if you try to cash in his soul, I guarantee that check will bounce.
Either way, the second you open Chase's jugular, just know that Old Lace here is gonna open yours.
Then it looks like this round belongs to you, Gertrude.

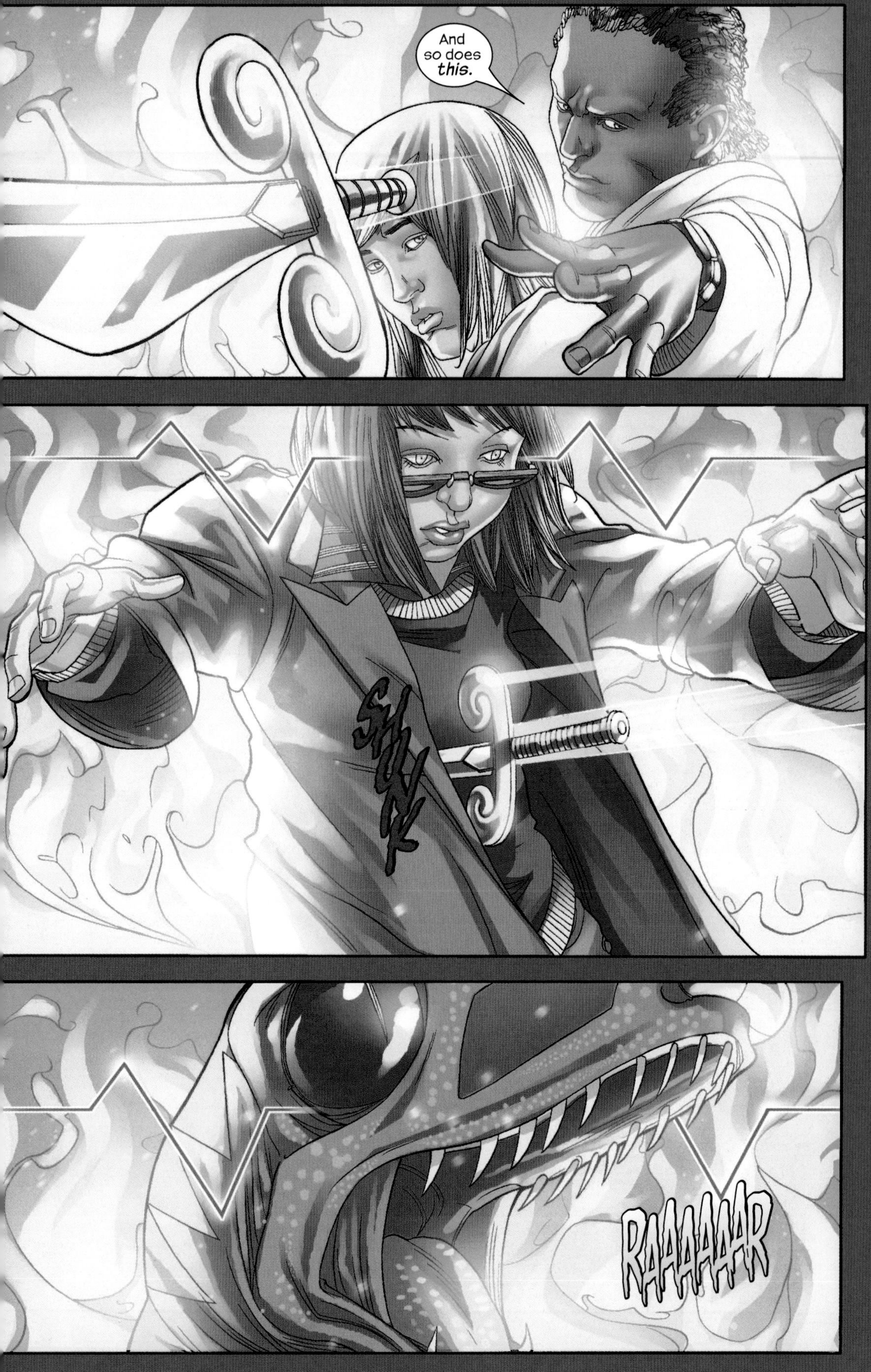
And so does *this.*
SHUNK
RAAAAAAR

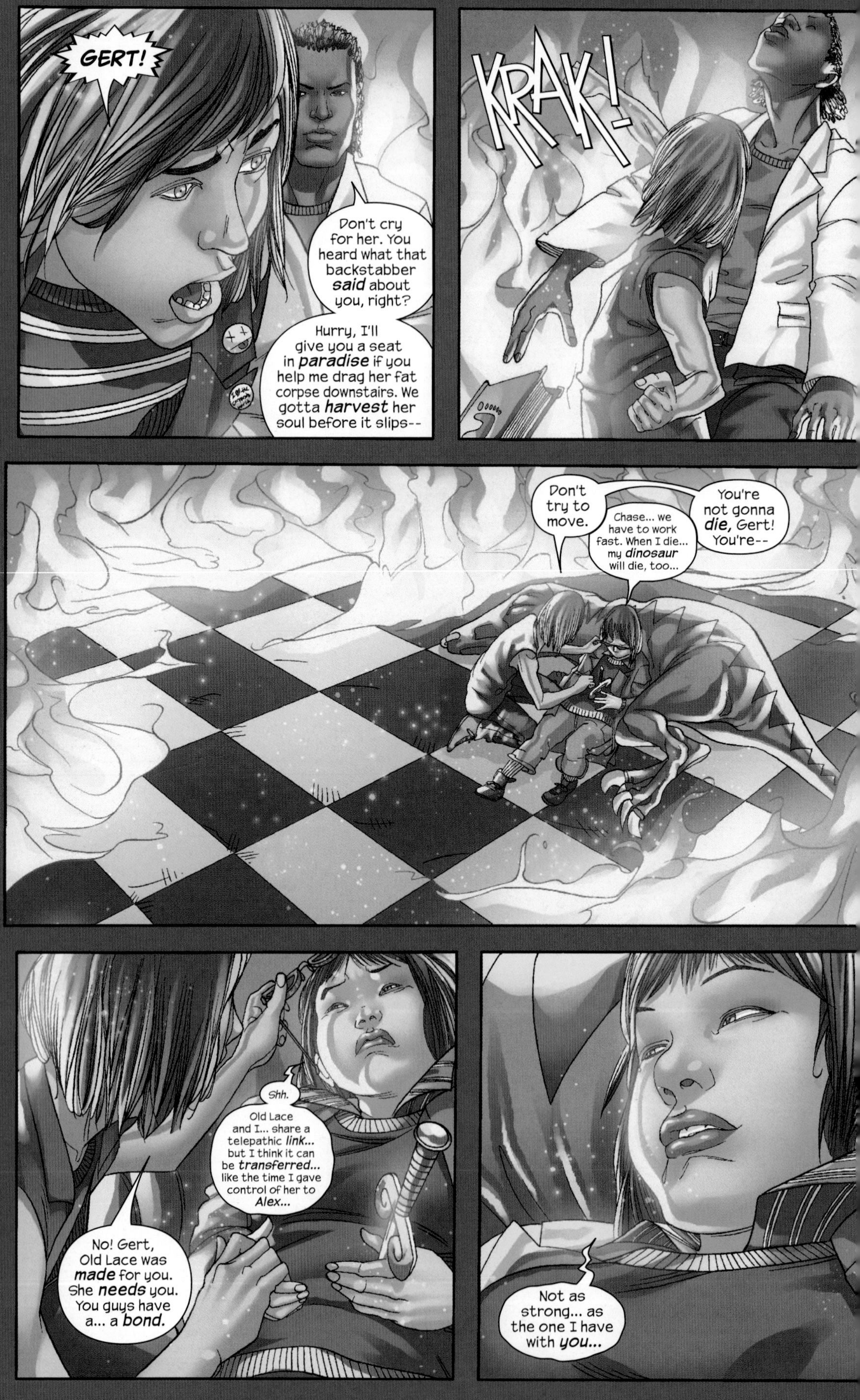
GERT!
Don't cry for her. You heard what that backstabber said about you, right?
Hurry, I'll give you a seat in paradise if you help me drag her fat corpse downstairs. We gotta harvest her soul before it slips--
KRAK!
Don't try to move.
You're not gonna die, Gert! You're--
Chase... we have to work fast. When I die... my dinosaur will die, too...
Shh.
Old Lace and I... share a telepathic link... but I think it can be transferred... like the time I gave control of her to Alex...
No! Gert, Old Lace was made for you. She needs you. You guys have a... a bond.
Not as strong... as the one I have with you...

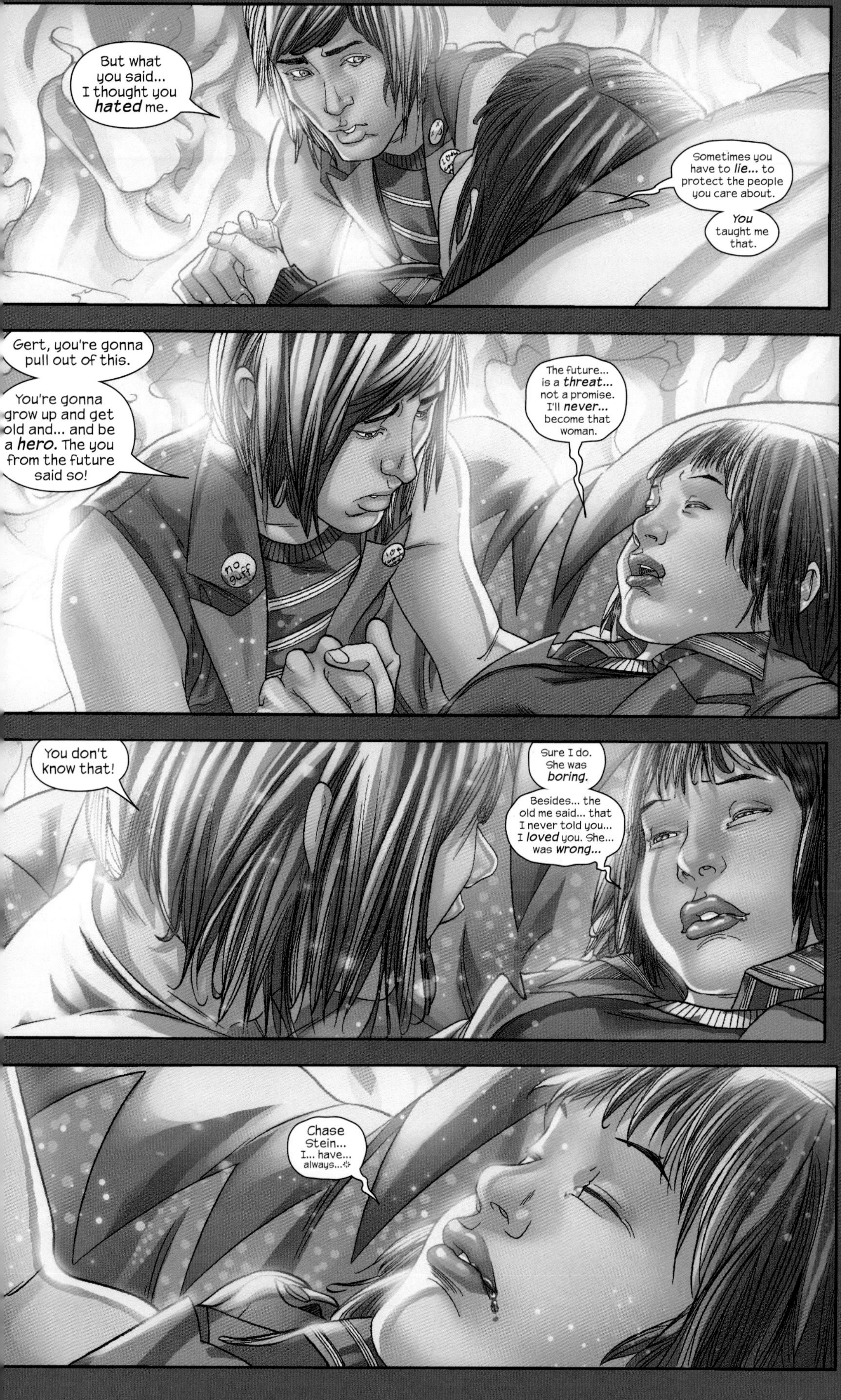

But what you said... I thought you *hated* me.
Sometimes you have to *lie...* to protect the people you care about.
You taught me that.
Gert, you're gonna pull out of this.
You're gonna grow up and get old and... and be a ***hero.*** The you from the future said so!
The future... is a ***threat...*** not a promise. I'll ***never...*** become that woman.
You don't know that!
Sure I do. She was *boring.*
Besides... the old me said... that I never told you... I *loved* you. She... was ***wrong...***
Chase Stein... I... have... always...

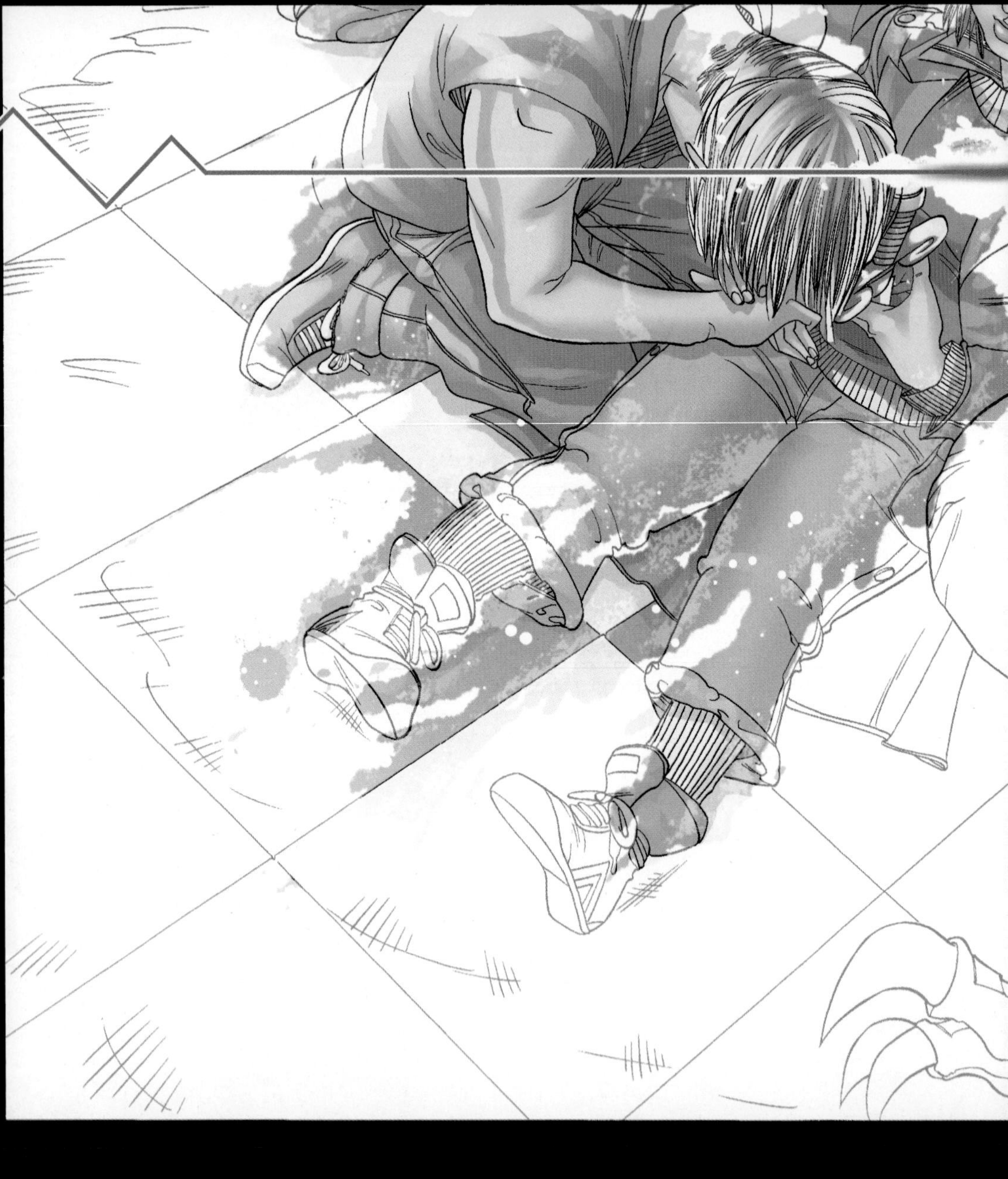

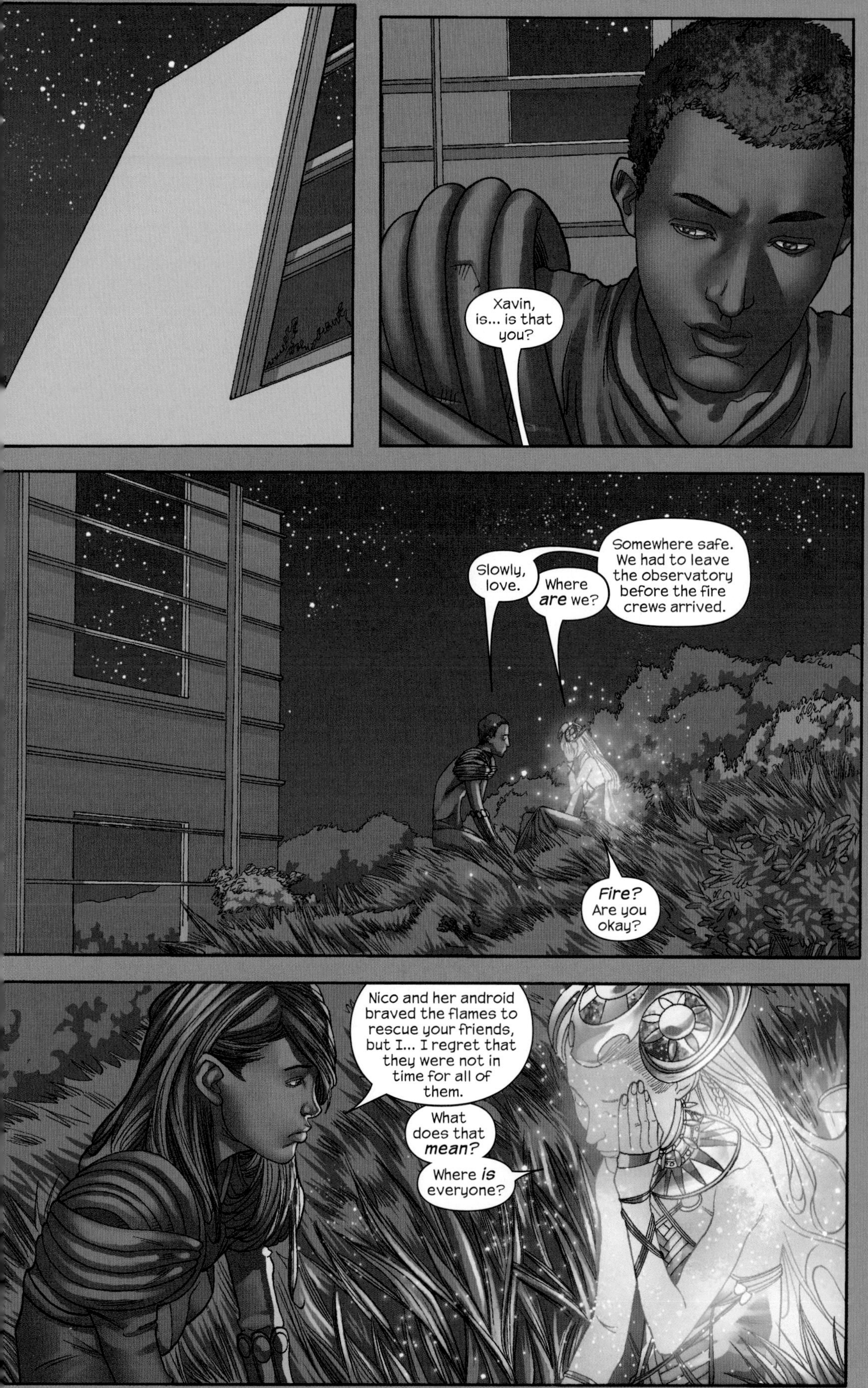

Xavin, is... is that you?
Slowly, love.
Where *are* we?
Somewhere safe. We had to leave the observatory before the fire crews arrived.
Fire? Are you okay?
Nico and her android braved the flames to rescue your friends, but I... I regret that they were not in time for all of them.
What does that *mean?*
Where *is* everyone?

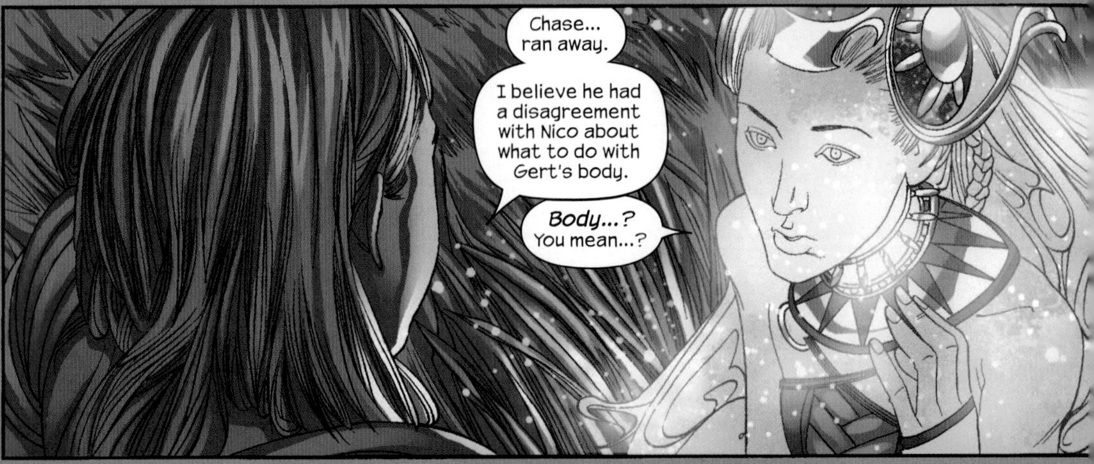
Chase... ran away.
I believe he had a disagreement with Nico about what to do with Gert's body.
Body...? You mean...?

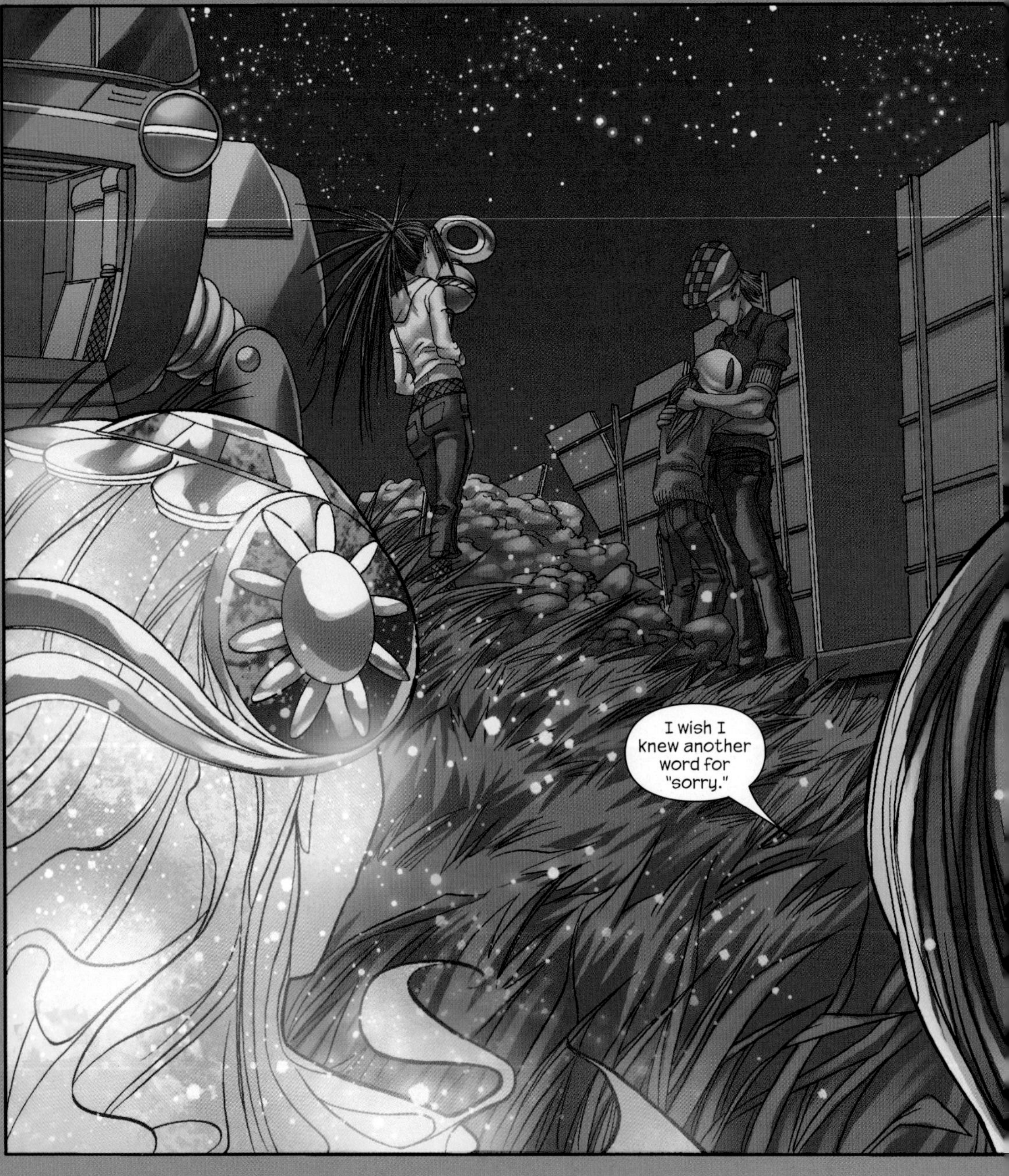
I wish I knew another word for "sorry."

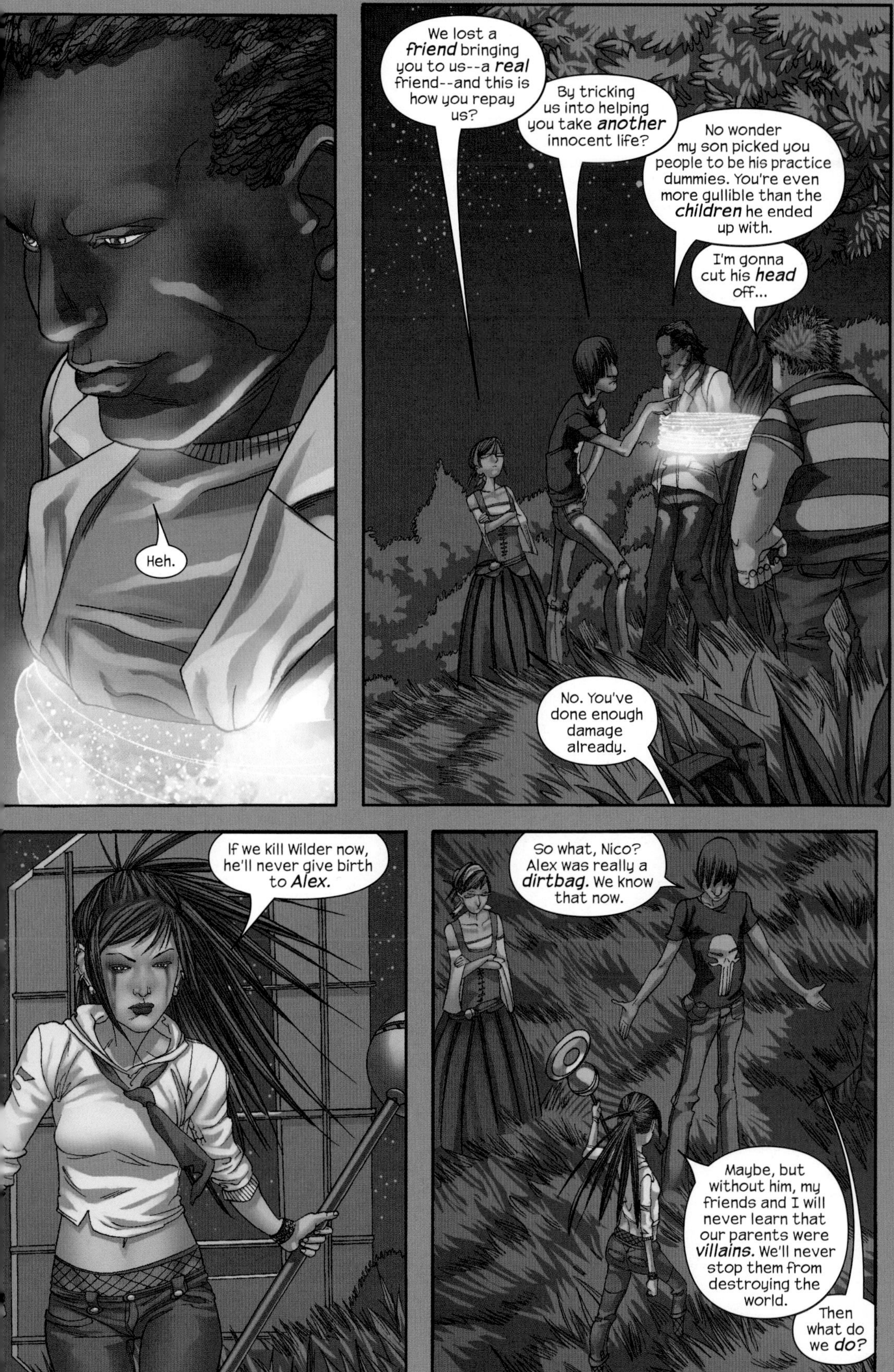
Heh.
We lost a friend bringing you to us--a real friend--and this is how you repay us?
By tricking us into helping you take another innocent life?
No wonder my son picked you people to be his practice dummies. You're even more gullible than the children he ended up with.
I'm gonna cut his head off...
No. You've done enough damage already.
If we kill Wilder now, he'll never give birth to Alex.
So what, Nico? Alex was really a dirtbag. We know that now.
Maybe, but without him, my friends and I will never learn that our parents were villains. We'll never stop them from destroying the world.
Then what do we do?

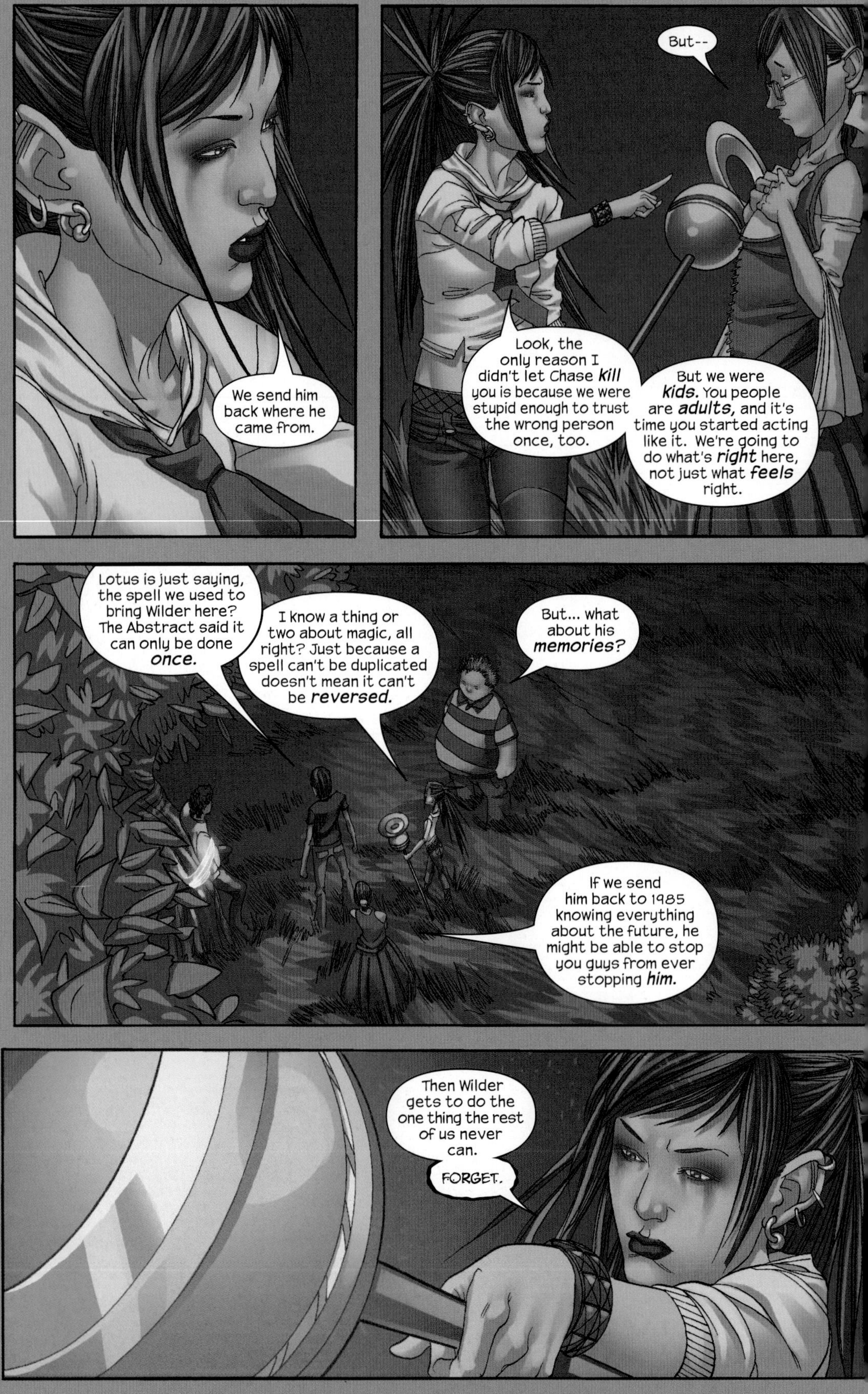
We send him back where he came from.
But--
Look, the only reason I didn't let Chase kill you is because we were stupid enough to trust the wrong person once, too.
But we were kids. You people are adults, and it's time you started acting like it. We're going to do what's right here, not just what feels right.
Lotus is just saying, the spell we used to bring Wilder here? The Abstract said it can only be done once.
I know a thing or two about magic, all right? Just because a spell can't be duplicated doesn't mean it can't be reversed.
But... what about his memories?
If we send him back to 1985 knowing everything about the future, he might be able to stop you guys from ever stopping him.
Then Wilder gets to do the one thing the rest of us never can.
FORGET.

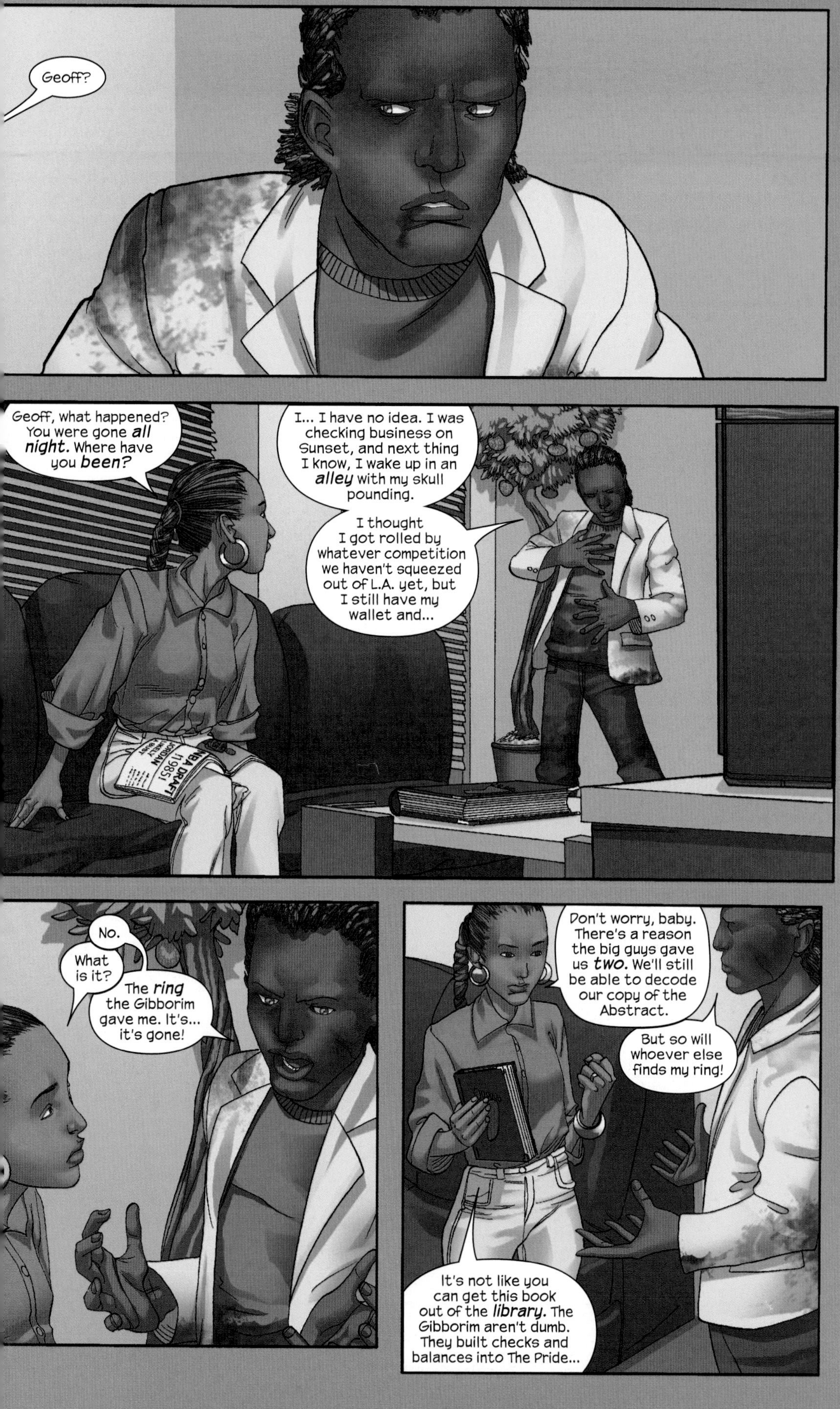
Geoff?
Geoff, what happened? You were gone all night. Where have you been?
I... I have no idea. I was checking business on Sunset, and next thing I know, I wake up in an alley with my skull pounding.
I thought I got rolled by whatever competition we haven't squeezed out of L.A. yet, but I still have my wallet and...
NBA DRAFT
No.
What is it?
The ring the Gibborim gave me. It's... it's gone!
Don't worry, baby. There's a reason the big guys gave us two. We'll still be able to decode our copy of the Abstract.
But so will whoever else finds my ring!
It's not like you can get this book out of the library. The Gibborim aren't dumb. They built checks and balances into The Pride...

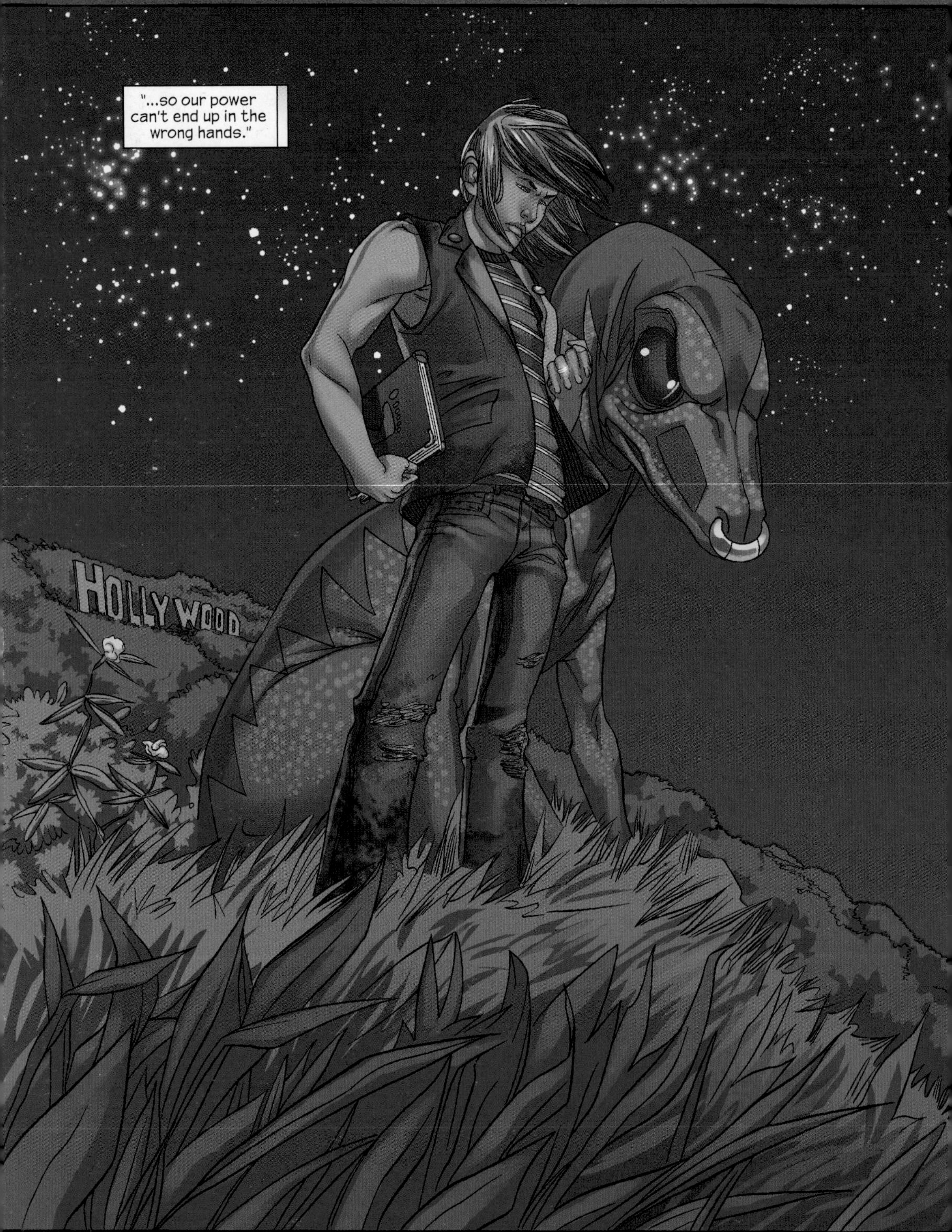
"...so our power
can't end up in the
wrong hands."
HOLLYWOOD